Books by the Same Author

Kiefer Sutherland: Living Dangerously

Johnny Depp Photo Album

Mickey Rourke: High and Low

Depp

Ten Thousand Bullets: The Cinematic Journey of John Woo

Dreaming Aloud: The Life and Films of James Cameron

Christopher Heard

BRITNEY SPEARS
Little Girl Lost

ISBN: 978-1-926745-74-9

Cover design: François Turgeon
Text design and composition: Nassim Bahloul

Cover photo:
© Reuters/CORBIS

Transit Publishing Inc.
1996 St-Joseph Boulevard East
Montreal, QC
H2H 1E3

Tel: 514-273-0123
www.transitpublishing.com

Printed and Bound in Canada

DEDICATION

For Isabelle (IHQOW)

Acknowledgements

My thanks first and foremost to the finest group of publishing people anywhere, the Transit Publishing team. Transit is a Canadian publishing house with guts and drive and spirit, all of which are woefully lacking elsewhere in publishing in this country and it is Pierre Turgeon who deserves a ton of credit for this. Thanks also to Francois Turgeon for his energy and determination. Thanks to Dwayne and Christine and Isabelle and Sarah, who get behind their books with a savage intensity that ensures everyone out there knows about them. And thanks to Gratia Ionescu who keeps all of the above in line.

Special thanks to my editor, Timothy Niedermann, who edits with a surgeon's precision but with a sculptor's vision. I am very lucky indeed to have someone of your skill in my corner.

A special word of thanks to brother Ian Halperin, a good friend who is always there when I need a bit of advice.

Thanks to everyone who spoke to me on the record or off during this process, from the good people of Kentwood, Louisiana, on up to the clinical psychologists who tried to give me as much of an understanding of the seriousness of postpartum depression that is possible for a male to grasp.

Thanks to my family: my father, Bill, my mother, Marie and my brother Peter. It is through them that the confidence to dream begins.

Thanks to my other family, the special people that surround me in my home in the beloved Royal York Hotel, from Melanie Coates to Heather McCrory to Mike Taylor to Kolene Elliott to Josh downstairs in the health club—you all create a wonderful atmosphere that has made me extremely and most enjoyably productive.

Heartfelt thanks to the beautiful Rhonda Thain. Once again, you saw to it that work was balanced with comfort and warmth and support—all deeply appreciated.

Table of Contents

PROLOGUE

Not long ago, my three-year-old daughter, Isabelle, was visiting me in the grand old hotel I live in. Like Eloise at the Plaza, Isabelle loves to run along the hallways and skip and dance across the spacious mezzanine overlooking the chandeliers and the ornate lobby. On this day, Isabelle and I explored the old Imperial Room—a venerable nightclub/lounge that has played host to performers like Marlene Dietrich and Tony Bennett. The room was deserted, quiet; Isabelle wanted to go onto the stage, so I lifted her up there. She began to sing and twirl and dance. I sat at a front-row table and watched, beaming proudly as my beautiful little girl performed for an imaginary audience.

When she had finished her act and become bored with the dark empty space of the Imperial Room, we returned to the lobby. An old British lady was sitting there by herself. As we passed by, she looked at Isabelle and said to me, "She is adorable! You should put her in show business." I thanked the lady, but her words struck an ominous chord. I stopped and hugged Isabelle for a second and thought of little Britney Jean Spears. I wondered to myself, did someone say something like that about their little girl to Lynne or Jamie Spears? Is this how the Britney odyssey started, how the end of her innocence began? Or would it have happened anyway? Was making Britney a superstar what her parents had always intended and vowed to achieve?

Staggering, sustained success of the sort achieved by Britney Spears is never an accident. She had sold nearly a hundred million albums before she turned twenty-eight and she is the only female artist to have had her first four albums debut at number 1 on the Billboard charts. While chance certainly plays a role in the careers of most recording artists, Britney did not get to where she is by mere happenstance.

* * *

This book is about the tumultuous life of a smart, talented young woman named Britney Jean Spears, born in the Mississippi mud and raised in Louisiana's sweltering Southern Baptist country. It traces her meteoric rise to the very heights of pop-culture success. But, like Goethe's Dr. Faust, who sells his soul to the devil in exchange for everything he wants on this earth, Britney has had to pay an enormous price to achieve her desires.

Though manipulated by an ambitious mother, controlling managers and greed-driven entertainment executives, Britney has, perhaps naively, been a willing party to it all. Others may have dangled the carrot of fame before her, but she allowed herself to become mesmerised by it. She began to channel all of her gifts and focus all of her energies towards one thing: churning out product to feed the cash machine that bore her name. And, despite everything that has happened to her, despite all of the obstacles in her path, she has never let that machine falter. She achieved the dream every little girl has of being a star. But once she got there, the bill came due in many ways.

This book follows her rise to the heights of fame and fortune and her descent into personal hell; it also details her recent return to stability and relative happiness. A new Britney has emerged. The question we may find ourselves asking is: What Britney is this? The one we thought we knew, or the one who is truer to herself? But, in the end, all we can do is hope that the little girl inside Britney who loves to sing and dance finally finds happiness.

A Kid in a Candy Store

"I don't like defining myself. I just am."

–Britney Spears

On September 26, 2009, Britney Spears was reported to have spent over $3,000 in a candy store at the Las Vegas Mirage Hotel. The tabloids got onto the story and, naturally, blew the incident way out of proportion, presenting it as yet another example of a rich, spoiled, profligate star carelessly throwing her money around. To be fair, anyone who has strolled around the high-end shops in the Las Vegas super hotels knows that spending three grand in one of them would not be difficult and certainly wouldn't take long. Spears was in Las Vegas with her two young sons, Sean Preston and Jayden James and her agent and then boyfriend Jason Trawick on the final North American leg of her wildly successful *The Circus Starring Britney Spears* tour.

"She was staying in one of the very comfortable Mirage Villas," a worker at the Mirage relates. "She wasn't wild or crazy or anything like that. She spent money like there was no tomorrow, but she's got it and she was enjoying it." Did she in fact spend $3,000 at the Sugar Factory? "Yes, it was ten bags full of stuff, lots of stuff for her boys, shirts and toys and candy. She also bought a ton of stuff like couture lollipops and higher-end fun stuff that she said she was giving to her dancers on her tour." It turns out that the actual amount of the Sugar Factory binge was closer to $6,000. "Well, she spent three grand in the store but then the store and the hotel arranged for another $2,500-plus worth of stuff to be sent to her suite, so she didn't pay for that stuff."

Britney Spears has become such a fixture of the daily pop culture miasma that even when she steps into a candy store and does a little bit of self-indulgent shopping, it becomes a news item. Everything to do with the visit to the candy store was splashed across the nation's tabloids and examined under the dubious microscope of manifold gossip columns: Oh, look, she's with Jason Trawick! Weren't they quits? Didn't Britney dump him after many public squabbles? Are they back on again? They must be—here they are shopping in Las Vegas together. And look, she has her two boys in tow. Does that mean she's getting custody again? She has the boys outside the jurisdiction of the California courts. That must mean something, but what?

All this wild speculation because of a trip to a candy store. Britney was in Las Vegas because she was concluding the final North American leg of her 2009 tour, *The Circus Starring Britney Spears*. The tour marked her comeback from an abyss of drugs, alcohol, marital discord, custody battles, mental instability and public crack-ups. Her father, Jamie Spears, had taken control of her affairs and she was putting a new veneer on everything in her life. She looked healthy and fit. The tour and album were Britney's way of telling the world that she was back and stronger than ever.

The Circus Starring Britney Spears tour began in March 2009 in her home state of Louisiana. After doing thirty shows through May in the U.S., it was over to Europe in June and July, then back to the U.S. and Canada for twenty-four more shows; the tour finished up in Australia in November. But there was something missing. Barbara Ellen of the London *Observer* described the show thus: "What a shame then that the Circus Show, while not calamitous like the infamous MTV Awards 'comeback,' was so . . . well, so-so. Not bad, just boring, lackluster, underpowered, which, in my book, is far worse."

While all modern popular culture has a manufactured quality to it, Britney the pop star seems to be an almost entirely manufactured entity. The *Circus* album and *The Circus Starring Britney Spears* tour just seem to highlight it, but this is not to say that the venture hasn't been successful. John Meglen, president of the tour promoter, AEG Live/Concerts West, gushed, "It is one of the biggest and best-selling tours of the decade. Response and reaction has been phenomenal worldwide. European fans couldn't wait for her to get there, many, many venues sold out instantly and we've had to juggle dates to add more shows to meet the demand."

The tour was a dazzling financial success. The critical response was generally positive, but only grudgingly so. Jane Stevenson, long-time music critic for the *Toronto Sun*, was suspicious of the whole thing: "You have everything from martial arts displays and clowns and bicycles riding around the stage, [and] it is hard to really look at her performance amidst all the commotion . . . Britney looked great. I wrote that she looked like she was trying to look like a cross between Pamela Anderson and Madonna but she didn't seem to be fully into it, fully committed to it in terms of passion and excitement and the pure joy that you see from some performers to be doing what they love doing and sucking up all that positive energy from the audience at the same time."

James Montgomery of MTV News described the show as a "huge, loud, nonsensical three-ring affair." He said that Britney "looks great in her myriad of outfits," but that she is also "lost in the sheer hugeness of the production around her."

Jennifer Chancellor of the *Tulsa World* may have expressed it best when she wrote, "Even with the sex, the innuendo, the crassness, the bombast and the million dollar production, there is still a subtle naiveté about Spears and her stage presence. It peeks from beneath her curtain of hair extensions and her torrid lash-batting, but it's there. She is still the child-like Disney Mouseketeer."

Still a Disney Mouseketeer. This is the image of Britney Spears that persists, despite her attempts to break free of it. And it is probably the closest to the real Britney in many ways. But ever since she left the confines of the Magic Kingdom, she has attempted to sculpt a far different image for herself, edgier, sexier, more like her idol Madonna. And she has been successful, unbelievably successful. Her image and her music have gone through transition after transition and her fans have followed. But it has been a struggle, not just to break the mold cast around her by Disney, but against those who have sought to control her and to dictate her interests. And she has struggled against herself, in particular against the person success has made her. She is emerging now from depths many sink into forever. It is a story of talent, perseverance, arrogance, despair and repentance. There is now a new Britney Spears unfolding, driven by the same drive and determination that created her original success, but this time tempered by experience. One thing is sure: she won't disappoint.

Dancing and Tumbling

"I'm from the South, and down there we are all about high standards, about respecting people and being polite to people no matter what they might be doing to you."

–Miley Cyrus

Britney Spears grew up in the American South. Those who live there tend to describe the region with pride. To them the South is the part of the country that, faced with all the pressures of modern life, still adheres to strong traditions and solid values; down South, life has a comfortable, human rhythm. But, as with much of what we hold dear, there is more to it than that. The South is a zone of contrasts and conflicts and it always has been. The solid Christian values and genteel traditions exist— and indeed still characterise the region—but they coexist with the notorious tensions between white and black, rich and poor. Lately, parts of the South have experienced dynamic economic growth, which has created opportunities that have cut across old racial and economic divides, but life can still be a struggle in the small-town South, where the old ways are most deeply rooted.

McComb, Mississippi, is the largest town in rural Pike County, with a current population of just over 13,000. Demographically, it is a lot like any town in the South. While the county is almost evenly divided between white and black, McComb itself is almost sixty percent black. Lynne Irene Bridges and Jamie Parnell Spears were born here. Like many couples in McComb, they were high-school sweethearts and married at eighteen, just after graduation in 1975. A son, Bryan, arrived three years later. By that time, they had moved to the tiny town of Kentwood, Louisiana, current population 2,200, located ten miles south of McComb. Jamie was employed as a building contractor and sometime chef and Lynne taught elementary school.

On December 2, 1981, Lynne Spears gave birth to their second child, a girl. They named her Britney Jean. Like her parents, Britney was born in the McComb hospital. Little Britney immediately attracted attention. Hazel Morris, who wrote birth notices for the local paper, the *Kentwood News Ledger*, is likely the first journalist to have written about Britney Spears. This is what she had to say about her: "Britney Jean Spears, the Baby of the Week, is an active, precious, bundle of joy." Years later, Hazel would become the curator of the Britney Spears section of the Kentwood Museum.

Lynne Spears was thrilled. She had badly wanted a girl—a child, as she put it, to "dress up like a little doll." The woman who runs the beauty shop in the Walmart mall where Britney and her family shopped (and still do, from time to time) said, "She was a nice kid, very full of life and bubbly, they all were, but her mother, Lynne, she was gorgeous, she could have been a movie star herself she was so pretty."

The family lived in a comfortable home with the Greenlaw Baptist Church on one side and a bar on the other. Jamie Spears was able to find regular work as a contractor and construction worker. They eventually installed a large piano in the living room so that Britney could plunk out notes and practice her singing. She had a typical little girl's bedroom. Here, in her small private world, she would arrange her dolls and stuffed animals as an audience and sing and dance for them. Watching herself in a large mirror, she'd pretend to be her idol, Madonna. How many other little girls were doing the same across the country? But the ambitions of most little girls change; they eventually abandon their dolls and stuffed animals and find other playthings. Britney's childhood bedroom, though, is carefully preserved in the Kentwood Museum.

There is a local story about the first time Britney Spears took the stage. She and her cousin Laura Lynn Covington, daughter of Lynne's sister Sandra, had begun taking classes from Renee Donewar. Renee's dancing school for kids was located in Hammond, Louisiana, nearly thirty miles away, but on weekends she would teach in communities throughout Tangipahoa Parish.

For their first dance recital, Britney and Laura Lynn did a routine together. Both wore frilly pink costumes and they had their hair done the same way. Nervously waiting their turn to perform, they looked like two adorable peas in a pod, but when the music started, that abruptly changed. Laura Lynn giggled and repeated the dance moves she liked over and over. But Britney, a look of intense determination on her face, completed the routine exactly as she had learned it, even though she was out of time with the music.

Renee would describe Britney as being "a perfectionist right from the start. Whenever I would introduce a new step to our classes, Britney was always the first one to get it." Renee commented later that she could see even then that little Britney wanted to be a star. She didn't seem attracted to the notion of stardom or fame, but she clearly loved it when people watched her perform and cheered her on. It was in Renee's dance class that Britney earned her first award: the best attendance prize. Britney was just three years old.

* * *

Performing seems to have come naturally to Britney at a very early age and not just on stage. She has been described as having "always been an athletic little girl," and when she started doing back flips on the living room carpet, her father decided that she had the makings of an athlete and signed her up for gymnastics lessons at a local gym five nights a week. It was 1987 and Britney was five years old. She took to gymnastics readily. Jamie Spears set up a balance beam in the middle of the living room so that Britney could train at home as well. The Spears clan indulged little Britney as they tried to watch television or do their homework. Soon, she was entering local gymnastics competitions. Her natural enthusiasm for the sport convinced her parents to invest further in her development as an athlete and before long she was competing regularly farther and farther away from home.

Then she started to win. As she has consistently done with everything, Britney applied herself to gymnastics and in 1990 she took first place at the Louisiana State Gymnastics Competition. Wearing her lucky white leotard, she executed a perfect back flip followed by a somersault to win. Her father got it into his head that the eight-year-old Britney could be the next Mary Lou Retton. The next step was clear.

On a 500-acre ranch in New Waverly, Texas, seventy miles north of Houston, there was a special gymnastics camp run by legendary Olympic gymnastics coach Bela Karolyi. In the 1970s, Karolyi had almost single-handedly turned a team of skinny Romanian girls into an Olympic juggernaut, exploding onto the scene at the 1976 Olympic Games in Montreal, where his star athlete, Nadia Comaneci, became the first gymnast ever to score a perfect ten. Karolyi continued to lead the Romanian national team until just after the 1980 Olympics, when, following a disagreement with Romanian authorities, he defected to the U.S. Switching allegiances, Karolyi became the individual coach for a number of U.S. athletes, including Mary Lou Retton, who won the all-around gymnastics gold medal at the 1984 Olympics in Los Angeles. Four years later, he was appointed head coach of the U.S. women's gymnastics team.

Since arriving in the U.S. in 1981, Karolyi has also run the camp for the advanced training of U.S. Olympic hopefuls. Karolyi will not take on an athlete unless he feels that the person has what it takes—or at least has a realistic chance—to excel at this demanding sport. Athletes have to have won a competition or be endorsed by a recognised coach or gymnastics organisation before he will even consider them.

First, he looks at a young athlete to see what level of natural talent he or she has. Then he invites the athlete to spend a week at the camp so that he can determine whether he or she has the drive and discipline to become an Olympian. Athletes who demonstrate that rare combination of abilities are asked to join the camp for serious training.

Karolyi would later say that Britney "was one of the little girls who really excelled." But Britney, at age eight, was not prepared physically or emotionally for this level of training. Karolyi and his coaches didn't applaud the girls' efforts and tell them how cute they looked. They drove the girls hard and then drove them some more. Very quickly it became a negative, punishing experience for young Britney. As she would later describe it, "Almost right away, when I had to go to training I would start crying because it was so hard. I was good at gymnastics because it was fun, but this was not fun. This was painful."

Despite Jamie Spears's dreams, Lynne Spears recognised that Britney was just not meant for the cutthroat world of big-league athletics. She may have been filled with drive and ambition, but not for that. Britney abandoned gymnastics in the spring of 1991. Right away, she found other things to apply herself to.

TALENT

"I don't mind training and working hard, I just don't want that to be ALL I do."

–Britney Spears

Kentwood, Louisiana, is deep in the Bible Belt, a huge swath of the American South where religious worship is not a choice but an immutable and unquestioned way of life. As Britney's first real boyfriend, Reg Jones, described it, "We all really believed in God and were all very religious and believed in what it said in the Bible. We were afraid not to."

While the Spears family lived just a few hundred yards down the road from the Greenlaw Baptist Church, they attended services at Kentwood's First Baptist Church, five miles away. Many members of the congregation still remember the night in 1985 when a four-year-old Britney wowed a packed house with a rendition of "What Child Is This?" during the Christmas service. Britney was already a member of the First Baptist Church junior choir and sang like a little songbird every Sunday. But this was her first solo performance. A parishioner from McComb who remembers the evening and the performance said, "Man, I will tell you she belted it out. We all knew her and her family from the church, of course, but this was . . . a special night in the little girl's life. And I will tell you further, even though all the things she's gone off and done now, that night she was scared skinny. She was very nervous, but then once she started singing, you would have sworn she was twice as old as she was."

In the fall of 1988, when she was six, Britney entered first grade at McComb's Parklane Academy, a private Christian school. Like many private schools in Mississippi, Parklane was founded in 1970, after the state mandated the desegregation of public schools. For many years, including the time Britney was there, Parklane was an all-white institution; it graduated its first African American student in 1999, but the student body remains ninety-nine percent white.

While the Parklane tuition fees were not high by most standards, paying them put a lot of pressure on Jamie and Lynne Spears. It cost an average of $150 a month to send a student to Parklane and there were also books and supplies and extracurricular activities to pay for. Britney's older brother, Bryan, was enrolled at Parklane as well, so the family had to come up with over $5,000 a year in school fees. For Jamie, a struggling contractor with a young family, it was a stretch. But somehow they made do.

Like all Southern Baptist institutions in the area, Parklane began instilling Christian values in its students from the moment the first bell rang at 8:00 a.m. The school day started with a devotional reading from the Bible. The students then recited the pledge of allegiance and sang the national anthem.

From time to time, a representative from the True Love Waits movement would come in to give an inspirational, cautionary talk to the students. This movement grew out of the Lifeway sect, which had been established in Tennessee in 1891 and which held that solutions to all of life's problems could be found in the Bible. The True Love Waits credo reads: "Believing that true love waits, I make a commitment to God, myself, my family, my friends, my future mate and my future children to be sexually abstinent from this day until the day I enter a Biblical marriage relationship."

Kelly Burch, a classmate of Britney's, remembers that "Christian moral values was a big thing there—not that that was a bad thing. The word 'love' was used a lot. The idea behind the school was that young Christian men and women were being challenged to love each other as they love themselves. Nothing wrong with that."

Although the school offered a good variety of extracurricular activities suitable for young Christians, Britney did not participate. During her early school years, she did gymnastics training up to five days a week and dancing lessons three days a week at Renee Donewar's school in Hammond, Mississippi—nearly a ninety-mile round trip.

She also took singing lessons. When asked many years later at what moment she had realised she didn't just like to sing but that she was a real singer, Britney said that it was her mother who had first had that realisation. Britney was only three at the time. "I was in the backyard jumping up and down on a trampoline," she said. "I was singing a Sinéad O'Connor song and my mother said that the higher I bounced, the higher the notes I hit." Lynne Spears has also cited this incident as the moment she recognised her daughter had "perfect pitch."

On those long drives to and from her dancing and singing lessons, the car radio would be on and Britney would sing along. An early singing teacher, Bob Westbrook, opined that "she practiced and practiced and sang and sang and since she had a good voice to start with all that practice developed her voice just the way that working out for hours every day will just naturally develop your body."

On weekends, Britney often sang in shows or performed in gymnastic competitions. When she was six, her mother entered her in her first talent contest, at the Kentwood Dairy Festival. It was a typical tot performance—sporting a cute little costume, top hat and cane, blonde curls bobbing, she sang and danced her way across the stage—and at the end of it all the winner was . . . Britney Spears.

Over the next two years, Lynne and Britney travelled throughout the region to whatever local contests they could find. Britney would win virtually every single one of them. She entered more and more competitions. Although she was bringing home plenty of ribbons and trophies, she was missing a lot of school. When Britney turned eight, Lynne thought it was time to ratchet up the intensity, so she entered her in a major competition: the Miss Talent Central States Competition, held in Baton Rouge, Louisiana. Britney would have to compete against girls from four neighbouring states: Mississippi, Louisiana, Texas and Alabama. The little contestants would don elaborate costumes and wear makeup that would make them appear far older than they were. They had to sing, dance and display whatever other talents they possessed to make a big impression on the judges. Britney chose to include gymnastics in her routine and by the end of the weekend competition she had won every category she was entered in.

Lynne Spears had always been absolutely convinced that Britney, now in the third grade, was a special child with a special talent, but this competition proved it to everyone. Parklane Academy music teacher Mary Ellen Chamberlain remembers, "Her voice was so much more mature and developed than [those of] other little girls her age." Chamberlain chose Britney to perform a solo in a musical revue she had organised for students and their parents; she sang the Old English folk song "Lavender's Blue." Then Britney was asked to perform in the annual high school musical, "Give Thanks, America" in the role of a schoolteacher.

By now, Britney Spears was known as the best singer in the school, so whenever "The Star-Spangled Banner" needed to be sung, she would get the nod. When she sang the national anthem, "she was awesome," said former teacher Darlene Hughes. "It is funny, but she sang that song with such power and such depth that a lot of people who saw her sing it were sure that she was just lip-synching to a recording."

Then a fateful thing happened. One day in the school lunchroom, a friend of Britney's approached her with a newspaper article about an open audition for young singers and dancers in Atlanta, Georgia, for a new Disney Channel show called *The All New Mickey Mouse Club*.

Britney raced home from school that day to tell her mother about it. She insisted to Lynne that this was the perfect opportunity—just what they'd been waiting for. Lynne agreed and was impressed by Britney's initiative, but this represented a challenge. Atlanta was about five hundred miles away and they would have to drive the distance. The trip would be costly and what were the chances of success? Britney would be one of perhaps thousands of girls vying to impress the casting people and those casting people would also be visiting other cities to meet with thousands of other young hopefuls. Lynne worried that it wouldn't be worth the expense and that it would just set Britney up for a disappointment—something young Britney had thus far very little experience with.

Britney was undaunted, though. She begged and pleaded and came up with every conceivable argument to convince Lynne that this was a trip they had to make, a chance they had to take. Finally, Lynne gave in. They packed up and headed to Atlanta.

ALMOST

"I wanted it sooooo bad!"

−Britney Spears

The original *Mickey Mouse Club* is an American institution. It was a monster television hit that lives on in TV lore, but in fact it only ran for four years. It was first conceived as a promotional feature for the 1955 opening of Disneyland. Americans loved the popular song and sketch format and the teenaged "Mouseketeers." These fresh-faced kids were supposed to embody the wholesome, prosperous image of 1950s America that the U.S. wanted to believe in and project to the world.

The enduring appeal of *The Mickey Mouse Club* is its timeless, youthful enthusiasm, which the Mouseketeers were intended to reinforce. But this was a challenge. Children grow. The most popular of the original Mouseketeers, Annette Funicello, was cast when she was a gangly fourteen-year-old, but she quickly developed into an attractive and voluptuous young woman before the eyes of the nation. Funicello confides that the show's creators borrowed a trick from the movie business: "Yes, from Judy [Garland] doing the little girl in *The Wizard of Oz* on up to my part in *The Mickey Mouse Club*, young women would have to wear these strange tension bandages wrapped around our breasts to make us appear less developed . . . At the end of the run of the show, I was eighteen years old and quite independent but we were supposed to play it like we were pretty much still fourteen and still quite innocent—because that was what the show was about."

* * *

Matt Casella, the casting director for *The All New Mickey Mouse Club*, was looking for "An ordinary American kid with extraordinary talent." But he wasn't just looking for any talented kid. He was on the hunt for someone who could project an image that would in turn reflect the larger corporate image of Disney—a tall order. The rules were simple: because Casella would be seeing thousands and thousands of kids (not just in Atlanta, but also in Dallas, Miami, New York, Detroit, Chicago and Los Angeles), each would have just one shot: she'd come with a song prepared; she'd walk on stage, perform the song, walk off the stage and go home to wait for the call.

Lynne and Britney arrived in Atlanta to find two thousand kids lined up, all vying for the same spot. Britney knew she'd have to impress Casella with something truly special. She had decided to sing "Sweet Georgia Brown," and she was electrifying: she sang and danced and strutted and back flipped and never missed a beat. Although he sat through countless auditions, Casella still remembers this one clearly: "We saw her on the first day and she blew me away. I could not believe this kid was just eight or nine years old. She commanded the stage with a comfort and authority that I didn't see in seasoned professional young performers twice her age. She scored tens across the board from everyone. She was going to stick around so we could see her again." What he meant was that Britney was one of just six call-backs from among the hundreds who auditioned that first day in Atlanta. The six were asked to return the next day to audition again. This time, their performances would be taped and viewed not just by Casella but also by several Disney Channel producers and executives.

Britney and, even more so, Lynne were stunned—and then gleeful. But their glee did not last long. In the end, the producers and executives nixed Britney because she was too young. "Their thinking was that having a little girl like Britney in the cast alongside other performers who were all in their early teens would upset the balance of the show," Casella explains. "And they were quite right about that, but I was really pushing for Britney. She was stunning, so there was no way I was going to give up on her."

Matt Casella persisted. He had his assistant call an agent he knew in New York, a virtual legend on Broadway who handled and developed young talent ripe for launching. The agent, Nancy Carson of the Carson-Adler Agency, recalls, "I got a call from Matt's assistant telling me Matt had a little girl with him and that the little girl was absolute dynamite. And what made me sit up and take notice of this was the fact that I had known Matt a long time and he rarely ever suggested I represent anyone; he didn't see that as his function. So I knew that he thought this girl was extraordinary." Carson has represented child performers for over twenty-five years and she's the author of the book *Raising a Star: The Parents' Guide to Helping Kids Break into Theater, Film, Television, or Music*. Among her young clients were actors and writing partners Ben Affleck and Matt Damon.

Nancy Carson agreed to speak to Lynne Spears on the phone. Lynne asked her what the next step for Britney should be. Normally, if Carson was convinced during a phone call with parents that the child was not only very talented but also had an independent desire to perform—that is, the motivation was coming from the child, not the parents—the next step would be for the parents to bring the child to Carson's office for a face-to-face meeting. In this case, however, that wouldn't be practical, because the Spears family lived so far from Carson's midtown Manhattan office. So Carson suggested that they put together a package and send it to her. Included in the package should be a letter describing Britney in detail and explaining why Lynne and Jamie believed in Britney's commitment to becoming a professional performer; they also needed to send along any tapes or other materials that might give Carson a clear picture of what kind of talents Britney possessed. Carson would then decide if it was worthwhile to ask the family to make the trip to New York.

Lynne and Britney returned to Louisiana full of excitement and determination and Jamie set pen to paper. He wrote the letter to Nancy Carson, carefully explaining how singing and dancing were Britney's passions in life; he assured Carson that his daughter was enthusiastic and determined to pursue a professional career—she longed to see just how far she could take her dream. He added that they had initially thought Britney's future lay in gymnastics but finally realised that she really didn't have the same passion for gymnastics that she had for music. Jamie included a videotape with the submission and asked Carson to look at the material and share her opinion with them.

Carson annually receives hundreds of tapes like the five-song performance tape that the Spears family made for her, but she closely scrutinises each one. Production values mean nothing to her. She looks for talent that has the power to jump out and grab her. "The funny thing about the Britney tape was that it was only fifty-fifty," remembers Carson. "Half of it was not very good at all in terms of her performance, but the half that was good was very good—good in a way that I had not seen in a long time."

On the tape, Britney sang "Shine on Harvest Moon," then the difficult Johnnie Ray song "Cry." She followed this with "Somebody Loves Me," then "Nothing Compares 2 U," a Prince song that a favourite singer of Britney's, Sinéad O'Connor, had recorded brilliantly. The final song was "This Is My Moment."

Carson was impressed by one thing in particular: "[What] struck me dumb about this tape was that this little girl was not just singing, she was performing and not in a rehearsed, schooled kind of way, but a natural way. Her physicality was not practiced but a natural extension of how she was expressing the song—the way she moved her hands, the way she closed her eyes and emoted at the parts of the songs that needed it. She had a sophistication in the way she performed that was way beyond what I see in young girls."

And while the tape was rough and clearly shot by a nonprofessional, the choice of material allowed Britney to demonstrate all aspects of her repertoire. The selections showcased her vocal range, they showed how she could infuse a song with emotion and they highlighted her ability to dance and bounce around a stage while flawlessly carrying a tune. It was enough. As soon as she had finished viewing the tape, Carson picked up the phone and called the Spears home.

"I called and Lynne, who was very pregnant at the time, answered," she recalls. "I told her that what I had seen on the tape was wonderful and that I would love them to come to New York so we could meet and talk about what we could do together."

When Britney heard she was going to New York to meet with a legendary Broadway agent who specialised in making the dreams of young performers come true, she was ecstatic. But, even with all that she had accomplished in her short life, she didn't really have a clear idea of what she was getting into. Her first question on hearing the good news was, "Do they have cows in New York?"

Turning Pro

"Living in New York gives people real incentives to want things that nobody else wants."

–Andy Warhol

The elation the Spears clan felt at hearing that New York agent Nancy Carson was interested in representing Britney was tempered by the hard reality of their financial situation. There was no way in the world they could afford plane tickets to New York City, which would have run them over five hundred dollars each. So they began to scramble around looking for alternative modes of transportation.

According to a family friend from Kentwood, paying the bills "was no joke for them. Jamie wasn't working regular. He had to travel a lot to find contracts. He was not lazy, not at all, he is a good guy, and it was just that things really slowed down here. But I will tell you this: Jamie and Lynne would do anything for their kids. I mean, like, anything. A lot of people say that they pushed Britney into show business so they could have a better life, too, and maybe that was part of it, but they really made lots of personal sacrifices for her as well."

As Lynne explained in the VH1 documentary *Driven*, things were beyond just tight for them. "We would often have to rob Peter to pay Paul. And we were always late paying bills. It was very tough." Their telephone service was cut off due to non-payment. Their house began to fall into a state of disrepair and they couldn't afford to fix or replace anything. There were also, of course, Britney's singing and dancing lessons, transportation costs and school fees for both Britney and Bryan. Furthermore, Bryan had asthma and that meant doctor and pharmacy bills were piling up. In one frightening incident, Bryan had a seizure that was so serious he needed to be taken by air ambulance to a New Orleans hospital for emergency treatment. The airlift bill was added to the pile.

During this time, the family kept their spending to a bare minimum. Britney often had to wear hand-me-downs. But to Jamie and Lynne's credit, they shielded their children as much as they could from these difficulties. To add to the stress, they would soon have another mouth to feed.

Jamie and a pregnant Lynne decided to travel to New York with their children by train. The group soon grew to include Jamie's friend Hunter and Jamie's sister Jeanine and her little daughter, Tara. To conserve money in New York, all seven members of the traveling Britney clan shared a single hotel room and tried to walk everywhere instead of taking taxis. The weather was not ideal and they were often caught in the rain.

The first thing Jamie and Lynne did on arriving in New York was to take Britney to Nancy Carson's West 57th Street office. "I liked her right away," says Carson of Britney. "She was friendly, but very polite, always referring to me as 'Ma'am.' This was the little girl on the tape." Carson spent some time alone with Britney to confirm that this was *her* dream, *her* decision. "I spoke to her at length," Carson says. "You become almost like a psychologist when you do this long enough. You are not just looking at her and listening to her, you are looking beyond the words, you are trying to get a real sense of what this little person is on the way to becoming. Immediately with Britney I got the sense that she was not answering my questions with what she thought I wanted to hear or what her parents had told her to say. She was answering me very sincerely. I could see that performing and singing were something inside her. This was something innate, even though she was still just a young girl."

Carson was indeed interested in taking Britney on as a client, but she knew that Britney needed some training to turn her innate talent into something marketable. What Carson proposed was an intensive, several-months-long training camp to smooth the rough edges off Britney's technique and expose her to other young professional performers. She would no longer be just a cute little Southern ingenue; once she signed on with Carson, she would start preparing to earn a living through performing.

While Britney was very excited—hopping up and down—at the prospect of becoming a real-live performance artist, Carson saw that her parents were struggling with the implications of this. The proposed training regime would require Britney to move from small-town Louisiana to New York City. It had been enough of a financial hardship for the family to get themselves to New York for this one meeting. How would they manage a move to the Big Apple, even just for a short while? They were standing at a major fork in the road and they had to make a decision that would affect all of their lives drastically.

"I suggested that they go back to Louisiana and just think about it," says Carson. "But I also told them what I tell every parent I speak to about this kind of thing: Do not sell your lives out from under you to come to New York, because this is always a gamble and the odds are always long against you."

The family headed back to Kentwood after assuring Carson that they would think hard about everything and contact her very quickly with their decision. On April 9, 1991, however, almost immediately after their return, the Spears family's situation changed once again. Jamie Lynn, Britney's baby sister, was born and the family suddenly had other things to think about. Once life had settled down a bit, they thought long and hard about Britney's future. In early May, 1991, Lynne called Nancy Carson and told her that they weren't sure how, but they were going to do it; they were convinced that if they didn't, they would always wonder what might have happened and end up regretting their decision not to take that leap of faith when the opportunity presented itself. Lynne planned to recover from giving birth until the school year ended then bring Britney to New York for her summer of professional coaching.

Carson found an apartment for them to sublet and arranged voice lessons for Britney from an instructor named Gene McLaughlin. McLaughlin taught Britney how to control her voice better and how to use breathing methods to increase her power and resonance. "Gene was struck by how Britney could naturally belt out a song," says Carson. "He taught her how to use her muscles in her throat to project and to deepen her voice." Sadly, McLaughlin died of AIDS not long after training Britney.

Next, Carson set Britney up with another coach, Robert Marks, who specialised in presentation rather than inner vocal technique. Marks is blunt in his assessment of the young Britney:

"She could sing well, but she was not singing properly." But he emphasises that he never had a single problem with her. She was like a little pro from day one: she would always show up ready to work, she would have all the necessary materials and she would follow instructions without question.

Carson also arranged for Britney to work with Broadway dance choreographer Frank Hatchett. Hatchett ran the Broadway Dance Centre and was renowned for his innovation and his determination to create unique dance moves that projected and reinforced the musical number they accompanied. Initially, Britney was a bit intimidated by the powerful black man who shouted out instructions to her, but after a while she relaxed and began to soak up everything he said. Hatchett was impressed. "She was a tiny little thing," he recalls, "but she was a real dedicated little professional. She understood what the purpose of the lessons was, and she was determined to get better and better all the time." Hatchett's specialty was jazz, a particularly difficult and abstract form of dance that is highly interpretive and hard for most young children to master. But Britney took to it readily—she seemed to understand the connection between lyrics and music and dance movements.

Carson was very pleased with her progress. "She was like a little sponge," he remembers. "She picked up things very quickly, and over that first set of lessons and classes she made remarkable strides forward."

At the end of that first round of Britney's professional instruction, Carson had a video made of her performing. The contrast between that video and the one Lynne and Jamie Spears had submitted to Carson is remarkable. In the second video,

Britney, dressed in a little black swimsuit, dances and vamps her way around a studio singing an impressive version of the Whitney Houston hit "One Moment in Time." In a few short months, Britney had clearly progressed by leaps and bounds.

The next step, however, was to get Britney some professional experience. "One of the things that I key on when working with a child performer is motivation," says Carson. "Failure and disappointment are and always have been a part of every career in any facet of show business. When a performer gets knocked down, that is not important at all; what is important is that they get up and try again. If they can't do that, they will go nowhere." To give Britney and Lynne a little taste of that, she sent Britney out to audition for the massive Broadway hit musical *Les Misérables*. Britney tried her hardest during the audition and acquitted herself well, but she did not get the part.

To balance things out, Carson had Britney audition for a few jobs that she knew she could get—little gigs that would give Britney a taste of a professional working environment without heaping too much pressure on her too quickly. Britney did a walk-on in a syndicated version of the classic television show *Candid Camera* and had little parts in a car commercial and a barbecue sauce commercial. In August, she auditioned for the high-profile talent show *Star Search*, but she wasn't called back.

At the end of the summer of 1991, it was time for Britney to return with her mother to Kentwood. Before they left, Carson told them that she would continue to try to secure more auditions for Britney and that they should be prepared to return to New York almost at a moment's notice. The strain on the family was mounting, however. As much as Lynne and Jamie wanted success for Britney, this project was costing more than they had anticipated and their relationship was beginning to suffer. Due to the building financial pressure, the couple had begun to argue more and more frequently over money.

RUTHLESS

"Onstage, I'm the happiest person in the world."

–Britney Spears

It didn't take long for Carson to call Britney back to New York. A casting call had been announced for a fairly high-profile off-Broadway musical based on the classic four-time Oscar-nominated 1956 film *The Bad Seed*, about a family of psychopaths. The musical spoof of the original tells the story of an eight-year-old girl, Tina Denmark, who yearns for stardom. Desperate to play the lead in a school play, Tina is instead cast as a poodle named Puddles. She decides that the only way she can get what she wants is to murder the little girl who has won the lead role. When her crime is discovered, she is shipped off for treatment to the Daisy Clover School for Psychopathic Ingenues. When she is finally released from Daisy Clover, she heads for Hollywood.

The audition was an open one, meaning that no roles had been filled and the director, producers and choreographers would be looking at a legion of little girls to see which ones suited which parts. Carson wanted Britney to audition for this show. With her looks and abilities, there was every chance that she would be noticed and cast. Lynne and Jamie didn't hesitate—there was no question that Britney had to grab this chance. So, once again, they found themselves scrambling to come up with travel money and cheap accommodation in New York City.

The show had been renamed *Ruthless! The Musical* by the time the audition process began. Each young aspirant was asked to sing a song from the score called "I Was Born to Entertain." Even the ever-pragmatic Carson believed Britney had a shot at the lead—monstrous little blonde anti-angel Tina Denmark. But the producers thought otherwise. Even though she was seriously considered for one of the lesser roles, the producers felt that her lack of real stage experience weighed against her and they ultimately turned her down.

Dejectedly, Britney and Lynne returned to Kentwood. Once again, Britney had to explain to her friends at Parklane Academy what had happened in New York. Putting a brave face on it, she focused on the wonderful things that she had experienced rather than her failure to win the role. However, she didn't have to bear her disappointment for long. Within days, the girl chosen over Britney to fill the supporting role dropped out. The producer and director asked Nancy Carson if Britney could audition for the role again.

Girding themselves for yet another trek north, Lynne and Britney headed off to New York. This time Britney dazzled—so much so that not only was she offered the supporting role but she was also made understudy to the lead, Laura Bell Bundy.

It was both a moment of triumph and a moment of terror for Lynne. It was what they had been working so hard for, what they had been dreaming about, but it also meant that they had to make some momentous decisions almost immediately. Britney would have to relocate to New York, which would present all kinds of logistical problems. The family quickly decided that Britney,

Lynne, Jamie Lynn and a babysitter would move to New York City for the run of the show—and beyond, if necessary—leaving Jamie behind in Kentwood with Bryan.

When word of this got around Kentwood, reactions were mixed. Some people thought that it was a very cold thing for Lynne to do. One woman who worked at the local Walmart said, "When Lynne and Britney just up and moved to New York, it kind of raised some eyebrows around here. [Lynne] had a very young daughter who she was dragging off for this show business thing. It put quite a strain on Jamie, but he had lots of folks around him who cared very much about him and his family and were always willing to help out." Others, however, were completely supportive: "I thought it was awesome," said Britney's fourth-grade teacher, Darlene Hughes. "It would have been such a waste not to get to try with the talent that she had, especially since her mother was so supportive. When Lynne came to me and told me that she was taking Britney out of school and moving to New York to do a show, the first thing I did was put together a package of lessons for them so she could keep up with her studies."

Once again, financial issues weighed on Lynne and Jamie's minds. It helped that Britney would be earning a decent, but not spectacular, salary. They would use the money to live a semblance of a normal life in New York. Britney enrolled in the Professional Performing Arts School on West 48th Street. PPAS was founded in 1990 for children who wanted a career in the performing arts. It was a challenging environment for Britney. Virtually every child in the school had the same lofty ambitions she did; some came from show business families. Consequently, all shared similar experiences. For the first time, Britney was surrounded by her peers. On the downside, she was used to being the centre of attention—the only star around. At PPAS, she was just one very talented kid among many.

As Britney was learning her lines and getting ready for the premiere of *Ruthless!*, Carson called to tell her that the *Star Search* people had been in touch. They wanted her to perform in the junior section of the show. A quick check of her schedule revealed that Britney could fit in *Star Search* before *Ruthless!* began its run.

Star Search was a serious talent contest. A number of today's bright lights—including Beyoncé Knowles, Alanis Morrisette, Christina Aguilera and Justin Timberlake—made successful appearances on the show before they hit the big time. The host was Ed McMahon, the long-time sidekick of Johnny Carson on *The Tonight Show*. The show was structured as a head-to-head competition with seven categories, including male vocalist, female vocalist, vocal group and junior vocalist—the category in which Britney would compete. Two performers or groups of performers would do a routine and the winner would be invited back to compete against another performer, creating the kind of tension that would draw viewers back week after week.

As with all reality shows, a good deal of this tension was manufactured. It seemed like the competition went on for weeks, but it was actually shot over a few long days in a Los Angeles studio. Performers and their parents signed a nondisclosure agreement forbidding them to reveal the identity of the winner before the final show aired. While the airwaves are currently filled with shows like this, in the early 1990s, *Star Search* was the only one of its kind to draw such a huge audience. Nancy Carson had placed a number of her young clients on the show; even the losers benefited from the massive exposure.

In April 1992, Lynne and Britney Spears flew to Los Angeles for their first taste of Hollywood. Britney's main competitor in the junior vocalist category was another product of the rural South, a boy named Marty Thomas, who hailed from Missouri. (As it happened, Marty was also a student at PPAS.) Each contestant had to come equipped with enough songs and costumes to maintain the illusion that this was a weekly competition. For her debut appearance, Britney sang a tune called "I Don't Care," pouring everything she had into it. Afterwards, she awkwardly bantered with McMahon, who asked her if she had a boyfriend back home in Louisiana. She said she didn't. Then McMahon asked if he would be a suitable boyfriend for her. She looked embarrassed and sheepishly replied that she would have to think about it.

By the time Britney reached the final stage of the contest, she was flying high. Then the producers threw her a major curve. She was assigned the Grammy Award-winning "Love Can Build a Bridge" by the Judds to sing in the grand finale. But Britney was not familiar with that song, nor was she comfortable singing it. An upset Lynne urged the organisers to allow her to sing another song, but they refused. Lynne then called Nancy Carson in New York to ask what could be done. Carson said she would talk to the producers but that there was probably little she could do. In the end, Britney had to comply with the producers' choice.

The problem stemmed from the nature of the song itself. "Love Can Build a Bridge" is written from the point of view of someone who has experienced a good deal of life's pain. It would be extremely difficult for a ten-year-old girl to perform it in any real, meaningful way. Britney did her best, but the result was almost preordained: young Marty Thomas from Missouri ended up taking the big prize at the end of the show. Carson was upset because she felt the playing field had not been level—it almost seemed as though the finale had been rigged against Britney. As it happened, Carson represented Marty Thomas as well, but her disappointment for Britney was sincere.

Carson's reaction was nothing compared to the collective funk that Britney's loss caused in McComb and in Kentwood. Virtually every local television set had been tuned to *Star Search* for the entire run of the show. For years, Lynne Spears replied, "It just wasn't fair" when asked about the competition. Britney took the loss very hard, although it was hardly a loss at all: she had come second in a national talent show. She'd grown used to winning every talent competition she entered and she couldn't make the intellectual leap required to understand the huge difference between the Kentwood Dairy Festival and *Star Search*.

Marty Thomas hasn't risen to the heights that Britney Spears has, but his career is thriving—he recently appeared in the long-running Broadway hit *Wicked* and the musical *Xanadu*. Their shared *Star Search* experience had the interesting effect of bringing the Thomas and Spears families together. It's as though they had all lived through the same traumatic event. Marty was also appearing in an off-Broadway show—*The Secret Garden*—and after *Star Search*, his mother invited Britney and Lynne to share an apartment with them in the Strand at 10th Avenue and West 43rd Street.

Money was very tight. Although both Britney and Marty were

working off-Broadway, off-Broadway doesn't pay very much. Both children were earning just enough for their families to get by on. Interviewed for *Driven*, the VH1 documentary, Marty said, "We were just living off our boot strings. We lived in the littlest apartment. Britney didn't go out and play after class; she went to more classes. Sometimes she didn't get along with the other kids because they weren't as driven as she was."

On May 6, 1992, *Ruthless! The Musical* opened at the Players Theatre, an old, 248-seat MacDougal Street venue. That particular run of the play has become legendary and not just because it marked the off-Broadway debut of Britney Spears. A very young Natalie Portman was also featured and the star of the show, Laura Bell Bundy, made a lasting impression playing the little blonde demon. She went on to carve out a successful theatre career, appearing in, among others, the recent Broadway production of *Legally Blonde: The Musical*. In 2004, Bundy mounted a one-woman off-Broadway show called *Shameless! The Life and Times of Laura Bell Bundy*, in which she tells her own story by playing different characters: Judy Garland, Marilyn Monroe and . . . Britney Spears.

Playing the lead role in *Ruthless!* quickly got Bundy noticed and in the fall of 1992, she was offered a small part in a Disney film, *The Adventures of Huck Finn*. It paid fifteen times what she was making in the off-Broadway show, so she jumped at the opportunity. She left *Ruthless!* for just over two weeks and Britney, her understudy, took over the role of Tina Denmark during her absence.

Britney threw herself into the role with an almost excessive exuberance, but this was the perfect approach. Nancy Carson claims that she had refused to go to the play until Britney assumed the lead role because that was how she had envisioned her client's New York debut—as a star. She wasn't disappointed. "I thought she was great," Carson says. "It wasn't just me. Everyone in the audience thought she was great, too. She really displayed a wide range of her natural abilities in this production."

It was over almost before it began. After fifteen days, Britney had to return to her supporting role. This didn't sit well with her. She had enjoyed hearing the applause and commanding the stage—having everything centred on her. Now, waiting around to play her small part in every performance was starting to bore her. She was anxious to do something else. And Lynne was growing tired of New York City as well.

Just before Christmas, 1992, Laura Bell Bundy announced that Britney could take over the lead role again for a while, as she and her mother were returning to Kentucky for the holidays. But this time Britney was not so thrilled at the prospect. She missed her home and her brother and her father; Christmas wouldn't be Christmas without them. She, too, wanted to go home.

Lynne asked Nancy Carson to intercede. Was there any way she could get Britney out of the show so they could go home? They had been away too long. They were feeling lost. The routine drudgery of appearing in an off-Broadway show had set in; the initial excitement had worn off and Britney was tired. She was still a little girl and she had been working very hard. Carson was indeed able to negotiate Britney's way out of the show and Britney, Lynne and Jamie Lynn headed south to Kentwood.

MICKEY MOUSE CALLS

"I want to be an artist that everyone can relate to, one that's young, happy and fun."

–Britney Spears

Four years after launching *The All New Mickey Mouse Club* (now simply called *MMC*), casting director Matt Casella was again on the hunt for talented kids to join the Mouseketeers. Some cast members were now in their late teens and needed to be replaced. Starting in L.A., Casella worked his way across the country. By the time he arrived in New York, he had seen and evaluated almost twenty thousand hopefuls.

One of the first people he called when he got to the Big Apple was his friend Nancy Carson. He asked her if she had any standouts he might see before he waded into another sea of starry-eyed, but mostly untrained, aspirants. Her response was immediate: "What about Britney?" After all this time, Casella needed to have his memory refreshed, but as soon as he recalled Britney he got very excited. "I told Matt that Britney was not the diamond-in-the-rough little girl who had grabbed his attention a few years before," says Carson. "I told him that she was grown up, had a lot of training under her belt and had some professional stage experience." Now, with Britney's image clear in his mind, Casella realised he'd seen her on *Star Search*. He told Carson he wanted to meet with the eleven-year-old right away. She put in a call to Kentwood and asked Jamie, Lynne and Britney if they were ready to go on another adventure—possibly the adventure of a lifetime. They could hardly say no.

The auditions were structured a bit differently this time around. Casella and his team were, as always, looking for kids who had charisma and looks and singing and dancing talent, but they were also on the lookout for kids who could tell a story on camera. The initial crop of Mouseketeers had included a couple of very talented singers and dancers who could not speak coherently on camera. Since *MMC* was a variety show, this was unacceptable.

The Spears troupe returned to New York for the audition. "I recognised Britney, of course," says Casella. "She was still the tiny little cutie with the lovely manners. But this time she had a confidence about her—the confidence a good performer gets when they have some experience and know that they can get it done when given the chance."

Britney sang "Running Back to You," a Vanessa Williams hit and she followed it with a highly energetic dance routine that was technically spot-on. She finished by telling the assembled adults a story called "The Tooth Fairy." She had clearly blown away Casella and his team. Britney, Lynne and Nancy Carson were very excited. They had a collective feeling that this was it: Britney had finally broken through. But their excitement was muted by the announcement that, while Britney had been fantastic, the final casting decision would be made by higher-ups in the Magic Kingdom. Casella said he was certainly going to endorse Britney, but it would be weeks before the Disney brass could view all the finalists' tapes and make their choices.

Whenever the Spears family came to New York, Carson tried to maximise their time by arranging other auditions or readings for Britney besides the one she had been specifically summoned for. So, after the *MMC* audition, Britney met with the producers of the 1995 film *Gordy*, about a talking pig in search of his missing family. When Britney was eventually offered a role in the film, though, she turned it down. This was probably a good move, since another talking-pig movie appeared the same year—the Australian megahit *Babe*—which would consign *Gordy* to cinematic oblivion. Although the money Britney would have earned from the role would have been a godsend, the family decided to take a gamble and keep her schedule open in case a call came in from Disney.

The call came. "Britney was selected out of the thousands who auditioned to be in the final twenty-three," emphasises Carson. "But that meant more auditioning. Only six of the twenty-three would be selected." The next round of *MMC* auditions would take place in Orlando, Florida—an exhaustive, three-day process. Those vying for a spot would be evaluated in six different categories on a scale of 1 to 10. One of the categories was appearance and because Britney was smaller than average, she was docked a point going in. Among the young stars to be she was up against were no less than Justin Timberlake, Jessica Simpson and Christina Aguilera.

The star of the three-day event was Aguilera. Her booming voice was already developed and she received the highest score of anyone for her singing. Aguilera's complete domination of the singing category led a young Jessica Simpson, who was slated to perform right after her, to demand that she be allowed to sing later in the program. She knew she could never match Aguilera's prowess and was afraid of underscoring the comparison by coming right on Aguilera's heels. When her demand was not met, Simpson had an onstage meltdown and walked off.

Britney scored high—the highest of all, once everyone's scores were tallied. She received an 8 for appearance, 8.5 for on-camera persona, 8.5 for dance, 8.5 for vocals, 8.5 for acting and 8.5 for personality. The contestants were sent home to await the casting decision. The Spears clan returned to Kentwood and Britney resumed her studies at Parklane Academy. She came home from school a few days later to find her mother on the phone with Nancy Carson. There was some good news. "It is always wonderful to call a family and a young person with good news," says Carson. "So much more often it goes the other way, and the news is disappointing. So this was a pleasure, a wonderful day."

Britney had made the cut. She was invited to join the cast of Disney Channel's *The All New Mickey Mouse Club*. Lynne was thrilled and thanked Carson profusely. She hung up the phone and told Britney that she was now a Mouseketeer. Breaking her professional demeanour for once, Britney squealed, jumped up and down and ran around the house screaming that she was so excited she could hardly stand it.

Lynne told the news to anyone in town who would listen—which was virtually everyone. The reaction was swift and a bit fanciful. The Town of Kentwood decided to throw Britney and her family a little going-away party. April 24, 1993, was officially declared Britney Spears Day and the declaration came with an official proclamation:

WHEREAS, this year for the first time, the State of Louisiana has had a participant chosen, and she is one of ours, we have watched her grow and watched her talents mature and have seen her performances given with such warmth and noticeable enjoyment and,

WHEREAS, the people of Kentwood and the surrounding area wish to give tribute to this well-deserving young lady as she continues her work in Orlando, Florida,

NOW THEREFORE, I, Bobby Gill, Mayor of the Town of Kentwood, do hereby proclaim, Saturday, April 24, 1993,

BRITNEY SPEARS DAY

Residents of Kentwood and the surrounding area were invited to come on down and "applaud Britney's accomplishments and wish her great things as she takes this next step in her promising career."

The day was filled with celebrations. Local businesses and many homeowners posted good-luck messages in their windows or on their porches. At the Kentwood Lions Club ballpark, the Little League team formed a kind of honour guard and presented Britney with a cake. She took to a makeshift stage to thank everyone and belt out an animated rendition of Whitney Houston's "I Will Always Love You." It was a special day for all involved. And it looked like the Spears family was about to get a reprieve from the financial hardship they had endured for so long, thanks to the hard work of an eleven-year-old girl.

The family published a thank-you letter addressed to the mayor and the people of Kentwood expressing their heartfelt appreciation:

Dear Kentwood,

Britney has many memorable moments to remember in her short, little life.
But April 24 has to be the most sentimental yet. It's so exciting to have these new experiences but what makes it so wonderful is to have so many loved ones that you can share them with.

Thank you Kentwood for your support and encouragement.

We love you.

The Britney Spears Family

Lynne, Britney and one-year-old Jamie Lynn soon left for Orlando, where Britney's new adventure would begin. Jamie and Bryan, as usual, stayed behind. Bryan, now sixteen, was still attending Parklane Academy, where he was a popular athlete and Jamie continued to pick up work wherever he could.

The family had waited a long time for this. They had done without to help Britney attain her dream, a dream they all shared. Now it looked as if their sacrifice was going to pay off. After years of struggle, relief was in sight. Yet in one sense their struggles were just beginning.

MMC

"All our dreams can come true,
if we have the courage to pursue them."
"If you can dream it, you can do it."
"It is kind of fun to do the impossible."
　　　　　　　　　　　　　　　　–Walt Disney

At the end of April, 1993, Britney, Lynne and Jamie Lynn moved into an apartment at a Disney-owned property in Kissimmee, just south of Orlando. *The All New Mickey Mouse Club*, taped at the Disney-MGM Studios theme park (now Disney's Hollywood Studios), was on a six-month production schedule, from May through October.

At the first production meeting, the fledgling cast members and their parents met with Disney executive producer Dennis Steinmetz. The class list of that 1993 group of Mouseketeers, who beamed up at Steinmetz that day with excited faces, contained a pantheon of contemporary American entertainment figures: Christina Aguilera, Justin Timberlake, Ryan Gosling, Nikki DeLoach and of course, Britney Spears. Then aged eleven or twelve, they all sat expectantly waiting for Steinmetz to speak.

He started, surprisingly, by talking about school. He told everyone that the three-hour-per-day, fifteen-hour-per-week tutoring schedule had to be adhered to without question or exception. This was not just the law; it was Disney policy.

Furthermore, Disney expected parents to have their child's school provide a curriculum for additional home schooling. There was an intentional sternness to Steinmetz's message—he wanted it to be taken very seriously. He told the children that inspectors from the local education board would be stopping by without warning to check on how they were doing. He warned that if it was discovered that a cast member was falling behind or neglecting his or her studies then "that man right there"— Steinmetz pointed to a bespectacled man standing quietly to one side—"will tell me if you will be performing on this show or not." The man was Chuck Yerger, an educator who has made a career of tutoring professional child performers.

One of Yerger's first pupils was Shane Culkin, whom Yerger had tutored in 1991 while Shane's brother Macaulay was shooting the film *My Girl* on location in Orlando. After a short stint at Nickelodeon, Yerger moved to Disney, where he was effectively running what everyone informally called "the Disney School." "It is not as easy a job as one might think," says Yerger. "One of the toughest logistical parts of it is coordinating all the different schedules the kids are on and trying to make sure you keep in mind how tired or jacked up with excitement they might be. This is, like, hyper-teaching."

All the schooling took place in a little bungalow near the set. However, while the Disney people made a great show of being strict about educating the Mouseketeers and other child performers, their standards weren't very high. Britney scored straight As in social studies, English, math and history—but so did virtually everyone else. "You showed up, you got As," says Ryan Gosling. "The lessons seemed very easy, like a grade or two below our ages."

Which is not to say it was a sham. Schooling was important to Disney and Yerger, whom ex-Mouseketeer Tony Lucca dubbed "the Mouseketutor," was a firm and disciplined instructor. Yerger remembers that Britney stood out among the Mouseketeers because she was so . . . normal. "It was pretty tough not to notice Britney. She showed up for the first lessons with a fresh face, bubbling smile, lots of manners and holding hands with a little toddler [Jamie Lynn] . . . When I think back on it, I remember her being very professional when she was working, but when she was in class she was just this wholesome, lovely, lovable little girl that you just wanted to hug all the time."

Former *MMC* choreographer and director Sarah Elgart remembers, "Britney really took a liking to the Ernest Hemingway book *The Old Man and the Sea*. They were all required to read that book for class. She would carry it around and want to talk about it. She really seemed to get it and it moved her and touched her. I thought that was very interesting."

While the new crop of Mouseketeers was going through orientation, the older members of the troupe were recording a cast album called *The All New Mickey Mouse Club*—which, unfortunately, ended up being a very embarrassing and awkward attempt at white-bread rap. When production began in earnest, the directors had to create segments or sequences that would highlight each child's natural gifts and mesh the talents of the newer Mouseketeers with those of the older ones.

During early rehearsals and filming, Britney quickly established herself as the dancer of the new group. She could often be found in the rehearsal building trying out new moves. If the director and choreographer thought something was too complicated for her she would practice until she got it right. Elgart was impressed by her professionalism: "It was quite incredible. She would be in the rehearsal building trying out a new routine, then she would be on the set shooting and recording a half hour later."

* * *

A typical day for most of the Mouseketeers began when the cast van picked them up and delivered them to the bungalow for their lessons with Chuck Yerger. Others came by car to Disney-MGM Studios, where there was a special parking lot reserved for Mouseketeers and their families. After lessons and a bit of discussion about what they would be working on in the studio that afternoon, the entire cast would gather to have lunch together. This lunch tradition was started back in the days of the original *Mickey Mouse Club* because Disney felt that the children would perform better as a team if they ate together every day. After lunch, it was time to rehearse and then go to hair and make-up. Shooting would start between 3:30 and 3:45. Filming would last, in accordance with child labor laws, for three solid hours before a wrap was called; then it was back to the dressing room to remove make-up and costumes before returning home. The children put in five twelve-hour days a week.

Like the original *Mickey Mouse Club*, MMC was designed to reflect an old-fashioned, wholesome vision of America. Each episode began with the Mouseketeers rushing out to greet the audience over the theme music. Then three or four of them would sit at the edge of the set while the rest of the troupe dashed off to change for the first sequence. The seated Mouseketeers would tell the audience what was coming up on the show, then one of them would beam into the camera and kick things off by saying, for example: "Hi, I'm Britney! Welcome to the *Mickey Mouse Club.*"

Each day had a theme. Monday was music day and the focus would be on presenting musical numbers and creating and playing music; a young pop star or group would often be invited to appear. Tuesday was guest day; someone with an unusual background or an interesting experience to share would be invited. Wednesday was designated anything-can-happen day; Thursday was party day; and Friday was Hall of Fame day, when children with special talents or gifts would come on the show and be inducted into the Mickey Mouse Club Hall of Fame. And, of course, each episode would end with the entire cast holding hands and singing the iconic Mickey Mouse Club song: "M.I.C. See you real soon. K.E.Y. Why? Because we like you! M.O.U.S.E."

* * *

Disney took audience reactions to their products very seriously. *MMC* fan mail was answered (by staffers, not by cast members themselves—Mouseketeers were never shown the fan mail they received or even told how much there was) and used to determine which cast members should be given more airtime. As letters started pouring in praising Britney's dance skills, she was gradually given more dancing to do on the show. At Disney, the thinking was that a happy fan was a fan who would keep tuning in to the show and who would also buy products related to the show. The Mouseketeers weren't just hired hands, they were also part of an image Disney wanted to project, so the company spent a lot of time coaching them on how to court the public, how to behave, how to react to fans, even how to smile for maximum effectiveness (drop the lower lip and show as many teeth as possible and give your head a little toss when you smile to indicate enthusiasm and sincerity).

"The thinking was that whenever we were out in public, we were carrying the Disney flag," says Gosling. "They really wanted to make sure that we represented what they wanted projected— it was part of the deal going in." Disney PR professionals taught the young stars the proper way to answer interview questions. "When you're a kid, you think that is all just part of the job," Gosling explains. "We were told to stick to a simple set of answers and smile a lot. We all came off sounding like little boring robots, but that was the way they seemed to want it."

The image-making was constant. *Teen Beat* magazine occasionally published mini profiles of the more popular Mouseketeers, sharing such insights with its readers as Justin Timberlake likes chocolate-chip ice cream, or Christina Aguilera's favourite colour is turquoise. Britney's first *Teen Beat* profile revealed that her favourite singer is Whitney Houston, the best day of her life was the day she found out she had become a Mouseketeer, her favourite actors are Demi Moore and Tom Cruise and, oddly, her favourite movie is the violent thriller *The Hand that Rocks the Cradle*. Her movie pick might seem out of keeping with the wholesome image that the Disney PR team had cultivated for her, until you realise that the Curtis Hanson-directed film was produced by Hollywood Pictures, a Disney-owned company that made adult-themed films that Disney felt uncomfortable marketing under its own name.

* * *

It soon became clear that Britney's Southern-belle innocence and overall likeability had made her a favourite with the show's producers. Furthermore, she and Christina Aguilera were the show's hot new singers. But while Britney was wholesome, Christina was a dazzler. Her voice, which was a bit odd and very mature-sounding for one so young, earned her the nickname "Mariah" from *MMC's* singing coach, the late Robin Wiley (who died of cancer in 2006 at the age of forty-five). Known affectionately on-set as "Wiley Coyote," Wiley is legendary among *MMC* alumni for having helped to launch so many careers—in particular, that of Justin Timberlake and his band 'N Sync, for whom Wiley became lead vocal arranger after *MMC* was cancelled.

Wiley wanted her young charges to know that she took them seriously. She conducted her coaching sessions in a trailer that was located away from the main studio. The trailer was nothing luxurious: it was equipped with an electronic keyboard and a tape recorder and there was a small area where students could stand. They were there to get their voices into shape, nothing more. Wiley was also a recording artist and she had a smoky voice, so she naturally focused in on Christina, whose voice was the strongest and most distinctive. But she also recognised a steady improvement in Britney that was based in equal parts on natural talent and hard work.

Among the older Mouseketeers, it was Keri Russell whom Britney came to know best that first year. Sixteen-year-old Keri was often asked to babysit Britney and Jamie Lynn and Britney came to look up to her. The two would often go shopping together and for drives in Keri's car. When asked in a 2002 interview about her friendship with Keri Russell, Britney said, "I idolised Keri a lot. I wished I had her long beautiful curly hair. I wanted to look like her, I wanted to be her." Keri became her confidante, but that ended when the *MMC* season concluded and Russell left for L.A. to pursue her burgeoning movie career. Later, Russell would land the lead in the TV series *Felicity*.

* * *

The 1993 season of *MMC* wrapped in October, after they had shot fifty-five episodes. Between seasons, cast members were free to do what they wanted—within the confines of their contracts. Britney, Lynne and Jamie Lynn returned to Kentwood for a six-month breather. Back home, though, there was some adjusting to be done. First of all, Britney's *MMC* episodes were only just beginning to be aired. The Disney Channel was only available on cable and most people in the Kentwood-McComb area weren't subscribers. So Britney found that her homecoming was not really like that of a conquering hero—it was more like she'd just come back to town after another professional absence in some big city somewhere.

The second adjustment that Britney and her family had to make was that at the age of eleven, Britney had become the family breadwinner. Jamie was still struggling to find work without much success. Most of the jobs he did find were out of town—as far away as Jackson, Mississippi—which meant that he had to leave sixteen-year-old Bryan to fend for himself. All of this was hard for Jamie and it was hard for Lynne and Britney, who had become accustomed to a more cushy life in Orlando. During Britney's free time, she and Lynne would often go shopping at the kind of stores they could only dream about back in Kentwood. So everyone in the Spears home was a bit uncomfortable and generally felt that the start of the second season of *MMC* could not come fast enough.

BACK IN KENTWOOD

"When I'm offstage, I'm just like everybody else."
–Britney Spears

Britney was no longer a Mouseketeer. In June 1994, after the *MMC* wrapped for good, she returned to Kentwood and took a well-earned break. She spent the summer at home, for once, living the life of an average Southern girl transitioning from her preteen years to that hormone-wracked stage of life known as adolescence. The dream was not forgotten, but it was on hold. Lynne called Nancy Carson in New York and put her to work finding auditions for Britney. She regularly asked Carson what they could do to "get things moving again," but the answer was always the same: "Keep positive and be patient."

Weeks, then months rolled by. In the fall, Britney returned to Parklane Academy. Lynne went back to work as a second-grade teacher at Silver Creek Elementary. With her career apparently on hold, Britney went three times a week to New Orleans to practise with a professional dance troupe, but her singing languished. Aside from singing at the occasional wedding or sporting event, she did not perform publicly.

Lynne had heard about a hotshot New York entertainment lawyer named Larry Rudolph whose firm, Rudolph and Beer, specialised in representing and managing young recording artists. Soon after *MMC* was cancelled, Lynne, Jamie, Jamie Lynn and Britney went to New York to meet with Rudolph. The lawyer saw something in Britney and agreed to represent her, but for a long time nothing happened. Lynne and Jamie often called Rudolph to check, but there was never any news.

It was a giant letdown. Before Britney joined the *MMC* cast, very few people in the Kentwood-McComb area had cable TV; once their local success story started to appear on the show, many had signed on so that they could watch her shine. Cable subscriptions soared. Two towns in two states had claimed Britney as their own. Now it seemed she was back permanently because her prospects had all dried up.

Gradually, Britney became a normal teenager. Her *MMC* memories faded and she became interested in other things—including, eventually, boys. She progressed from grade 7 to grade 8 and sometime that year, perhaps due to her lingering celebrity status, she attracted the attention of Mason Statham, a popular boy who was a year older than she and who had been unofficially dubbed "most handsome boy in school." To Mason, Britney may have just been another date, but to Britney, Mason was a first taste of that glorious agony called love. For several weeks, they went to school dances, to the movies and out for dinner at the local Ruby Tuesday restaurant, where to this day a photo of the couple adorns the wall with the caption "The Beauty and Beau."

Then they shared their first romantic kiss. It was just a chaste goodnight kiss, but, like all girls with their first kiss, Britney remembers it well. Shortly afterwards, it became clear that Mason had lost interest in her. "He didn't say two words to me," she recalls. "I started wondering if I did something wrong. I started analysing myself and of course you get over that kind of thing, but you sure beat yourself up over it."

As it happened, Mason had a sister who had just broken up with a friend of Britney's brother, Bryan. Reg Jones was a year younger than Bryan and was his teammate on the Parklane football team. Each held a glory position: Bryan was the quarterback and Reg was his favourite wide receiver. Reg came from one of the area's most successful families. He lived in a mansion and his father, Reginald Sr., was a lawyer who then became a judge one town over, in Liberty, Mississippi. His mother was a well-known artist and his stepfather was a successful doctor.

Reg had been hanging out with Bryan for a couple of years and the family knew him well. One day, Lynne Spears stopped to chat with Reg when she ran into him at the local Blockbuster Video store. In the course of their conversation, she casually asked Reg whom he was dating at the moment. Reg explained that he was on the prowl, as it were, having just broken up with Stacey Statham. Lynne mentioned that Britney had a rather serious crush on him. Did he know that? Reg didn't know what to make of this. He was seventeen and in his junior year at Parklane. Britney was just fourteen and in eighth grade, junior high, not even high school. Lynne, of course, knew that a seventeen-year-old jock wouldn't be looking to date a fourteen-year-old girl, but she still insisted that Britney was interested and that they would make a fabulous couple.

A few weeks passed. The 1995-96 school year was drawing to a close and Reg found himself without a date for the big end-of-school-year dance. Two of his friends, David Simmons and Wes

Holmes, had invited girls they had recently started dating. By sheer coincidence, one of the girls was Britney's cousin and the other was her best friend at Parklane. The idea of dating Britney suddenly didn't make Reg feel so uncomfortable. "A couple of the guys were dating girls a bit younger than they were and they seemed to be okay with it," said Reg. "So I thought, yeah, this will be fun, all of us hanging out together." When his sister mentioned that another boy was getting ready to ask Britney to the dance, Reg took the bait.

The next day, he stopped Britney outside the gym and asked her if she would like to go to the dance with him. More importantly, like the Southern gentleman he was, he asked if her dad would allow it. Britney recalled the moment for a journalist many years later: "I told him that I would love to go with him—he was a great guy—but I did need to ask my father. But I pretty much knew that he would be okay with it. It was all real exciting."

Britney duly sought her dad's permission, but Jamie had already been briefed by Lynne, of course, so there was no chance of him saying no. But the Southern way had to be followed. Jamie sent word to Reg that he wanted him to come and discuss the matter with him personally. Jamie was then working as a cook at his grandmother's restaurant, Granny's Seafood Deli, in McComb. Reg went there to find Jamie, but he wasn't worried: "I knew him, I had known him for a few years, so I wasn't scared of him or anything. I was okay with going to talk to him."

While shucking crawfish, Jamie explained to Reg that Britney was his little baby girl and if he allowed Reg to take her out that meant his baby girl's safety and well-being would be in Reg's hands. Jamie wanted to make sure that Reg accepted the responsibility. "I told him that of course I understood," says Reg, "and I certainly respected what he was saying to me, but I did find it kind of odd that we were having such a long and deep discussion about simply asking Britney out to a dance."

Then it was big brother's turn. "[Bryan] said he wanted to talk to me about dating his sister," remembers Reg. "I told him there was nothing to really talk about; him and me was friends, so he could trust that I would treat his sister right without needing to say anything about it." Reg says that despite all these social formalities, he and Britney had been "building up to something, because I knew she had a crush on me. I finally pursued that crush and we just fell right on into each other. It was fireworks right from the beginning right on to the end."

Reg and Britney saw each other a couple of times before the big dance. The first time, Reg picked up a couple of movies at Blockbuster and went over to the Spears home for dinner. "Miss Lynne," as Reg always called her, made a wonderful dinner of salmon and stuffed bell peppers. Then they made popcorn and all sat around the living room and watched movies together like a big family.

Reg and Britney continued to date over the summer and were an established couple by the time school began in the fall. It was during the fall term that Britney took her first driving test. In Mississippi, one can get a learner's permit at fourteen and a half. Britney failed on her first attempt, however and she was embarrassed and angry with herself. (She would get her permit later, when she was fifteen, in Louisiana.) To make her feel better, Reg sent her a bunch of flowers with a sweet and supportive note that concluded with the words "I love you." The following

Friday, after a football game, Britney and Reg were walking to the swimming pool when Britney stopped and threw her arms around Reg. She told him she hadn't thanked him properly for the flowers and the sweet words. Then she planted a heartfelt kiss on his lips. Recalling the moment, Reg says, "It was one sweet, sweet kiss."

Just before homecoming weekend, the football team chose the homecoming maids. Each starting player drew a name out of a hat. The name he chose would be his escort onto the field at the game. Reg, perhaps unsurprisingly, picked Britney's name and as they walked onto the field together that Saturday afternoon, there was a lot of chatter about how wonderful they looked as a couple.

On the night of the big homecoming dance, Britney got ready at her best friend Erin's house, while Reg and Erin's boyfriend, Wes, got dressed at Reg's house in McComb. Britney wore a simple black dress that made her look older than she was. When the guys arrived to pick up their dates, Erin's father told them that they had to have the girls home no later than 1:00 a.m. It was considered a big deal that girls of this age were going out with older guys. It's a Southern tradition that girls under fifteen are always chaperoned on dates. Tradition was dispensed with in this case, but the boys, mindful of propriety, had the girls home ahead of schedule. There was nothing remarkable about the evening— everything was very chaste. A little peck on the cheek was all that occurred when they parted company.

But appearances can be deceiving. According to Reg, it was sometime during this period that Britney, still shy of her fifteenth birthday, lost her virginity to him. This is disputed by her family, but he is quite clear about it. Their public image, however, remained pure. The two spent more and more time together, becoming inseparable. Within a year of when they'd started dating, Britney was the only person Reg wanted to see. He was not hanging out with his pals and not partying with his football and basketball teammates. Each morning, he would pick Britney up and drive her to school.

After almost a year of dating, Britney started telling Reg that she wished they could just go off and get married. Reg was more cautious. He reassured her that he felt the same way and was madly in love with her, but he reminded her that she was still just fifteen years old. They simply could not get married right now and they should probably not talk about it so much.

Lynne would no doubt have agreed with him. As happy as she was at having snagged such a good catch for Britney, she retained strict control over the relationship to ensure that nothing untoward happened that might damage Britney's career prospects. She was vigilant and highly reactive. One day, Reg and Britney were at the Spears home listening to a new CD. "We were just sitting around listening to the music," Reg remembers. "We were kissing a bit, but there was nothing happening beyond that." They were making noise, though and, hearing them giggling, Lynne burst into the room. "What are you two doing?" she demanded. "Nothing," was the truthful response. "Well this don't look good and I don't like it one bit!" Lynne bellowed. Britney protested that they were fully dressed with all buttons done up, so there was no reason to be upset, but Lynne would have none of it. She ordered them to move to the family room, where they could be watched. Naturally, they complied.

Reg graduated from Parklane in the spring of 1997 and to celebrate took a road trip to Vail, Colorado. The trip was organised by Reg's mother, Gay, who went along and Britney was allowed to go with them. They stayed in a rented condominium. It started out as a fun, romantic getaway. Reg and Britney played together in the pool and took long strolls through the picturesque town of Vail. Then, about halfway through the trip, Reg got a bad case of food poisoning and had to spend the rest of the time in bed in agonising pain. "I was deathly ill," he recalls. "But Britney stuck by me the whole time. She never left the condo except to go shopping. One day, she brought me back some boxer shorts and a very cool shirt. She would just lay with me in the bed and hold the garbage pail for me when I was heaving up into it. That made me feel real good."

Britney clearly took their love affair very seriously. It may have been a teen romance, but she had been working with adults and living up to adult expectations for a number of years. She had so far led a driven, focused life and she approached her relationship with Reg with characteristic intensity. To her it was—it had to be—a torrid, grown-up relationship, albeit minus (maybe) the sexual component. They were always together; they took care of each other. "We would say 'I love you' all the time to each other and we meant it," says Reg. He gave her a ring and a necklace and she was always at his football games, cheering him on. It put everything else out of her mind. One very cold game night Britney stood, as usual, on the fifty-yard line yelling encouragement to Reg. Gay saw that Britney was shivering with the cold, so she ran home to get a fur coat. There she was, recalls Reg proudly, "the only girl in the stadium wrapped up head to toe in a fur coat and she was all mine."

* * *

When one year and then another passed without movement in Britney's career, people in McComb and Kentwood concluded that maybe young Britney had had her fill of show business. She had seen her childhood dream come true and now she had returned to a more normal and balanced existence. But nothing could have been further from the truth. Britney still harboured a burning desire to be a star and the older she got, the more she understood what that would mean: it would make her distinct and special. Lynne couldn't let go of the dream either. She was constantly on Britney to keep moving forward, to keep her eye on the big prize.

In her book, *Heart to Heart*, Lynne describes the move back to Kentwood as a "comedown." She insists that Britney no longer felt that she belonged in Kentwood, that she had gotten used to working hard and meeting challenges, so Kentwood held no inspiration for her. So she said. But Britney was almost certainly conflicted about it. Part of her was content to be immersed in the familiar and comfortable environment of Kentwood, to be like everyone else; she was happy to have a regular boyfriend, to hang out with friends, to relax, to do whatever she wanted whenever she wanted. The other part of her was filled with ambition. She loved performing, being a star; she'd had a taste of it and she wanted more. Lynne, so driven and ambitious herself, was fighting to bring that part of her daughter into focus.

The two had always been very close and open with each other, but as Britney entered further into her teens, she began acting more independent and Lynne worried that her daughter would not rise to meet her expectations. A major bone of contention was that Britney had taken up smoking. Lynne was furious about this. She would reprimand Britney, telling her that smoking would damage her voice and make her look trashy. It all came to a head when Britney was caught smoking with a couple of friends in the school washroom. Lynne was called in to discuss disciplinary measures and it sent her over the top. Whether it was due to the fact that Britney was smoking in the first place or that she had broken the rules that her mother had laid down for her is an open question, but Lynne became convinced that she could no longer trust Britney.

This led to a few incidents. One morning, Lynne, driving to work, saw Britney smoking a cigarette as she waited for Reg to pick her up. She screeched to a halt and jumped out of the car to confront Britney. According to Reg, "She had a right fit on Britney," screaming at her in public. Another time, Britney was driving with Lynne beside her in the passenger seat along Highway 51 just outside of Kentwood when they got into yet another argument over Britney's smoking. Lynne demanded to sniff Britney's fingers to see if she could smell cigarettes. Britney, hands on the steering wheel, refused. Lynne became even angrier. She reached over, grabbed Britney's right wrist and pulled her hand from the wheel. Britney lost control of the car. They went into a spin and slid into a ditch. Neither was hurt in the mishap. Lynne had detected no lingering scent of cigarettes on Britney's fingers.

In the fall of 1997, Reg left for Southwest Mississippi Community College to continue his education. Soon, word got back to Britney that Reg was stepping out on her. Her reaction was not to nurse her pain but to retaliate. She started to cosy up to other guys and made sure the news got back to Reg, who, in turn, was hurt and angry.

According to Reg, there were two guys Britney "was going out with or doing whatever with, just to play games with me." One was Corey Butler, a boy in her grade. The other was Jason Alexander, whom Britney had known since they were in daycare together. Anger had turned Britney into a manipulator who felt no qualms about using her love struck guy friends to strike back at her boyfriend then sending Reg cute little notes adorned with smiley faces apologising for hurting him.

On top of all this, Lynne had also begun to cause problems between Britney and Reg. She loved that Reg was a good catch— he lived in a house so big that there were elevators to take you from floor to floor—but she was unsettled by the fact that the two had been spending every minute they could together and were talking about marriage. She and Britney argued often about Reg. Lynne had married and had children young and her life had been radically altered by it. She saw Britney heading down the same road and was determined to do everything in her power to stop her. She declared that if Britney and Reg's relationship was going to continue, then they would have to play according to her rules.

Lynne set to work to put Britney's career back on track. The first step was to take Britney out of Parklane and start home-schooling her. For all intents and purposes, this marked the end of Britney's formal education, even though she had only completed grade 9. The next step was to re-establish Britney's links to the show-business world. Fate intervened to help her out.

ALL THAT JIVE

"I can't sing the same thing all the time. That would bore me."
                                                    –Britney Spears

Not all the Mouseketeers had left Orlando. Justin Timberlake had stayed on to pursue his singing career. In late 1995, a year after *MMC* ended, he was contacted by now-notorious entrepreneur Lou Pearlman, who wanted him to join a fledgling boy band called 'N Sync. Pearlman had already struck gold with the Backstreet Boys and was looking to do it again. Justin accepted the offer and convinced Pearlman to take on fellow ex-Mouseketeer Joshua Scott (JC) Chasez as well. By late 1997, 'N Sync had hit big in Europe and were preparing to release their first U.S. album.

Then Justin's mother, Lynn Harless, had an idea. A girl band from England, the Spice Girls, had just scored a major chart success in North America with their tune "Wannabe." Harless went to Pearlman and pitched him the idea of putting together a female version of 'N Sync—an all-American version of the Spice Girls.

Pearlman, busy with the Backstreet Boys and 'N Sync, didn't have time to organise it. He liked the idea, however, so he suggested to Lynn that she pull it together herself. Once she had a group of girls and could show him something, he would decide whether he wanted to underwrite the project.

Inspired, perhaps, by her son's success and certainly motivated by the prospect of making a good deal of money herself, Lynn went to work. She turned first to her connections with proven talent: former *Mickey Mouse Club* cast members. Nikki DeLoach, who had been a pal of Britney and Christina Aguilera on the show, was still in Orlando as well; she was the girlfriend of 'N Sync member JC. Lynn approached her first. Nikki loved the idea. By this point, word was circulating that Britney Spears was looking for work, so Lynn Harless called Lynne Spears. Lynne Spears was intrigued by the idea and they set up a meeting at the Harless's home near Memphis, Tennessee. When Lynne and Britney arrived, they found Nikki DeLoach there, along with three other excited young singers whom Harless had selected: Amanda Latona, Danay Ferrer and Mandy Ashford. The enthusiasm among them for the project was palpable. Everyone seemed to be on the same page. The girls got dressed up and posed for pictures together as a group and then they posed for a few more with the members of 'N Sync. Britney had the chance to renew her friendship with Justin, who was now all decked out as a pop star with cropped, dyed-blonde hair.

So the girl band Innosense was born and with Lou Pearlman's money backing the venture and its close association with hot newcomers 'N Sync, it looked like a sure winner. Britney and Lynne headed back to Kentwood while the management contracts and paperwork were drawn up. The Spears family planned a second trip to Memphis to sign the papers and get started on Innosense. The day before they were due to arrive, however, Lynn Harless received a call from Jamie Spears. He told her that they had decided to turn down the deal. Britney Spears would not join Innosense.

* * *

On the face of it, the Spears family's decision was nothing short of bizarre. Some blame Jamie, some Lynne; others feel that lawyer Larry Rudolph bears ultimate responsibility. Britney, after a brief spell in the limelight on *MMC*, had had no luck getting work and now she was being offered the chance to team up with three other talented young women for a project backed by Lou Pearlman, a man with deep pockets and a proven formula for success. To say "No, thanks" to that seemed either colossally arrogant or colossally stupid.

But, of course, there was more to the situation than that. The decision had not been made lightly. After much reflection, Lynne Spears had decided that if Britney signed on for this project she would be repeating herself. On *MMC* she'd been part of an ensemble cast—a group, in other words—and Lynne believed that if she joined Innosense, the pattern would be the same: a lot of hard work, some shared glory and a bit of money. Then it would all end and they would be right back where they started. This feeling was reinforced by the photos that had been taken in Memphis. Britney did not stand out; of all the Innosense girls, she was the least noticeable. To allow her to join would be to set her up for obscurity, even if the band was successful. This was not part of the plan—both Lynne and Jamie wanted something more.

For his part, Larry Rudolph believed (correctly, as it evolved) that the boy-band phenomenon was already cresting and that the Spice Girls, with their worldwide exposure, were too dominant a brand. An American all-girl band would look like a manufactured imitation, a lame attempt to cash in on the popularity of others. But Rudolph did think there was a market for a solo artist, someone to deliver sugary bubblegum pop to the young teen and preteen crowd—the audience that Madonna had left behind.

So the decision was made: Britney would go solo. They would need some publicity shots and a new demo tape. Some of the solo pictures taken during the Innosense session could be used, but making a demo tape was a problem. They did the best they could—Britney sang a few songs into an ordinary tape recorder. Then they packaged everything up and sent it off to Rudolph. Although Rudolph had been representing Britney for a couple of years, nothing had come of it, but now things were different. Britney was no longer twelve and fresh from Disney; she was turning sixteen and was immersed in an active teenage lifestyle. She had matured physically and emotionally. Rudolph could see it in the pictures and hear it on the tape. As had Nancy Carson before him, he sensed something about Britney that made him listen to her tape again and again. He knew what to do.

The first thing Rudolph focused on was finding a song for her to sing. If Britney was going to be recognised as a fresh new voice, she had to be heard in a completely different way. He got in touch with a music producer friend who had just recorded an album with Toni Braxton. They were having second thoughts about one of the songs on Braxton's CD because it sounded too young to appeal to her audience. A deal was struck to let Britney use the Braxton song on a demo. Rudolph sent Britney two recordings of the song: one was just the music, without the lyrics; the other was the full version recorded by Braxton. He instructed Britney to study the music and study the way Braxton, a fantastic natural singer, approached it. He then booked a professional recording studio in New Orleans where Britney could record the demo. One last instruction: she was to sing that song like she had never sung a song before.

* * *

Zomba Music Publishing is a spectacular, if mysterious, pop music success story. The independent company was formed in 1971 by South Africans Clive Calder and Ralph Simon. In 1974, they reestablished Zomba in London, England, because they were opposed to South Africa's apartheid regime. They formed subsidiary Jive Records in 1981, which took off when they began recording hip-hop artists—notably, rap duo DJ Jazzy Jeff and the Fresh Prince (Jeff Townes and a young Will Smith). From there, Jive gradually expanded into the mainstream, signing the Backstreet Boys in 1991 and 'N Sync in 1998.

Jive became well known for taking total control of the marketing of their artists. Before he went into self-imposed seclusion after selling Jive to BMG (now Sony BMG) in 2002, Calder often said that he'd tried to model Zomba on Berry Gordy's Motown. Gordy was a genius not just at discovering raw talent—like Diana Ross, Stevie Wonder and Michael Jackson and the Jackson 5—but also at packaging performers and controlling how they were presented to the public. Says Will Smith, "I have been a millionaire since I was seventeen years old, man. That is because of Jive Records and Zomba—they got behind us and would not stop until we made it."

* * *

In late 1997, Jeff Fenster was a vice president at Jive Records. His job was to wade through submissions and demos in search of new acts. It was to Fenster that Rudolph sent the demo of Britney doing the Toni Braxton song. Fenster was impressed. He wasn't able to put his finger on exactly what had grabbed him, but he recognised that Britney had a special quality and he told Rudolph he wanted to hear more. Fenster still recalls that the demo was "remarkable. She wasn't even singing in her key, but there was something powerful and interesting about her singing. It wasn't until after he had impressed me with the tape that [Rudolph] sent me her picture."

But when Fenster told Rudolph that Jive was interested in hearing more of Britney, he wasn't asking him to send another demo. He wanted Britney to come to Jive Records in New York and sing three songs in front of the company's executive team. Boldly, Britney, with Rudolph and her parents, chose three songs that had been recorded by powerful-voiced women: two by Britney's idol Whitney Houston ("I Have Nothing" and "Jesus Loves Me") and one by Mariah Carey ("Open Arms").

Britney and Lynne were flown to New York for the meeting. They were understandably anxious. Apart from singing at the occasional wedding, Britney had not sung in front of an audience for years. This would be a whole new experience for her. Not only was she older—a different person, really—but also the kind of song she was attempting was different. Furthermore, she wasn't as sure of herself as she'd once been.

Britney has described that audition as "the most nerve-wracking I have ever done. It's so different performing in front of three people staring at you. Performing onstage is one thing, but this was strange and hard." Britney was now entering a new world. She was not being treated as a child anymore. She was, for all intents and purposes, an adult. When she auditioned, there would be only four other people present: three music executives and Larry Rudolph. No parents. She was on her own.

Though Rudolph felt that Jive was the company that would be most receptive to a young talent like Britney Spears, he had set up auditions at several other labels as well. Jive would be their last audition stop. The whole day Britney spent in New York was a blur. They went from one office tower to another. Britney sang the same songs several times over and was introduced to people whose names she instantly forgot, all of whom were dressed in suits and ties and had the same noncommittal expressions on their faces.

Her first two auditions elicited polite smiles and flat rejections. The suits at the third expressed only lukewarm interest. Then they went to Jive and made their way to Fenster's office. By this point, Britney was exhausted and disillusioned, but, encouraged by Rudolph, she went ahead and belted out her songs. She sang two with musical accompaniment and one a cappella. This time there was interest, but it was not overwhelming. "She had no material," said Fenster. "She wasn't a songwriter. She was fifteen years old. But her vocal ability and commercial appeal caught me right away."

Fenster knew almost immediately that he would sign Britney to a recording contract. He was very influential at Jive and his decisions always carried weight, but the procedures for signing artists were firmly established. As a new act, Britney would only be signed to a three-month contract—in effect, a probationary period. While all at Jive agreed that she had something, they needed assurance that it would translate into commercial success. They would record some songs with her and more executives would give their input. If, at the end of three months, it looked like she couldn't deliver, then they would not renew the contract.

The Spears family was elated, but once their excitement subsided, they realised there was a significant logistical issue. In order to do the necessary recording, Britney would have to move to New York again for an extended period. Up until this point, Lynne had travelled with her, bringing Jamie Lynn along. But this time Lynne didn't see how she could do it; Jamie Lynn was now five years old and in school and she needed her mother at home. Jamie was also unwilling to move to New York with Britney.

Since Britney was still only fifteen, she clearly couldn't live in New York on her own. The obvious solution was a live-in chaperone. Lynne Spears had a candidate in mind: Felicia Culotta, or Fe, as she was called. Lynne and Fe had met many years earlier when Fe was working in a children's dentist's office near Kentwood. The two had hit it off and Lynne had often invited Fe to watch Britney perform locally. Fe had moved to New York to work as a nanny, but she and Lynne had stayed in touch. As luck would have it, she had just left her job and was looking for work. She accepted Lynne's offer of employment. At thirty-two, Fe was old enough to project authority to fifteen-year-old Britney but young enough to be her confidante. Lynne was very pleased with the arrangement: "Every mother hopes that there is an angel watching over her little girl. We were lucky that our angel happened to be looking for a new job."

A dinner was arranged at a New Orleans restaurant to

reintroduce Fe and Britney. Providence seemed to smile on their reunion: the two showed up at the restaurant wearing almost identical blue jeans and white tops. Fe says that when she'd first known Britney, she'd seen "two different people in her": Britney "would skip onstage and perform like a real little pro and then once that was done she would grab your hand and want to show you her dolls." But the older Britney Fe encountered that night in New Orleans was "more anxious about having a career; she was more serious about making sure she succeeded."

Back to NYC

"I feel like a totally different person than I was two years ago. I feel like so much of my innocence is gone. I'm still me, but this business makes you grow up so fast."

–Britney Spears

Fe and Britney flew to New York in late September. On their way to the airport, Fe (whom Britney took to calling Fe Fe) had started taking pictures. Fe was never without a camera. She snapped photo after photo of Britney experiencing this next show business adventure and in 2000 published them in a book entitled *Britney: Every Step of the Way*.

Even though Britney was still on a probationary contract, once she arrived in New York, Jive Records treated her like the star they hoped she would become. They installed her in a spacious penthouse they owned on the Upper East Side, which had a spectacular view of the Manhattan skyline.

At Jive, Jeff Fenster's first order of business was to find the right people—writers, producers and arrangers—to help Britney create her sound. She was teamed up with songwriter/producer Eric Foster White, who had written for Whitney Houston and the Backstreet Boys, which meant that he had a feel for the sound of the day. He was also a very talented musician in his own right and could play virtually any instrument. Once the songs were written and ready to be recorded, Foster White and Britney would present to the Jive brass whatever material they thought was worth pursuing. As soon as she was settled in, Britney began commuting to Foster White's studio in New Jersey and putting in long days under his tutelage.

One of the first things she did upon arriving in New York was to call Reg Jones. "She was thrilled to be in a swanky [penthouse] like that," he recalls. "But she found it a bit too big. There was just the two of them in there and she was used to living in smaller places, but we immediately made plans for me to come visit her there." Reg stayed with Britney and Fe for a week at Thanksgiving. He and Britney did the touristy things, attending the Macy's Thanksgiving Day Parade and skating on the rink at Rockefeller Center beneath the giant Christmas tree.

Britney had to work most of that week, so Reg spent a lot of time in the recording studio with her. Foster White allowed Reg to hang out in the sound-mixing booth with him. To make Reg feel included, Foster White would send him next door to relay messages to Britney—instructions about what tone to aim for and what notes to hit. "That was a really happy time in New York," Reg says. "I was really treated well while I was there."

* * *

Stockholm, Sweden, developed into a pop music Mecca during the 1990s and among those most responsible for this was the dynamic songwriter/producer/arranger duo Max Martin (Martin Sandberg) and Denniz PoP (Dag Volle). PoP was the most prolific of the pair. He had begun his career in the 1980s as a very successful DJ and in 1992 established Cheiron Studios to record remixes of songs by everyone from Michael Jackson to Donna Summer. PoP hit his stride as a producer when he wrote and produced Swedish techno-pop band Ace of Base's debut album, *Happy Nation*. The album was released in April of 1993 and sold over 600,000 copies in Europe, a real achievement for a debut. For the U.S. market, the album title was changed to *The Sign* and sales took off, reaching a staggering twenty-two million copies worldwide. A day after the album's release, Max Martin showed up at Cheiron with some demo material and was promptly hired on as house writer and producer. A year later, PoP assigned Martin to help Ace of Base with their second album, *The Bridge*.

In 1995, PoP and Cheiron Studios were asked by the Zomba Label Group to help a band they represented record their eponymous first album. The band was the Backstreet Boys. Martin penned the group's hit songs "Quit Playing Games (with My Heart)," "As Long as You Love Me," and "Everybody (Backstreet's Back)." In late 1997, Martin wrote a song for the African American female pop group TLC, but they weren't recording or planning anything at that point, so they declined. Martin passed it on to the people at Jive, who told him they had a young female singer it might be a good match for. Martin sent a recording of the song to Britney's home address. Jamie opened the package, listened to the song, then played it for Lynne and Jamie Lynn. That night, they called Britney in New York and played the song for her over the phone. An excited Jamie declared, "That is it, Britney. That's the song that's going to make it for you!" It was called ". . . Baby

One More Time."

Eric White added ". . . Baby One More Time" to the list of songs he was recording with Britney and soon afterwards he and Jeff Fenster played some selections from Britney's sessions for Zomba and Jive Records owner Clive Calder, his close adviser Barry Weiss and other top company executives. Britney was not there—she was represented exclusively by her recorded voice. The men listened sternly to each cut. When the session was over, the consensus was unanimous: Britney would go to Stockholm and make an album. This decision cut short her three-month probationary period; her contract was now permanent.

In December 1997, as Britney and Fe prepared to leave for Stockholm, Britney sat down and wrote a letter to Reg: "Well, I am getting ready to go to Sweden and I am really excited. I wish you could come with me. That would be great. I will think about you when I am there. I hope you will do the same. I know it gets hard when we are apart (at least it does for me), but I just think about the future and I know I have something great to look forward to and that keeps me going. Tell your family that I miss them very much and can't wait to see them again. Be careful and please don't get hurt when I am away. I think I would seriously die. Please don't forget about me. I love you so much and miss you terribly. Love Brit. P.S. Be good!"

There is a sense of insecurity in the letter. Britney clearly wanted to go Sweden and welcomed everything the trip represented, but she seemed apprehensive about being carried too far from home by this new adventure. The flight, which Fe has described as "a complete nightmare," did nothing to relieve her uneasiness. There was extreme turbulence during most of trip and Britney, returning from the washroom, was thrown around so violently that she burst into tears and spent the rest of the flight curled up in a ball on her seat.

Once in Sweden, however, things started looking up for her. Britney and Max Martin hit it off right away. Early in their recording sessions, Martin realised that while Britney had a good voice and while she knew how to sing, she needed to learn the limits of her voice and her vocal range. "What we wanted was to take her own voice, which was interesting, add a little bit of Madonna and then add a Europop kind of sound," he says. "It was the hope that the combination would create a unique mix, a unique sound."

Martin was just twenty-six at the time. He had classic Swedish looks—angular face, blonde hair. Britney enjoyed working with this cool, creative young guy, even though she was allowed virtually no input in terms of the songs or the music. This was a Jive Records/Cheiron Studios project and she was just there to do what was expected of her. Her daily grind in Stockholm was as tough as it had been in Orlando when she worked on *MMC*. She got to the studio at around 2:00 p.m. and worked until at least 2:00 a.m., with a short break at around 7:00 p.m. for dinner. Producer/arranger/writer Per Magnusson remembers that there was no real sense of urgency about the project at that point: "There was nothing special about this going in. We knew very little about Britney. We all thought she was just another young teenage kid that showed some promise and was given a bit of a shot. Britney had not released even a single during that time; she had no sound of her own. So it was fun for us because we could take her talents and mold them without having to give up our own particular sound that we had in mind."

Because Britney was working so hard, she didn't communicate with Reg as often as she'd promised she would. She wrote, "I am missing you lots, but am too busy to talk to you as much as I want to. Love Brit." Reg became anxious and began calling her from Kentwood as often as five times a day. This was not well received in Stockholm. Martin and PoP issued instructions to staff to refuse calls from Reg Jones, as they were disrupting the sessions and knocking Britney off her game. As soon as Reg's mother, Gay, got the first $1,500 phone bill, she put a stop to the calls altogether. She later commented, "I felt bad about that. He just wanted to talk to his girl. But I told him that she was there to work and do her thing and if this relationship was going to continue, it would have to continue without him calling her five times a day. It was just making him miss her more."

Reg now agrees. "Her schedule was so strange—she would [put in] long hours over there. And the time change and all. When you are trying to keep a relationship going over that distance for that length of time little things start happening. You start imagining little things in the other person's voice that you blow up into something bigger than you should. You really can't connect the same way over the phone." Gay gently tried to impress upon Reg that this was probably the beginning of the end of their relationship: "I tried to tell him in very nonthreatening terms that Britney's lifestyle and his lifestyle were growing further and further apart all the time and very soon they would be completely incompatible." Reg remembers that conversation: "Yeah, I sure as hell didn't want to hear that, but she was right. We would find ourselves deliberately picking fights on the phone because we just didn't know where we were headed anymore."

It can be said that Britney Spears became "Britney Spears" during her time in Stockholm. She didn't have her mother by her side and Martin and PoP did not patronise or coddle her; they treated her in the same tough, businesslike way they treated every other young professional they worked with. During those winter months in Sweden at the end of 1997 and the beginning of 1998, Britney, barely sixteen, did a lot of growing up.

* * *

Britney and the Swedish pop team recorded what they judged to be six solid tracks for Britney to take back to New York. She took a short break in Kentwood then went on to New York to complete her first album. She asked Reg to come and join her there. Her time apart from her boyfriend had been professionally productive but personally difficult and isolating. Fe had reported to Lynne Spears, however, that Reg was not a positive force in Britney's life. She said that when Reg was around or when he and Britney talked on the phone, Britney became distracted and lost focus on her work. Lynne didn't believe that Reg would actually be permitted to go to New York, but Reg's father, despite some misgivings about Reg leaving college to travel north, arranged for him to stay with a friend of his just a block from Britney's penthouse.

Britney and Fe had already settled back into the penthouse when Reg arrived in New York. When he got to the apartment where he was supposed to stay, it was late and no one was home to let him in, so he decided to go to Britney's. Fe, however, wouldn't let him in. Britney was furious. She called Lynne and demanded that she order Fe to let Reg in off the street. Lynne complied, but things were never the same again. Reg explains, "It was Felicia who was pretty much responsible for Britney and I breaking up. We didn't get along and she did everything she could to either keep us apart or make sure people around Britney saw me as some kind of negative influence on her."

To keep Reg busy—and to keep him from hanging around Britney when she was working—he was advised to get a job. He eventually found work in a restaurant uncorking wine bottles. Reg being forced to take on such menial employment only served to emphasise to everyone that where Britney was headed Reg could not follow.

OCTOBER 23, 1998

"I would really, really, really like to be a legend like Madonna. Madonna always knows what to do next."

—Britney Spears

The first three quarters of 1998 were taken up with preparations for the release of Britney's single ". . . Baby One More Time" on October 23. The album of the same name would follow in early 1999. Finishing the album took a long time. The recordings made in Sweden in the winter and early spring comprised about half the album; the other half consisted mostly of material written and produced by Eric Foster White. Throughout the spring and summer, Britney commuted from New York to White's New Jersey studio, recording and rerecording the fifteen tracks that would be her music-world debut.

* * *

It was an odd time for the Spears family. Although big plans were being made for Britney, the situation was becoming desperate back in Kentwood. Britney's income was too small to support the family and whatever rewards awaited her were still a long way off. So, on July 17, 1998, Jamie and Lynne Spears filed for bankruptcy, citing debts of almost $200,000 on a yearly income of just $21,000. The debts they had incurred over years of investing in Britney's talent had caught up with them. People in the McComb-Kentwood area who knew the family were aware of their difficulties, but they all seem to remember first and foremost that Jamie and Lynne kept their heads up, never adopting a "poor us" attitude. They had gambled everything they had on Britney and they were holding on as best they could, waiting for something good to happen.

* * *

The video for ". . . Baby One More Time" was shot on August 7 and 8 in Los Angeles and Jive had hired British music video director Nigel Dick to do it. His mandate was to make Britney's video debut something that the general public would not soon forget. Dick's work with existential pop sensation of the eighties Tears for Fears and later Oasis, had cemented his reputation, but it was his work with 'N Sync and the Backstreet Boys that interested Jive. The videos he had produced for those groups testified to the fact that he had what it took to visually snare the young music consumers Jive hoped would make up the initial core audience for Britney Spears.

Dick's first order of business was to head to New York to meet Britney. He found her working out at the Alley Cat Dance Studio. "As I watched her move and jump, watched her use her body in a powerful way, I thought of something over the top," says Dick. "I thought of a big-budget, Britney-as-superhero kind of scenario."

Britney, however, nixed that. She had been told by Jive and by her manager that Dick was the man—the best there was—but the superhero concept left her cold. As she puts it, "He wanted to have me dressed up in a kind of Power Rangers costume. I had a different idea for the song that I thought would be cooler for the kids to respond to." Dick remembers her reaction: "Britney was very polite and I could tell she didn't like the idea but was having a hard time telling me that. So I let her know that I wanted to know her thoughts." Britney's idea for the video was totally different. She saw herself sitting in a classroom, thinking about guys, restless and bored. She would start daydreaming and in her daydream she'd suddenly break into song and dance. The effect would be energetic, rebellious and sexy.

Dick realised she was right: "The initial idea I had for the video was absolute rubbish. I was basing my ideas on my initial meeting with Britney and usually that initial impression and instinct is sharp, but not this time. This time I am glad I rethought and relooked at things." Dick prepared a script based on Britney's idea and asked what she thought. She liked it. Then she put forward the idea of the Catholic schoolgirl uniform. "That was Britney's idea entirely," says Dick. "And she was full conscious of the 'forbidden fruit' aspect of the imagery. It would grab the attention of her contemporaries and older guys would dig it as well. She was thinking of maximum exposure."

Dick and Britney presented the concept to the Jive suits. They loved it and promptly approved the budget and the schedule. Dick had chosen to shoot the video on location in Los Angeles at Venice High School, which had doubled as Rydell High for the film *Grease*. Rehearsals took place in New York. Reg Jones was hanging around the rehearsal hall trying to stay as close to Britney as he could, so Britney offered him a role in the video. He was cast as her love interest, a high-school basketball player and Fe Culotta had a brief role as a schoolteacher.

The rehearsals went very well. One day, Jive boss Barry Weiss stopped by the studio to watch and what he saw floored him. "I was blown away," he says. "I was pretty sure we had a hit on our hands going in, but what I saw exceeded my expectations. Britney was confident and sexy and in control. I left there comfortable that we had played the Britney campaign perfectly."

Weiss and the Jive team decided to send Britney on tour with 'N Sync as an opening act once the video was finished. This did not sit well with Reg, however and two nights before they were set to leave for L.A., the issue exploded. Britney told him that she was looking forward to "being with Justin again," and Reg, feeling threatened, accused her of seeing Justin as something more than a friend. The argument got very heated and Britney ended up firing Reg from the video. Reg quit his job and left New York, returning to Kentwood. It seemed they were through. Back home, after cooling down, Reg tried to ingratiate himself with the rest of the Spears family in the vain hope that they would plead his case with Britney, but the damage was done.

In L.A., the shoot got off to a smooth start. Reg had been replaced by Britney's cousin Chad Spears, who was a model for Abercrombie and Fitch in New York. The video's story unfolds in just under four minutes. A bored schoolgirl daydreams in class. She imagines herself dancing and singing to attract the attention of a guy she has a thing for. In each dance number, she struts and pouts, executing a well-choreographed series of thrusts, spins and rolls. With every take, she becomes more and more provocative—even erotic. After the shoot wrapped, everyone knew that people would be talking about this video, but no one had the slightest idea of the impact it and its star would have.

* * *

As summer eased into fall, Britney tweaked her album and got ready for the PR tour that Jive was organising prior to the release of the single "... Baby One More Time." The tour would be nothing spectacular—just a cross-country jaunt to visit shopping-mall record stores and create some buzz about Britney and her song. The campaign had a simple slogan: "Britney. Get to know her on a first-name basis." The first stop was Nashville, Tennessee, where she would perform her material and get feedback from Jive personnel and executives at distribution giant BMG. The strategy that Jive mapped out for her was pretty much the one they'd used for the Backstreet Boys: generate buzz in Europe by releasing a few singles; use that momentum to take on the United States and the target demographic—American adolescents and kids in their early teens.

* * *

By the time Britney came along, MTV had gained the power to make or break a new artist. On September 14, 1998, the channel launched a new show: *Total Request Live. TRL* was a live, top-10 music video show that based its playlist on audience input. The first new video shown on the debut episode was "... Baby, One More Time." The show and the song immediately took off. In no time, *TRL* was boasting over a million regular viewers and, with the show's help, Britney's first new single debuted five weeks later at number 17 on the Billboard Hot 100.

Britney had very little time to relax and savour her first wave of major success. She embarked from Orlando on her first tour, as an opening act for 'N Sync, on November 17, 1998. 'N Sync were white-hot. They had several hits under their belts and had paid their dues, having toured as an opening act for Janet Jackson. They were now bona fide rock stars. The stadium was filled with screaming girls clamouring for the guys when a very nervous Britney took the stage to sing three songs. She and her dancers broke into ". . . Baby, One More Time," and soon the whole audience was chanting the lyrics. They knew the song. Britney relaxed almost instantly. "It was so cool to look out and see people singing along with me," she says. "It really helped me because I started to really enjoy playing for them when I saw that."

Lynne, Jamie and Jamie Lynn were part of that audience. Reg Jones was also there, as much for appearance's sake as anything else. Tensions had eased between him and Britney since the summer. Their romance was clearly over, but Reg was still struggling to accept it. The situation was made even more awkward and painful for him when Justin Timberlake came over to greet Britney, Reg at her side. It was obvious to Reg that Justin and Britney were very happy to see each other. At the post concert dinner, Lynne Spears fawned all over Justin and dismissively introduced Reg as a "friend from back home." Reg remembers, "Jamie would say I was Britney's boyfriend, but Lynne did everything she could to put some distance between Britney and I. I knew she was hoping that Brit and Justin would get together."

Reg was, in effect, the first victim of Britney's new star status.

"[Lynne] told me that very night that Britney could not be a huge star if fans ever thought she had a serious boyfriend," he explains. "It was all bullshit, of course, but I knew then that things had changed forever." Events soon confirmed this. On December 2, Britney's seventeenth birthday, the tour hit Kalamazoo, Michigan. After the show, Justin and the rest of the band surprised Britney in her trailer with a big birthday cake and they all sang "Happy Birthday" to her. Justin and Britney hung out talking for hours and Justin gave her a special gift—a gold friendship ring. Their long association was growing into something deeper.

A little over a week later, on December 11, the 'N Sync tour rolled into Nashville for a scheduled date. Jamie Spears and his work crew, which included his younger brother, Austin and Reg Jones, were on a job nearby and stopped by to cheer Britney on. Everyone had been drinking and Austin and Reg were clearly intoxicated. They went backstage before the show and acted like drunken hillbillies, hooting and hollering and yelling at Britney. She was mortified. She burst into tears then screamed at them all to get away from her. Ripping into Reg, she told him that getting drunk and embarrassing her had only pushed her further away from him. As Jamie started to pull the drunken duo out of the theatre before they upset Britney any further, Britney declared that she never wanted to see Reg or her Uncle Austin at a show of hers again. Reg confesses, "It got even worse after we left. Jamie was real mad at Austin and they got into a hell of a fight. I thought Jamie was going to literally gouge his brother's eyes out. I remember at least one of the guys had a gun that he was waving around. It got real ugly." Britney was able to pull herself together and perform without any noticeable effect.

She was leaving her past and many of the people in it, such as Reg, behind. Months before, she had been an unknown young artist battling to break out any way she could. Suddenly, she was a pop sensation. A large part of her life would now be spent on a tour bus with her four-person dance troupe and her friend-chaperone, Fe. Britney opened for 'N Sync for three months, taking only a few days off at Christmas. With the exception of the drunken incident in Nashville, the tour went remarkably well. Each element of Britney's new career was feeding another: her single was fueling interest in her concert appearances and the video was selling her CDs.

In January 1999, the album . . . *Baby One More Time* was released and both the single and the album hit number 1 on the Billboard charts, where they stayed for two weeks. Not even a year and a half had passed since Britney had sung into a portable tape recorder to make a demo for Larry Rudolph. Now she had the top-selling album in the country. It was the kind of meteoric success that made everyone forget the years of toil it took to achieve. Britney and her family had paid the price of admission to stardom; what remained to be seen was whether they could afford the price of staying there.

LIKE A VIRGIN

"Just because I look sexy on the cover of Rolling Stone *doesn't mean I'm naughty."*

—Britney Spears

The U.S. cover of the . . . *Baby One more Time* CD shows Britney sitting on the floor, looking up at the camera, her head cocked to one side, a friendly, rather generic smile on her face. She looks all of fifteen, but she was nearly eighteen. The Jive PR people insisted that she was not being made to look like anything other than what she was—a young, healthy, American teen—but it seems evident that she was being packaged to heighten the ability of her audience demographic (the twelve-through-sixteen set) to identify with her.

But Jive was caught in a bind and they knew it. Britney's last appearance before the American public had been as a twelve-year-old Mouseketeer and *MMC* had been in reruns through 1997. The kids who were buying her CDs wanted to see the girl they thought they knew—a fresh-faced Disney graduate. The problem was that she was older and so were they. Britney's instinct about the video had been right on. She and her audience were now teenagers and she had to capture the essence of being that age, hormones raging beneath a well-scrubbed exterior palatable to adults. Dressed in her Catholic schoolgirl uniform (What better image of the adult world's attempt to stifle the teenage soul?), Britney was walking the same tightrope as every other teen and fighting for the same balance. And to help her cohorts through this turbulent period, Britney was offering them fantasy and song.

In the video, she's a prim schoolgirl who lets her mind wander in class; her daydream explodes into song and dance—a frenzied outpouring of emotion and longing. The bell rings, she wakes from her reverie and she's back where she started. The only thing that's changed is that she now wears a sly smile on her face. That first video established the Britney Spears image for the duration: on the outside, she was the still-chaste ex-Mouseketeer, but on the inside she was something else. No matter what was churning within her, no matter what mild sexual innuendo the video might contain, what it depicted was teenage fantasy and fantasy it would remain. It was all part of the allure—an allure that sold records. Twenty-five million of them. So, although Britney was now on the cusp of superstardom, she was still fundamentally a Mouseketeer. More grown up, yes, but still the same virginal Southern belle. But how long could such an image be maintained?

That eighteen-year-old Britney had a budding relationship with Justin Timberlake was an issue, but this was quickly spun: they were "just good, close friends." Justin and the members of his band were already old hands at this. By the time Britney had scored her first hit, the 'N Sync boys had been stars for three years. Their faces were plastered all over teen magazines in many parts of the world and with the adulation had come the inevitable intrusions into their personal lives. *Seventeen* once asked band member Lance Bass what he looked for in a girl and he'd answered that he liked girls who were sincere, down-to-earth and funny.

Probably true, but Lance was gay. He was carefully hiding his sexual orientation and he continued to do so until long after 'N Sync had split up. It just didn't fit the 'N Sync fantasy.

Justin's own story had more than a few similarities to Britney's. His success was also largely due to a dedicated mother, though his life had been easier than that of Britney, with her hardscrabble upbringing. He was from the comfortable Memphis suburb of Shelby Forest. His parents had married young but separated when he was just two. Both had remarried and remained in Shelby Forest. Like Britney, Justin was exposed to the limelight very early. He won the 1992 Universal Charm Pageant held in Nashville, Tennessee, collecting $15,000 for being best dressed, best dressed in sportswear, best model, most handsome and supreme winner. Also like Britney, he'd bombed out of *Star Search* when he was forced to sing a tune that was way out of his comfort zone.

When Justin and Britney had reconnected at the start of the 1998 'N Sync tour, Britney was coming to the end of her relationship with Reg Jones and Justin was involved with Veronica Finn, Britney's replacement in Innosense. But, as Reg himself admits, "[Justin] said this and he said that, but I knew—I knew they were either already together or would be together real soon." Someone who worked with 'N Sync also picked up on what was going on: "You could see it. You could feel it whenever they were in the same room. It was almost like they didn't even have a choice; they were drawn together because of the very unique things they had in common."

As early as January 1999, Britney and Justin had to finesse questions about their relationship. Asked by MTV News if they were dating, Justin smiled and said that they were, but then added, "We've been dating seriously for the past seven years and I'm dating two of her backup dancers too." Justin was taking a page out of Marlon Brando's book: Brando liked to give journalists who asked personal questions outrageous replies that they couldn't print. Britney was not quite as savvy and merely spouted the rather transparent party line supplied to her by Jive and her manager: "People just say that Justin and I are together because we were on *The Mickey Mouse Club* together, but it just isn't true. ['N Sync] are all like brothers to me."

Two weeks before she'd said that to MTV News, however, she and Justin were spotted dining together in a West Hollywood restaurant. They were giggling and holding hands and sampling food from each other's plates. Britney was reportedly wearing the gold ring that Justin had given her for her birthday the month before. Also, Britney moved to Orlando, Florida, in early 1999 to work with director and choreographer Johnny Wright, who was based there and who was in charge of creating and organising her first solo tour. Of course, Justin was based in Orlando as well.

But Britney didn't have a lot of time to fuel the rumour mills by hanging out with Justin in public. She was too busy. By February 1999, her debut single, "... Baby One More Time," and the album of the same name were certified platinum—that is, each had sales in excess of one million units. Britney was on the brink of being a millionaire seven months after her family had filed for bankruptcy.

Britney Spears was rapidly becoming very famous. She was booked to appear on *The Tonight Show with Jay Leno* and to be a guest and performer on the talk show *Donny & Marie*. Jumping to capitalise on her newfound fame, Larry Rudolph helped arrange endorsement deals for Britney with Sunglass Hut and Tommy Hilfiger. Meanwhile, Jive was drawing up plans for her second video—for her song "Sometimes"—and scrambling to organise what would be her first solo tour.

The pace was frenetic. Something was bound to give and it did. On February 11, 1999, while in Los Angeles rehearsing the big dance number for her "Sometimes" video, again directed by Nigel Dick, Britney suddenly heard the ominous popping sound that all dancers and athletes dread. Her left knee had given out. She crumpled to the floor and rolled around screaming, gripping her injured leg. Dancers and crew members rushed to her side and tried to calm her. They helped her to a couch and put ice on her elevated leg.

A doctor examined her and determined that the injury was more than just a twist. She had cartilage damage and would need corrective surgery. Britney contacted orthopaedist Timothy Finney, team physician for the New Orleans Saints of the National Football League. Dr. Finney performed a minor arthroscopic procedure to remove a small piece of cartilage that had been torn off when Britney twisted her knee. The surgery was quick and painless, but Dr. Finney was adamant that to recover properly, she would need a solid month of rest. She returned to Kentwood to recover.

Britney remained out of the public eye for almost two months. One of the only times she emerged was to make an appearance on MTV's *Total Request Live*. Probably as a gag, she showed up for the live telecast wrapped in blankets and sitting in a wheelchair. The day after the show, she ordered the limo Jive had rented for her to drive her and her bodyguard Big Rob to a Jack in the Box restaurant for burgers and fries. She then ordered the driver to take her to Cartier so she could look at jewellery. There, wearing slippers and still confined to a wheelchair, she lingered over an $80,000 diamond bracelet but didn't buy it. She looked, by her own admission, "nasty"—she hadn't showered in a couple of days. Joke or no joke, Britney was becoming self-indulgent in the way only a pop star can.

When her convalescence was over, she returned to work on the "Sometimes" video, which was finally shot on April 9 and 10. But something was different about her and people quickly picked up on what it was: her breasts were about three cup sizes bigger than they had been before her injury. And although the "Sometimes" video doesn't emphasise that area of her body, her profile does indeed seem to have been augmented, at least in comparison with the "... Baby One More Time" video, shot some six months before.

Reg Jones later revealed that Britney had been talking about getting breast implants for a few years: "She started talking about getting a boob job when she was sixteen. I tried to talk her out of it. I tried to tell her to wait until she was at least eighteen. She believed that she would be a more popular performer if she had the smoking hot body ... I wasn't in the operating room myself, of course, but she did it, I know she did it." For his part, Timberlake was evasive: "I don't know about her breasts, I was always too busy looking at her fantastic butt." Britney herself called all the discussion about it "retarded." "I did not have breast implants," she insisted. "It was just a growth spurt."

Britney was indeed growing up. And those who hadn't yet

figured that out were set straight by the cover of the April 1999 *Rolling Stone*. It featured Britney reclining on purple satin sheets, wearing a wide-open shirt, push-up bra and tight, shorts-style underwear. In one hand she held a phone receiver with a spiral cord extending out of the shot, in the other, a Teletubby doll. The cover sent a message that had been carefully crafted to confirm her image. She was scantily clad, but she was also clutching a doll. The photographer was David LaChapelle, who is known for his nudes and his surrealistic sensibility. The shoot took place in Kentwood over a period of two days and the sheets were stitched on Lynne's sewing machine. In the article that accompanied the cover shot, Britney denied that the "Sometimes" video exuded sexual energy: "All I did was tie up my shirt. I'm wearing a sports bra under it. Sure, I'm wearing thigh-highs, but all kids wear those. It's the style. Have you seen MTV, all those girls in thongs?" She also bristled at the fact that some were interpreting the lyrics to ". . . Baby One More Time" ("Hit me baby one more time") as having rough-sex overtones. "I didn't mean I wanted to be physically hit—it just means give me a sign, basically. I think it is kind of funny that people would actually think that's what I meant."

People were beginning to ask whether Britney Spears was a one-shot wonder or a star with staying power. Even *TRL* host Carson Daly had his doubts. "The loyalty factor with teens is dangerous," he said. "As quickly as they come, they will leave. But Britney should make enough money this year not to have to worry about what the teens do to her a year from now."

Jive Records executives had their fingers crossed. Marketing boss Kim Kaiman described Britney as "so very Southern, so sweet and gracious. And that really warms programmers' hearts." Jive vice president Jeff Fenster was upbeat and set the tone for the next step in Britney's career: "She's got the opportunity to become someone who combines the best elements of Madonna in terms of versatility with the serious singers that she looks up to like Whitney Houston and Celine Dion."

Oops! . . . She Did It Again

"There are so many teenagers out there that dress more provocatively than I do, and no one says anything about them."

–Britney Spears

On March 9, 1999, Jive announced the ... *Baby One More Time* tour. The main sponsor was Tommy Hilfiger. A secondary sponsor, Nestlé, dropped out when the April *Rolling Stone* appeared, citing the provocative nature of the Britney Spears cover and the photos accompanying the article. Among the few who voiced objections to the spread were members of the Christian right; the most outspoken belonged to the Mississippi-based American Family Association. AFA president Tim Wildmon released a statement: "Her disturbing mix of childhood innocence and adult sexuality is troubling."

Britney's response to such criticism was disingenuous: "I didn't really know what was going on during the photo shoot, we were all just having fun; it was like playing dress-up for me." Maybe, but photographer David LaChapelle has said that Britney recognised and enjoyed the risqué element: "I said to her, 'You don't want to be buttoned up, like Debbie Gibson . . . Let's push it further and do this whole Lolita thing.' She got it. She knew it would get people talking and excited."

A Jive Records executive put it this way: "She did it her way and she pretty much always got her way right from the start. That doesn't mean she couldn't make stupid decisions; she did that a lot. But, to be fair, this was all happening very fast with no idea where it was going, so a lot of what she did in terms of denying being a part of the whole picture was pretty much knee-jerk reactions to fast-moving circumstances by someone who was young and lacking in worldliness and sophistication." In short, while Britney felt the need to backpedal a bit for the press, she—together with her manager and parents, of course—was controlling her own image, for better or for worse.

* * *

The . . . *Baby One More Time* tour kicked off in Pompano Beach, Florida, on June 28, 1999. Between then and September 15, Britney performed fifty-six shows in the U.S. and Canada, finishing up with a show in Hong Kong on October 23. In November, she travelled to Sweden to record a major part of her second album, *Oops! . . . I Did It Again*, with Max Martin; she had begun the process with Eric Foster White in New Jersey in September. In January, she completed the album in Florida, New York and California.

On December 17, 1999, a couple of weeks after she turned eighteen, Britney called in to *Total Request Live*, which was debuting the video for her latest single, "From the Bottom of My Broken Heart," to announce that in March 2000 she would be doing a series of solo concerts entitled the *Crazy 2K* tour as a "continuation of the . . . *Baby One More Time* tour." She also disclosed that she would be doing a solo world tour later that year based on her new album, *Oops! . . . I Did It Again*.

In February 2000, Britney was nominated for Grammy Awards in the categories of best female pop vocal performance and best new artist. At the awards ceremony on February 23, she performed two of her songs: ". . . Baby One More Time" and "From the Bottom of My Broken Heart." She was enthusiastically received by the crowd of industry insiders, but she did not win a Grammy that evening. The award for best new artist went to a different Mouseketeer—Christina Aguilera.

* * *

Another Spears family milestone occurred that February: the twenty-four-year marriage of Jamie and Lynne Spears came to an official end in a small courthouse in Livingston Parish, Louisiana. The terms of separation were quietly arranged. Someone close to the family revealed that Jamie "fell on his sword so Britney would not get caught up in yet another public controversy." Jamie had to assume 100 percent of the family debt (though Britney subsequently paid everything), but he was allowed to keep the family home in Kentwood. Lynne had filed a petition for divorce in 1979, but she had withdrawn it. Now, in 2000, she decided she'd had enough. Jamie was convinced that now Britney was a star, Lynne was dumping him so she could attach herself to Britney's fame, but in her memoir, Lynne states that she could no longer stand the "cruel words" or "alcohol's evils," referring to Jamie's behaviour and substance abuse. Unsubstantiated reports even surfaced that the split was Britney's idea—that in early 2000, she had asked her mother how much longer she could stand living that way.

* * *

The *Crazy 2K* tour began on March 8, but after just seven performances, Britney took a break from it to fly to Hollywood to shoot the video for "Oops! . . . I Did It Again." Once more, Nigel Dick was the director. The video was filmed on March 17 and 18 on a Universal Studios soundstage and in it Britney meets and falls for a handsome young astronaut on Mars. When she first donned the red cat suit she was supposed to wear for the shoot, she found it too uncomfortable. She disappeared into her trailer and emerged wearing her preferred choice—a skimpy stripper outfit. This time, Dick did not agree. "Britney always had an equal say in the creative presentations of her songs," he says. "When she had an idea she wanted to include, the idea was listened to, explored and in a lot of cases adopted. But in this instance the idea was strange and didn't work." Neither Dick nor the Jive people who were on hand liked the stripper costume. Jive wanted to keep her image consistent and did not want her to flaunt her sexuality so overtly, especially since she was still insisting publicly that she was chaste. The line in the song "I'm not that innocent" was provocative enough for Jive, but Britney was champing at the bit. She wanted to develop a sexier image fast.

When Dick refused to allow the costume change, she stormed back to her trailer. Dick went to talk to her and she told him that she wanted to look risqué and thought the cat suit wouldn't help her achieve that. After some discussion, they compromised on a third costume—another snug red bodysuit. Shooting resumed.

While they were filming a dance number, a lens housing fell on Britney's head, resulting in a trip to the hospital and four stitches. She went right back to finish the video then flew off the next day to Grand Rapids, Michigan, to resume her tour.

This video would be the last Nigel Dick would ever do with Britney. He says that this was because "I argued with her about the costume and the attitude on that video and that bothered her. Britney was already expecting everyone to agree with her and to always get her way. I was hired to do a good video, not just to take orders from Britney."

* * *

The *Crazy 2K* tour continued through April 20. The eleven-song set was generally well received by audiences comprised mainly of screaming teen and preteen girls, many of whom came dressed like little Britneys. The tour schedule was punishing: for three solid months, Britney did a show virtually every night in a different city—places like Grand Rapids, Michigan; Moline, Illinois; Greensboro, North Carolina; and Roanoke, Virginia. The North American leg ended with an energetic show at the Hilton Hawaiian Village in Honolulu on the beach at sunset. Admission for this one was free and over ten thousand fans showed up, making it the biggest live beach concert of all time. The show was recorded for TV and, under the title *Live and More!*, it was released in DVD format later in 2000. Britney was also handsomely paid to allow a Japanese television station to record one of her performances to be aired exclusively in Japan.

Britney's first solo outing was marred slightly by allegations of lip-synching. Stadium rock and pop acts claim that the practice arose because productions were too complex and venues too large for singers' voices to be properly heard; furthermore, lip-synching would permit performers to infuse their acts with more energy and physicality and thus enhance their entertainment value. But after the 1990 Milli Vanilli debacle—the multimillion-CD-selling duo had their Grammy revoked when it was revealed that their vocals had not been used on their record—the public became less tolerant. *Rolling Stone* levelled the first accusation against Britney. Her initial denial was fairly credible: "There's a delay in the screen above me," she explained. "So if you listen to the music and watch the screen, they don't sync up. I think that confuses people. But I am singing every song; I am singing my ass off." When pressed, she added, "There are times during the show, when I am dancing so much, where I get out of breath and we have a signal where I'm dying and they'll help me out." She didn't explain what "help me out" meant. Accusations of lip-synching have dogged her ever since.

* * *

There was a two-month break between the *Crazy 2K* and *Oops! . . . I Did It Again* tours, but those few weeks were hardly restful for Britney. When she wasn't preparing for the tour, she helped her mother promote the book they had written together: *Heart to Heart.* To that end, on May 10, Britney appeared on *Late Night with Conan O'Brien*. Three days later, she did her first stint as guest host on *Saturday Night Live*. When she was introduced at the start of the show, she strutted out sporting a huge set of fake breasts and she poked fun at her innocent image in several sketches. Her message was clear; she was winking at everyone, sharing the joke, as if to say "Y'all get it now?"

* * *

The *Oops!... I Did It Again* tour would be Britney's first official European tour. The main leg of the tour was scheduled to end on November 21, but there would be a final performance in Rio de Janeiro, Brazil, on January 18, 2001. By this time, it was clear to all but the most naive that Britney could no longer be passed off as a perennially budding teenager. She still looked young and well scrubbed, but she was almost nineteen and due for an image change.

A telling moment had come as she was kicking off the *Crazy 2K* tour in March 2000. She mentioned to an interviewer that she "adored" Justin Timberlake and made a giggly remark about what a good kisser he was. Instantly realising her blunder, she slyly added, "My manager is going to kill me if that gets out." This just added to the now-rampant public speculation about whether she was a virgin. In a way, she'd been set up for it. Like Annette Funicello, who'd had her breasts strapped in when she was on the original *Mickey Mouse Club* to make her look forever fourteen, Britney was trapped by her image in a time warp and she was ready to burst out of it.

Many people couldn't understand what the big deal was. Years earlier, when Britney was dating Reg Jones, their community had seen them as a healthy young American couple. They had spent lots of time together and were obviously in mad, passionate teenage love. To assume that they had never even experimented with sex would require quite a stretch of the imagination. As one Kentwood native puts it, "Of course they did it and why not? Nothing wrong with two people in love celebrating that by enjoying each other that way. Why she kept denying it was a bit hard to understand."

In fact, Britney kept denying it because she was told to. Her very young audience wanted their idol to be just like them. Jive Records was quite clear on this. Britney had to embody the ideal teen: clean, happy, healthy—and innocent. Her family and friends helped maintain the facade and Reg—even after their relationship ended and even though he was pressed again and again on the subject—maintained that such information was not for public consumption; he was a Southern gentleman and Southern gentlemen do not speak of their women in that way. The Spears family was grateful. Jamie even called Reg after one such public refusal to comment and said to him, "Thank you for saying what you said in the proper manner."

Britney, of course, had no choice but to play the ingenue to the hilt. In an interview she gave to the German magazine *Bild* early in 2000, she again stated that she had never been sexually active and didn't "believe in smoking cigarettes and [did] believe that everyone should serve God." The interviewer urged her to describe the challenges that this posed, given her pop-star lifestyle and she responded, "I am as interested in sex as any young woman is, but I am choosing to save myself."

As time went on, fewer and fewer people took her purity mantra seriously. The press hounded everyone involved in her life, desperately seeking the slightest defect in her wholesome veneer, but it held fast. The ever-evasive Justin Timberlake offered statements like, "I am not going to say anything because anything I do say will be blown all out of proportion." To the relentless celebrity press corps, no one was off-limits, not even Timberlake's grandmother. Badgered by an entertainment journalist to speak about the true nature of the relationship between Justin and Britney, she responded that not only was Britney a virgin but so was Justin; they were Christian kids and their line of work did not change who they were. So there was frustration all around.

* * *

At this point in the Britney Spears story, the transition she and her family had begun to make from bankrupt clan to rich entertainment-world family gained momentum. For the previous year and a half, since her debut, Britney had been well taken care of by Jive Records; the company was investing in their rising superstar. But now, finally, her cut of the record sales was coming in. Britney asked Reggie Covington, a banker who was married to her mother's sister, Sandra, if he would take charge of her finances for her. He agreed and she gave him power of attorney. He charged her a token 1 percent administration fee (an established show-business money manager would have taken 15 to 20 percent). In 2002, however, after Britney had moved to California and engaged a more experienced management team, Covington bowed out of the job.

What Britney wanted to do more than anything else was set up her family so they would never have to worry about money again. A Kentwood resident says that Britney, experienced in such things as having your utilities cut off when the bills aren't paid, clearly saw this as her responsibility: "You can say what you want about Britney, but . . . she seemed to take the blame for that, that all these sacrifices were being made to help her with her dream and part of that dream for Britney was repaying all that sacrifice." At her request, Covington found a seven-acre tract of land six miles outside of Kentwood; Britney bought it for $29,000 and built a nice house on it for her mother.

* * *

On June 20, 2000, having had practically no downtime, Britney launched her *Oops! . . . I Did It Again* world tour. The single had set a record for most radio airplays in one day and the album established a record for most albums sold by a female solo artist in one week (1.3 million). The sophomore effort of a successful recording artist is always subject to special scrutiny; everyone wants to know whether the artist is going to sink or swim. *Rolling Stone* rated Britney's second album 3.5 out of 5 and called it "fantastic pop cheese," adding, "Britney's demand for satisfaction is complex, fierce and downright scary."

This tour was, if anything, more gruelling than the previous two: Britney did ninety shows in six months on three continents. But for her and her crew, all three tours seemed to blend together into an eighteen-month-long marathon. This outing, however, was the most lucrative. The concert promoter, SFX, contractually guaranteed Britney that she would make at least $200,000 per show.

The tour kicked off in Columbia, Maryland, just after an online

People magazine poll had ranked Justin Timberlake and Britney Spears numbers 1 and 2 on its most beautiful people list and just after Britney had shot a McDonald's commercial with Justin and the rest of 'N Sync. Interestingly, Britney agreed to have the band she'd walked away from, Innosense, as her opening act for much of the tour.

She interrupted the tour for a few days to perform at the 2000 MTV Video Music Awards, held on September 7 at New York's Radio City Music Hall. Now eighteen, she was starting to push the limits of what her public would accept. She took the stage in a modest black suit. Partway through the number, she tore it away with a dramatic flourish. The audience gasped. For a split second it seemed as though she was naked. In fact, she was wearing a skin-tight, nude-coloured bodysuit studded with tiny, glittering crystals.

For virtually the rest of 2000, Britney was on tour. The North American leg ended in New Orleans with a show at the Superdome on September 20. On October 8, the European leg began in Birmingham, England and then moved on to London, where three shows were scheduled. There, Britney had her first brush with the notorious British tabloid press. With her entourage, she checked into the posh Royal Garden Hotel in Kensington then headed out for lunch and a much-anticipated shopping trip to Covent Garden. Leaving a restaurant, Britney was assailed by a pack of aggressive paparazzi. They surrounded her on all sides, cameras flashing, yelling her name, grabbing at her so she would turn their way. Britney was gasping and terrified. The mob rapidly became more and more physically aggressive. Even her bodyguard, the 289-pound Big Rob, was startled by the suddenness and intensity of the onslaught. He swooped in to shield Britney and half-carried her to their van. The paparazzi pack, in hot pursuit, descended on the van like monkeys swarming a jeep on an African safari, clicking pictures and screaming questions at Britney. As they drove off, she collapsed in tears and kept repeating, "Why is this happening? What is happening to me?" Britney Spears had been exposed to another dark facet of the superstar life.

In fact, Jive Records had helped to stoke the flames. Jive's PR department had leaked to the British press that Britney had a crush on Prince William, had exchanged e-mails with him and was going to Buckingham Palace to meet him. The media went predictably berserk. At first, Britney played along, saying she and William had "exchanged a few notes," but then that became, "I don't know where these stories come from" once Buckingham Palace had issued a sternly worded statement that Prince William and Miss Spears had had no contact with one another and that there would be no meeting at Buckingham Palace or anywhere else.

The experience was a wake-up call for Britney. From that point on, as she continued to tour Europe, her preconceptions about the superstar life were shredded, one by one. Perhaps she had imagined herself as a pop princess, revelling in wealth, luxury and ease after working so hard and so long. Wealth, yes, luxury, certainly—but Britney was a pop product now, a brand and it fell to manager Larry Rudolph to bolster that brand, to see to it that this gold mine stayed productive.

Because Britney was suddenly such a hot commodity, having broken recording industry records almost right out of the gate, she was first on every media outlet's request list. In every tour city—

from Cologne, Germany, to Helsinki, Finland, to Gothenburg, Sweden—there were press conferences, one-on-one interviews with large media outlets, meet-and-greets with dignitaries and promotional visits to record stores. "I was just being hustled from one place to the next," Britney recalls. "I didn't get to see much or do much but the stuff that was on the agenda." A Jive PR person reports that one day Britney and Rudolph got into a heated discussion. "Britney was asking why she had to have all her downtime booked up with interviews and appearances. Rudolph told her quite specifically that it was part of the business and part of what builds a long and successful career. He told her it was her job to present herself as 'Little Miss Perfect' whenever she was in public . . . Britney was really worn out and frustrated and said, 'I just want to sing and dance, that's all.' "

Although her entourage was growing—she was now supporting a large number of people on tour—Britney was increasingly isolated. If she ventured out to get a coffee or take a walk, Big Rob was never more than a couple of feet away. And these little outings usually had to be late at night when no one was around. She would return to her hotel suite and, as one of her dancers puts it, "kind of retreat into a little make-believe world to calm herself down. She would talk about making so much money that she could step away from this grind." She said to Fe that "Once this is all done with, we should open up a little shop in Venice [California] and just live real simple."

Lynne Spears was now back with her daughter full time and though Britney didn't need a chaperone anymore, Fe stayed on as her personal assistant. But Britney no longer had real friends. She took to saying, "My dancers are all my best friends; a girl can never have enough best friends." But they were her "best friends" only because they worked with her and spent so much time with her.

There was the odd exception. Trey James Esperanza, or TJ, had been part of her core group of backup dancers since her very first mall tour and Britney adored him. She felt close to TJ and it helped her to have someone around in whom she could confide. But Britney's management decided that TJ didn't have the talent to master the world tour's more complex choreography, so they dropped him, over Britney's protests. She had lost a friend because she didn't have enough "diva cachet" to prevent it. It was a lesson in the limits of personal power and the workings of show business that she wouldn't forget.

* * *

The gruelling 2000 tour schedule ended where it started, in Birmingham, England, on November 20. Since the end of June of the previous year, Britney had been either on the road, filming videos, or recording songs. She had done 171 concerts and released two albums and a number of singles. Both of her albums had debuted at number 1. Her second tour would gross over $40 million. Britney Spears was a bigger star than she'd ever dreamed possible, but everything had happened so fast that she was only now starting to realise what living her dream would entail. She had begun saying to journalists that she knew a person had to "sacrifice some freedom" to get what she wished for in life. She was gradually coming to appreciate how very difficult it would be to get any of that freedom back again.

BLAME IT ON RIO

"I am not ashamed to say that I love [Justin Timberlake] from the bottom of my heart."

–Britney Spears

On January 18, 2001, Britney was scheduled to perform the last show of the *Oops!* . . . *I Did It Again* tour in Rio de Janeiro, Brazil, as part of the Rock in Rio pop music festival. Justin Timberlake and 'N Sync were also on the card. Britney's portion of the concert was to be taped as a Brazilian TV special called *Britney Spears: Live from Rock in Rio*, which would be broadcast worldwide via DirecTV.

At a preliminary press conference, a British reporter managed to shout out a couple of questions to Britney before Big Rob got between them. He wanted to know whether she was sharing a suite with Justin and whether they were real, dyed-in-the-wool Southern Baptists and thus committed to remaining chaste. Britney and Justin were still publicly claiming to be just good friends who loved each other, but in Rio a weary Britney was overheard saying "It's getting harder and harder for me to keep saying that stuff" before she was whisked into a car. Several months later, when that comment appeared in print, it had been changed to, "It's getting harder and harder for me to stay a virgin."

The fact was, Britney and Justin were sharing a hotel suite and they did so for three nights. Kitchen staff at the Rio Intercontinental had been instructed on how to prepare Southern fried chicken, as Britney and Justin would be ordering it (with French fries and Coke) on a daily basis.

Between November 21, 2000, when Britney's European tour ended and January 18, 2001, the date of the Rio show, Britney and Justin were rarely apart. Both were now highly paid entertainers, but in the previous year or so Britney's star had begun to eclipse Justin's. Though very popular with the teen crowd, Justin was still just the front man for a boy band that had peaked and was starting to fall off, while Britney was a global sensation with record-breaking sales who could command world media attention with a wave of her hand.

In December 2000, Britney turned nineteen. On the first of the month, she made a quick trip to San Diego to surprise Justin, who was there with 'N Sync for the last North American date on the *No Strings Attached* tour. Britney took the guys by surprise, strolling onstage wearing big sunglasses and a wig. It was a fun moment for Justin and Britney, but it turned a bit awkward when Justin asked the crowd to sing "Happy Birthday" to Britney. His request was met with booing. The screaming girls were there to see 'N Synch and Justin's girlfriend was an unwelcome disruption of their fantasies. Britney, a bit miffed, left for the venerable La Quinta Resort and Club in Palm Springs, California, where she planned to celebrate her birthday. Her spirits picked up when she discovered that Justin had arranged for twenty-six dozen roses to be placed in her suite and the petals from ten dozen more scattered on the floors.

Three days later, Justin met Britney in Las Vegas at the 2000

Billboard Music Awards, where 'N Sync would perform. It was a stellar evening for the young couple. Britney received the album artist of the year award for *Oops! . . . I Did It Again* and the award for the highest one-week album sales figures ever achieved by a female artist. 'N Sync picked up album of the year, Top 40 artist of the year and the award for highest one-week album sales.

Britney and Justin were trying to carve out an emotional oasis for themselves away from the glare of the media and the machinations of record companies and business managers. When they were alone, they indulged in typical young-love silliness: Britney called Justin "Stinky," and he called her "Pinky." Later in December, after Britney had visited Justin at home in Tennessee at Christmas, she surprised him by arranging a weeklong Caribbean vacation for the two of them. Britney later described the trip as "pure heaven," and Justin said it was "something right out of *Blue Lagoon*." Not to be outdone, Justin planned a romantic New Year's celebration for them at a private log cabin in Vail, Colorado. Then both returned to work for a couple of weeks before hooking up again in Rio. Ten days after that, they got together again, this time at Super Bowl XXXV in Miami; MTV had put together a star-studded halftime show featuring Aerosmith, 'N Sync, Britney Spears, Nelly, Mary J. Blige and Tremors featuring the Earthquake Horns.

For the rest of the year, though, the two could only steal away together on rare occasions, as their schedules kept them extraordinarily busy. 'N Sync worked on a new album, *Celebrity* (their last, as it turned out), from January through April. It was finally released on July 24, in the middle of their *Pop Odyssey* tour, which had begun on May 23 and would end on September

1. (An extension, called the *Celebrity* tour, ran from March 3 to April 28, 2002.)

From February through August 2001, Britney was also working on a new album, her third, to be called *Britney*. Max Martin again served as writer and producer, so Britney had to spend much of this time bouncing between studios in the U.S. and Sweden. Justin wrote and produced one song for the album: "What It's Like to Be Me." Britney wanted to try her hand at songwriting, but though she received credit for five tracks, the experience taught her that she wasn't a natural songwriter; she leaned heavily on her co-writers. In all, she recorded twenty-three tracks, twelve of which she selected for the album.

Meanwhile, what can only be called the "Britney Spears empire" was taking shape. *Forbes* had ranked her one of the top-earning celebrities of 2000 based on the proceeds from the *Oops!* tour, her record sales and her endorsement deals; the magazine calculated that she was already worth nearly $50 million. Lynne Spears was sticking close to her daughter and in April 2001, the pair came out with their second book—a novel entitled *A Mother's Gift*. It recounts the struggles and adventures of a young girl who leaves home to search for success in the big world—essentially, a fictionalised version of their memoir *Heart to Heart*.

Endorsement deals were now pouring in. Britney signed a contract with Pepsi through which she stood to make tens of millions of dollars for a minimal amount of work. The deal included TV commercials, Internet campaigns and point-of-purchase promotions. The campaign kicked off with a commercial that established a new record for most expensive TV commercial ever made. After the deal was signed, unfortunately, Britney was photographed carrying a huge bottle of Coca-Cola. Her manager, Larry Rudolph, was angry. He explained to her in a forceful fashion what personal endorsement deals mean: she was expected to help sell Pepsi's products, not the competitor's. Britney retorted that she made their commercials and posed for their posters and that Pepsi would have a major product placement arrangement in her upcoming film, *Crossroads*, so what more did they want? Rudolph shouted back, "Loyalty!"

* * *

The next logical step in the marketing of the Britney Spears brand was to make a movie. Given her level of fame, movie scripts were pouring in, but everyone seemed to want her to play a vapid pop princess or a rebellious teenage vixen. She was offered a lot of parts in horror movies, as well. Even the King of Hollywood himself, Steven Spielberg, wanted her for a project that was being developed by his production company, Amblin Entertainment. It was described as a cross between *Dirty Dancing* and *The Flamingo Kid* and it would feature an ensemble cast. Rudolph read the script and though he was attracted by the idea of a Spears-Spielberg collaboration, he was concerned that Britney would not have the major starring role in her first film effort. Her team felt strongly that they had to pick a winner for her right off the bat, so they turned Spielberg down. Britney would hold out for a starring role or, better yet, convince a studio to build a movie around her.

Paramount Pictures was the first to step forward with a plan. They agreed to build a movie around Britney; it would be written for and with her. She was given script and director approval, unheard-of for a neophyte. But, as a Paramount studio executive says, "In the context of the time, there was no downside at all, Britney was everywhere, super popular, even if the movie was mediocre, which it turned out to be, it would still be profitable. In fact, because of licensing agreements and foreign distribution arrangements, it was in profit before it came out."

Crossroads would feature a few original songs by Britney and most importantly for the studio, it would be cheap to produce. Young screenwriter Shonda Rhimes was hired to write the screenplay. Rhimes had previously written the brilliant screenplay for *Introducing Dorothy Dandridge*, which became a film starring Halle Berry; she has since become best known as the creator and a main writer for the TV series *Grey's Anatomy*. Rhimes spent a little time with Britney to get a feel for who she was, what her skill level was and what she would and would not do onscreen. She then went away and crafted the screenplay to Britney's abilities and comfort zone. Britney would play a Southern girl who travels to L.A. with two high-school friends to audition for a recording contract. The movie begins in the South (it was partially shot in Louisiana) and develops into an adventure-filled road trip and bonding story before ending in Hollywood. The film would receive a PG-13 rating, but it was hardly risqué.

The film was assigned a budget of $12 million (in 2001, the average price of a studio film was $55 million) and given a twelve-week shooting schedule, wrapping up in May 2001. Ace music video director Tamra Davis was brought in to direct. She had made a name for herself by making videos for the likes of Depeche Mode and the Beastie Boys (Davis is married to Beastie Boy Mike D). This was Davis's first feature film and she was quite open about her reasons for taking on the project: Britney Spears was the hottest star on the planet and she seemed to succeed at everything she attempted. It was an attractive place to start. The two got on well. Davis commends Britney's professionalism: "Britney worked very hard on every aspect of the project. It was very impressive to see this young girl with so much power, surrounded by people talking to her and fussing with her, yet she remained focused on the job at hand at all times."

The rest of the cast was a mix of veterans and new faces. The veterans included Dan Aykroyd and Kim Cattrall; the up-and-comers were Zoe Saldana (who would achieve worldwide renown in 2009's *Avatar*), Justin Long (perhaps best known as Mac in the Apple computer TV commercials) and Anson Mount, who played Britney's love interest in the film.

Mount describes how the role came to him and why he accepted it. "I was doing a film called *City by the Sea* with Robert DeNiro and he saw me reading a script one day and asked me what it was. I told him it was a script for a movie starring Britney Spears and said I didn't think I would do it. DeNiro reacted strongly—asked me if I was crazy. He really liked Britney's music and said that the movie would be seen by many millions of people and that it was a great shot." At first, Mount thought that DeNiro was kidding him; then he realised that he was dead serious. Mount explained to DeNiro that he didn't actually have the role but that they wanted him to read. If he read well, then he'd be offered the role. "So DeNiro, who is a fantastic guy to work with, offers to help me with the lines. I read my character's lines and DeNiro played Britney."

As shooting progressed, young Britney's power became

more and more evident. Co-star Saldana reports that it was "a fun shoot but a strange one. Britney had never done a film before, but everything on the set revolved around her. And that was not at her insistence; she wasn't being a diva at all, at least not then. It was the managers and PR people around. They would be telling the producers and Tamra when Britney was available to shoot, when she needed more time to prepare for scenes, when she was not available at all. Britney seemed a bit embarrassed by it all, but she was treated like she was royalty. I don't know if that helped or hurt the film, it was just how it was."

The perks of fame were beginning to inundate Britney. Everyone deferred to her; everything was made to revolve around her. It was an intoxicating experience, but it would inevitably distort her perceptions and judgment. And the parasites were swarming.

Years before, after the sudden cancellation of *MMC*, Lynne Spears had engaged manager-agent William Kahn to help Britney find TV or movie work, but nothing had ever come of their association. Now that the money was rolling in but not coming his way, Kahn sued for punitive damages of $75,000 plus 15 percent of Britney's earnings. Britney shrugged it off: "When everything is going so well, along comes a, you know, a kind of a stomper." The incident was expeditiously settled out of court.

* * *

On September 6, just after completing her new album, Britney made another appearance at the MTV Video Music Awards ceremony, held that year at New York's Metropolitan Opera

House. Again, she chose a very revealing outfit for the occasion, but it was another element of her performance that really grabbed the audience's attention this time. She sang part of her new song "I'm A Slave 4 U" in a cage with a real tiger and another portion of it with a live albino Burmese python wrapped around her shoulders. This drew the ire of the militant animal rights group PETA, which accused Britney and MTV of mistreating the animals. At the ceremony, Britney was able to spend a little time with Justin, who was there with 'N Sync. The band's *Pop Odyssey* tour had just ended and their video "Pop" won five awards.

A few days afterward, on September 11, Britney boarded a plane for Sydney, Australia, where she was scheduled to do some more PR to coincide with Jive's announcement of her tour dates. By the time she landed, news of the attacks on the World Trade Centre was everywhere. Britney became hysterical: her brother, Bryan, was living in her condo in New York and she was desperate to get in touch with him; as it turns out, he was fine. Back in the U.S., she did an interview with CNN in which she was asked what she thought of President George W. Bush's handling of the crisis. She replied, "He is our president and we need to support him in whatever he decides." This earnest but rather naive statement was used by Michael Moore in his film *Fahrenheit 9/11*.

* * *

At the end of September, with the world still reeling from the events of September 11, Britney and Justin felt in need of a break. They rented a mansion in Destin on Florida's Emerald Coast and settled in to relax for a few days. But on September 22, burglars broke into the house while they were out. They took clothing and jewellery, as well as some video cameras, tripods and video players—total value, about $5,000. Almost immediately, though, rumours started rocketing through the media that the thieves had gotten their hands on a tape featuring Britney and Justin having sex.

Jive snapped into controlled panic mode. They considered three possible scenarios: first, there was no tape and the rumours were nonsense; second, the burglars were just kids and took the tape by accident along with the other loot; and third, the robbery had been executed specifically to get the tape to sell to an Internet celebrity porn site or to extort money from Britney, Justin and Jive Records.

The four young thieves were quickly apprehended and the stolen items were recovered, including a video tape. But, according to Rick Hord, a spokesman for the Okaloosa County Sheriff, the tape was "very boring"—just a bunch of vacation scenes. Britney only appeared on it for a few moments. Case closed. But the media chatter would not die down and Jive inadvertently kept it going when a company representative mentioned a "nonexistent tape of Britney and Justin innocently kissing and making out." The remark seemed to suggest that there was in fact a tape of the two of them together—just not a sex tape of the Pamela Anderson or Paris Hilton variety. Finally, when nothing further surfaced, the media moved on. For the time being.

Dream Within a Dream

"I'm rich, freakin' rich. It's crazy."
—Britney Spears

Money was now flowing. Big money. And Britney was generous to those who had helped her. Without blinking an eye, she made $1 million available to her father, Jamie, to wipe out the family debts. She also had the plans drawn up for her mother's new house—a $4 million Tudor mansion near Kentwood.

But others benefited from her largesse, too. She established the Britney Spears Foundation for children. Perhaps because her own childhood had been so strange and challenging, she had a deep empathy for children in need. One of the foundation's first initiatives was to give $200,000 to create a performing arts summer camp for underprivileged children in the area of Washington, D.C.; New York; Boston; and Hartford, Connecticut. Kids who wanted a future in the performing arts could attend free of charge and learn from professional singers and dancers. The first such camp was held in the Berkshire Mountains of western Massachusetts and eighty lucky kids got to attend. The next year, it took place in Cape Cod and there were more than 140 campers, plus one special guest: Britney Spears.

One of the dancers in Britney's troupe, Chase Benz, talks about her compassion towards children: "I saw it time and time again. If we were backstage after a show and there were local dignitaries wanting to meet Britney or media people wanting to talk to her, she would always step away from them if a little kid wanted to meet her. One time in particular, we were performing in England and a little girl in a wheelchair was brought backstage to meet her idol, Britney. Britney went right for her and made that little girl feel like she was the most important person in the whole place. She talked to her, signed all kinds of things for her— she even gave her the shirt off her back. I swear to God, there was Brit in a sports bra draping her shirt around the little girl's shoulders."

* * *

Britney, on the verge of turning twenty, was starting to look at the world in a different way. She was beginning to ask herself questions like: "Why me? What does all this mean? What should I be doing with it?" The stress of constantly recording and touring and promoting herself, as well as her parents' divorce—all of which she had seemed to be taking in stride over the previous year and a half—was weighing heavily on her now. She suffered from insomnia and anxiety attacks. Benz remembers, "It was tough on her, she had a lot going on. A lot of people were counting on her, and she had a lot of obligations to meet. She felt very anxious about not wanting to disappoint anyone."

She retreated a bit into herself but appeared to gain strength from the example of Madonna. She saw the similarities between them; Madonna had grabbed the big golden chalice, just like she had. Only Madonna was tougher. Madonna was in control. If you screwed with Madonna, she would screw you right back. Britney listened to Madonna's albums *Ray of Light* and *Music* over and over. She particularly loved "What It Feels Like for a Girl," which Madonna had dedicated to "all the pop bitches out there."

At the same time, Fe Culotta observes, "She was in this weird place emotionally. She was enjoying the fun stuff, but it was so surreal. It was like she was gorging herself on life. The only way she would ever get any rest was if she completely collapsed with exhaustion." No breaks for Britney. Instead, she started gearing up for her next effort: the *Dream within a Dream* tour, which would kick off on November 1 to coincide with the release of her third album, *Britney*. With this album, Britney left the teenage bubblegum sound behind and although the critical reception was mixed, the album sold 750,000 copies in the first week (less than her previous effort, but still impressive). *Britney* immediately rose to the top of the charts, making her the first female artist in music history to have her first three albums debut at number 1 on the Billboard 200 list.

A few days into the tour, the show arrived in Toronto, where at a press conference a reporter asked about the meaning of the tour title. Britney replied that it was the title of an Edgar Allan Poe poem: "It kind of means that we all have dreams, but not everyone can be in control of their dreams, make them live within them each day. Dreams are like magic, but real." The name of the tour and the album's song mix revealed Britney's state of mind. She was in a transition period, but she had little time to reflect on it.

The 2001 portion of the tour was typically intense—thirty-one shows in just seven weeks in locations spread across North

America (including a sold-out show in East Rutherford, New Jersey, on Britney's twentieth birthday). When the 2001 portion ended—on December 21, 2001, Britney announced that, with the exception of an April show in Tokyo, she would be taking "six months off from my career." This might have been wishful thinking. In fact, her break lasted just five months (the tour resumed on May 24, 2002, in Las Vegas) and it was a break in name only. *Crossroads* was opening in early 2002 and Britney had to promote it; she had a number of other commitments as well.

Britney's management and Jive Records had, in fact, been the ones to convince her that she needed a respite in the first place. They told her that she no longer had to push herself so hard, she had made it in spectacular fashion and she had little left to prove. She, did, however, have to keep growing and maturing as an artist and in order to do that, she would need some rest. All concerned were also worried that if Britney kept up her current pace, she'd eventually burn out completely.

Justin and Britney reconnected in L.A, where they were spotted doing some major Christmas shopping. Britney had let slip in October that she and Justin were going to get married, "probably sometime in 2002." As if to stoke the rumours, Justin bought her a ring that cost in the neighbourhood of $100,000. According to celebrity journalist Janet Charlton, the pair hit Rodeo Drive, in Beverly Hills and went "in and out of one shop after another buying leather pants, leather jackets, cashmere sweaters; and she bought Justin a diamond-encrusted watch that she had inscribed with the words 'To My Justin, Love You Always.'"

To the public, Britney and Justin were a dream couple: two

young success stories in a fairy tale relationship. What people didn't know was that when not on tour or travelling for other work-related reasons, they were living together in a large house in the Hollywood Hills. They'd planned to buy the house together, but Britney decided at the last minute to buy it herself. It was all very neat: both were co-managed by Johnny Wright; both recorded for Jive; and they were living together as comfortably as, in the words of one close contact, "an old married couple."

Jive was pleased with the misconception. The company continued to deny that its two star recording artists were in a sexual relationship and reaped the benefits that came from the media's interest in the squeaky-clean duo: their names were constantly in the news. It was a surreal situation. The press portrayed them as happy, lovey-dovey youngsters, but they were leading extremely busy and stressful lives. It was all wearing thin, especially for Britney. In January 2002, she revised her earlier statement, telling British journalist Cat Deeley, "Justin and I plan to get married sometime in the future—not in 2002, though."

* * *

Britney's first foray into acting, *Crossroads*, premiered on February 11, 2002. In interviews leading up to the release, she was asked if she wanted to leave music behind and pursue acting. "Acting is another form of expression that I enjoyed," she replied, "but music, that is in my soul. I will always go back to music."

The reviews the film garnered were predictably negative. Roger Ebert said, "I went to *Crossroads* expecting a glitzy bimbofest. What I got was the bimbos but no fest." The film pulled in an acceptable $15 million on its opening weekend, but then its take dropped precipitously. Britney's movie debut was still considered a success, but not nearly the success she, Paramount and Team Britney had hoped it would be. The soundtrack album wasn't a big hit either, in part because the film's three main Britney songs—"Overprotected," "I'm Not a Girl, Not Yet a Woman," and "I Love Rock 'n' Roll"—were all on her new album.

Despite getting panned, however, *Crossroads* wasn't all that bad. Though clearly inexperienced, Britney tried very hard not to merely play herself. The movie was nominated for a handful of awards, some frivolous, some unwelcome. She was nominated for an MTV Movie Award in the breakthrough performance and best-dressed categories; she won neither. She snared a Teen Choice Award nomination for best actress in a comedy or drama and best onscreen couple (with Anson Mount). It was at the ceremony for the notorious Golden Raspberry Awards, the Razzies, where *Crossroads* really cleaned up. It was nominated in eight categories—including worst original song ("Overprotected"), worst director, worst picture, worst screen couple and worst screenplay. Britney won worst actress (sharing the award with Madonna, for her dreadful performance in *Swept Away*); and the worst original song Razzie went to "I'm Not a Girl, Not Yet a Woman".

* * *

Justin had escorted Britney to the world premiere of *Crossroads* and to the Grammys on February 26, but he was visibly distracted at these events. Suspicions that something was wrong were confirmed when, shortly afterwards, he called it quits on their three-year relationship. Britney and Justin had established a rule: neither would allow more than three weeks to go by without spending time with the other, but by the time the *Crossroads* premiere rolled around, they had been apart a lot longer than that. Both had been spotted partying with other people. Justin had been seen ushering a bevy of models into his limousine after a party and had been linked to professional dancer Jenna Dewan. Britney was spotted in the company of Marcus Schenkenberg, a male model, though she insisted that "there's no hanky-panky." She publicly denied her split with Justin and even Justin's mother, Lynn Harless, said, "They are two young people involved in a very passionate relationship and they are having a bit of trouble right now."

USA Today quoted Britney as saying "I'm single right now," but it turned out that the quote had been taken from a skit taped for a British TV show called *The Big Breakfast*. Britney then went on the *Oprah Winfrey Show* and declared that she and Justin were not having any problems at all. Other rumours flew, as well. One was that Britney was Justin's beard—she was helping him to disguise the fact that he was gay. Another was that Justin was pretending to be Britney's boyfriend to help her hide her affair with a much older man. Each rumour was more far-fetched than the next.

Britney's most candid explanation came much later, on November 27, 2003, during an interview with Diane Sawyer on ABC's *Primetime*. When Sawyer mentioned the breakup, Britney smiled uncomfortably then completely lost control. Her face contorted in pain and she began to cry. Sawyer pressed on, asking her about allegations that Justin had left her because she was cheating on him. Britney composed herself a bit, but the tears were still falling. She answered, "I'm not saying he is technically wrong, but I am also not saying that he is technically right, either." This was as close to an admission of cheating as she would ever get. When Sawyer persisted with this topic, Britney, no longer able to contain her emotions, asked for a break in the interview. Sawyer complied.

In those early months of 2002, however, Britney kept saying that they were just taking a break and would sort out their problems like any other couple. But Justin was done. He was sure that Britney had been with someone else and had lied to him about it. He had been involved in two serious romantic relationships before meeting Britney and he'd ended both after becoming convinced that he was being cheated on. (Both of his former girlfriends—Danielle Ditto and Veronica Finn—deny that they cheated.) To Justin, Britney was now just like the others. In January 2003, he told *Rolling Stone*, "She has a beautiful heart, but if I've lost my trust in someone, I don't think it's right for me to be with them."

In fact, all signs indicated that Justin was right about Britney and that she'd been stepping out with her long-time friend—dance team member and choreographer Wade Robson. A talented dancer, Robson had worked closely with Britney and many credit him with being the first to urge her to shed her ingenue schoolgirl image and become an edgy, scantily clad vamp along the lines of Madonna. Robson had been nominated for an MTV Video Music award for his choreography on "I'm a Slave 4 U," the song Britney had sung with the python wrapped around her shoulders.

Britney had told friends for years that she had a crush on Wade. When rumours started to surface that she had cheated on Justin with him, neither she nor Robson would confirm or deny the stories. Justin was convinced that they were true. He had known Wade almost as long as Britney had and they were actually quite good friends. They had gone skydiving and motorcycling together. They had even collaborated on writing four songs for 'N Sync's *Celebrity* album and Justin acknowledged his friend in the liner notes: "Wade, never in my life have I clicked creatively with anyone like I have connected with you." But as soon as Justin broke with Britney, all contact between Justin and Wade ceased as well.

* * *

The media frenzy around the breakup made things more awkward and uncomfortable than ever for Britney because she was in the middle of a major publicity tour for *Crossroads*. Her behaviour became erratic and she tried to avoid the public eye. At the London press conference for the UK premiere, her PR people announced that the conference would end immediately if anyone brought up 9/11, virginity, or Justin Timberlake. At the premiere, on March 25, 2002, thousands gathered outside the famous Odeon Leicester Square Cinema to see Britney walk down the red carpet, but when her limousine arrived, over an hour late, she jumped out and rushed into the theatre without stopping to acknowledge her fans, as she usually did. Inside the cinema, when she was introduced to the audience, she was received with enthusiastic applause mixed with booing—some audience members were unhappy that she'd made them wait so long. Britney was upset by this and she exited the theatre as quickly as she had entered it. Her snubbing of her fans was all over the local media the next day. A similar scenario unfolded at the Paris premiere. A short concert had been arranged to open the film. At the last minute, Britney cancelled the show without explanation, leaving over three thousand fans angry and disappointed. She left the Paris screening of the film before it ended and was whisked away by limousine.

The adulation on which Britney had once thrived was now a burden to her. Each press conference was a potential assault on her privacy and an aggravation of the emotional pain she carried inside. To make matters worse, sharp-tongued critics and gossip columnists were starting to say she was spoiled and contemptuous of those who had made her a star. She felt hounded and resentful, barking at one reporter, "What is a person supposed to do when their life becomes entertainment for people?"

CRY ME A RIVER

"This is all just getting crazy."

–Britney Spears

The only international show on the *Dream within a Dream* tour agenda was held on April 25, 2002, at the Tokyo Dome. The reason for this choice was simple: the Japanese are the world's most rabid Britney Spears fans and hunger for all things Britney. MTV Japan was going to shoot the concert for a television special and, as if any further affirmation were needed, *Crossroads* became Japan's top-grossing film of 2002.

The next month, back in Kentwood, things took a sadder turn. The divorce of Lynne and Jamie Spears became final. Lynne was now living in the mansion that Britney had built for her, which they called "Serenity." She drove around in a new Lexus that Britney had given her for Mother's Day. Jamie was living in their old Kentwood family home, but after the divorce came through he went to New York to join Bryan in Britney's $3.5 million loft. To fill the time, he set about remodelling the loft.

Jamie rarely commented publicly on anything to do with Britney's career. He'd never seemed comfortable being the father of a famous pop singer and he fiercely guarded his privacy. On one occasion, four teenage Britney fans pulled up to the Kentwood family home and were set upon by three vicious dogs followed by Jamie carrying a large gun. One of Britney's PR people, Lisa Kasteler, explained that there had been death threats against Britney and her family and that Jamie was just being cautious; when Jamie realised that it was just another carload of fans, he had called off the dogs and gone back inside.

The *Dream within a Dream* tour resumed on May 24 with a two-date stop in Las Vegas and then it travelled across the country from west to east to do another thirty-two shows. After a show at the American Airlines Center in Dallas, Texas, on July 22, Britney and her squad flew to Toluca, Mexico, to unwind for a couple days before two concerts in Mexico City, on July 27 and 28. A throng of reporters was there to greet Britney at the airport. When they began calling out questions about Justin, she gave them the finger and the gesture was captured by photographers and shared with the world. During a preshow press conference, she was again asked about her personal life and she curtly replied that she would not take questions of that nature. If anyone had questions about her music or her shows, she would be happy to answer; if not, then the press conference was over. The assembled journalists booed and whistled at this, so Britney just shrugged and left with her handlers.

The first Mexico City show, held at the outdoor Foro Sol venue, went off without a hitch, but just after the second show started, a powerful thunderstorm hit. Britney stopped singing, said something to her dancers and then addressed the audience, saying, "Sorry, Mexico, I love you all." At that point, the whole troupe left the stage. Team Britney headed directly to the airport and left Mexico without offering an explanation. A spokesperson for Britney later issued a statement explaining that the stage had been hit by lightning (although no one in the audience could remember such a thing happening) and that the rain had made the stage dangerously slippery for the dancers (an odd comment, since the show's finale involved dousing the stage with water).

A month before the end of the tour and again in the midst of a torrential downpour, Britney's restaurant, Nyla, opened in New York City. Britney took a short break from the tour to attend the opening and say a few words to reporters. "This is gonna be, like, my hangout from now on," she announced enthusiastically. Jamie had worked on remodelling the premises, assisting Bobby Ochs, a restaurateur who had helped other celebrities to set up restaurants. Ochs would keep things running on a day-to-day basis and a woman named Jodi Wasserman would manage the floor.

Britney claimed that they had chosen the name Nyla because it combined the abbreviations of the states of New York and Louisiana (N.Y. and L.A.), but a reporter noted that Nyla was also the name of a Kentwood-area burger joint that Britney had frequented. The brightly decorated, two-floor restaurant was located in the Dylan Hotel on East 41st Street and had once been an upscale French establishment called Virot. Jamie converted it into an American-bistro-type space and the menu they adopted featured down-home Louisiana and Italian food. Britney had originally planned to call the restaurant Pinky, her nickname for Justin Timberlake, but she changed her mind for obvious reasons. On opening night, there was a party and a photo op and Britney was on hand to christen her new business venture. The weather was atrocious, but still a large number of fans gathered outside for a chance to see her in the flesh. Once again, though, Britney disappointed her fans. Arriving well over an hour late, she posed for a few pictures, made some brief comments and disappeared inside. She didn't even stay at the party very long, although she did pose for photos with wait staff, who had been hired based on their resemblance to Britney.

The next day, the New York media were brutally unkind. The *New York Post* and a local television news outlet both called the party one of the worst of the year and things didn't get any better for the venture after that. There were reports that Jamie often hung out at Nyla in the company of a busty, brassy "coke fiend," but Jodi Wasserman downplays all that: "[Jamie] would come in a lot. Britney was never there at all. I saw her opening night then maybe one other time, but her dad was in frequently. He seemed like a really decent guy, a down-to-earth guy, with no pretence about him. He would have a few drinks every now and then and he did come in with women a couple of times, but he never caused any kind of trouble." Trouble came in the form of bad reviews. There was also a widely reported (but unsubstantiated) case of food poisoning and a well-publicised stabbing that, even though it had nothing to do with Nyla, was reported to have happened outside "the restaurant owned by pop superstar Britney Spears."

The restaurant venture marked a turning point for Britney. She had grown used to seeing everything she touched turn to gold, but her golden touch was not proving to be permanent. She now seemed to have as many detractors as she had fans and she was not dealing with it all that well. Her psyche was showing more signs of damage with each passing month and unless she had some real guidance, she was headed for a breakdown. But Britney was now an industry. She was surrounded by people whose livelihoods derived directly from her earning power; and, although there were some in her inner circle who were quite concerned about her increasingly unpredictable behaviour, no one seemed willing to suggest that she be taken out of circulation, even for a few months. The cash river had to be kept flowing and Britney was the source.

* * *

The gaping wound to Britney's heart as a result of her breakup with Justin had not healed. And her pain and humiliation were about to be exacerbated by Justin himself. He was speaking publicly about their split, saying things like, "You know, we're just not perfect, and I am not going to judge anyone. It is just a situation of . . . it just is not enough anymore. It was a very intense relationship and it is finished." But inside Justin was hurt and angry as well and his way of dealing with it was through music. The second single from his first solo album, *Justified*, was an angry song called "Cry Me a River," and the video that accompanied it was even angrier. It doesn't take much imagination to see Justin's anger at Britney in every line and gesture. He sings, "You don't have to say what you did, I already know. I found out from him, now there is just no chance, for you and me, and now there will never be. Don't it make you sad about it?" The video depicts Justin breaking into his former girlfriend's house (the girlfriend is played by actress Laura Hastings, who bears a strong resemblance to Britney) and taping himself making out passionately with another woman. He then watches as his former girlfriend returns home to find the tape playing on her television.

Britney has said of the video, "I was shocked as shit when I saw it." It touched off yet another round of public speculation about Britney and Justin. *US Weekly* ran a cover story entitled "Britney vs. Justin: The War Is On." Timberlake coyly remarked, "It's not about her, it's about me." Britney told *Rolling Stone* that the whole thing was a publicity stunt; Justin had called her to ask if they could talk about getting back together and as the conversation was ending he mentioned that he was going to use a Britney look-alike in a video. "He said, don't worry about it, it's no big deal. So I told him to go ahead." Later, she would accuse Justin of calling her just so he could say he'd informed her about the video. After seeing the video, she'd called to ask him why he'd defamed her like that and he responded, "Well, I got a controversial video out of it, didn't I?" She commented wryly, "So he got what he wanted. I think it looks like such a desperate attempt, personally. But that was a great way to sell a record. He's smart. A smart guy."

Although 2002 was almost over, it still held one more nasty jolt for Britney. Her New York restaurant, Nyla, was an unqualified disaster. It was bleeding money, so before the place went bankrupt, Britney cut all ties with it. In financial terms, the failure was a minor issue for her. *Forbes* had declared her the most powerful celebrity in the world, ahead of Madonna. *People* reported that she'd sold just over fifty-two million albums in less than four years and had earned between $40 and $50 million per year in that time. So were the negative incidents of 2002 just passing clouds in an otherwise clear blue sky? Or were they a series of ominous tremors warning of the earthquake to come?

* * *

Britney's behaviour was getting harder to conceal or explain away. Some media outlets started to ask whether she was dabbling in drugs, either recreational or prescription. She was having mood swings—she'd be the high-energy performer one minute then cry uncontrollably for no apparent reason the next. She took to phoning her dancers or Fe or even Justin at all hours just to talk, just to connect. Lynne was going back and forth to Kentwood, so the situation wasn't as obvious to her, but Fe and Larry Rudolph were becoming alarmed. Rudolph was particularly worried about the rumours of drug use. He knew that they weren't true, but the fact that they were circulating was a liability—in the business of celebrity reporting, perception becomes reality very quickly if not kept in check. Fe worried that Britney wouldn't be able to handle the pressure much longer. They got her a prescription for Prozac to help control her anxiety and depression, but the problems persisted because Britney didn't take the drug regularly, reaching for it only when she felt anxious or depressed. So it was largely ineffective—in fact, it exacerbated her erratic behaviour. She tried to stifle her feelings by rehearsing or working constantly on anything vigorous or creative.

Then one of the things everyone in Britney's inner circle feared the most actually happened. In November 2002, supermarket tabloid *The Star* printed a story about Britney and some of her stage troupe partying in a Miami nightclub called Crobar and snorting cocaine. There was no photographic evidence or confirmation by a credible source, but the tale was out there for public consumption. Someone claimed to have been in the club with Britney and two of her dancers. They allegedly went into the bathroom together and one of the girls laid out lines of cocaine on a toilet seat. The informant said he didn't actually see Britney inhale the cocaine because he was looking at someone else, but he claimed he'd heard her sniff the drug. Rudolph vehemently denied the story and threatened legal action if there was no retraction, but in the end there was no retraction and no legal action.

When the story reached Kentwood, Lynne was confident that it wasn't true, but Jamie wasn't so sure. He had seen changes in his daughter and they upset him. Britney made a quick trip home to Kentwood to assure her family that everything was okay. Jamie, barely able to contain his emotions, told her, "Baby girl, you can come home anytime you want. You don't have to do this." But it was too late to reverse the flood. Way too late and everyone knew it. The show must go on, after all.

SEX SYMBOLIC

"You grow up fast in show business."

–Britney Spears

Britney had reached a career pinnacle after just four years. And, like many who rise too high, too fast in show business, she was ill-equipped emotionally and intellectually to deal with it. So everything was crumbling. First, her personal life began to fray around the edges, then her work began to suffer. To avoid becoming another show-business casualty, she would have to recognise that the time had come to reinvent herself. Britney knew that the schoolgirl sexpot thing, successful as it had been, was no longer something she could get away with. Working with the people around her—Larry Rudolph, the Jive Records team and Johnny Wright—she tried to develop new image ideas. They needed to hit on something that would get the public looking at Britney differently. She could be a hot, sexy, adult woman performer—someone like, maybe, Madonna.

On the personal front, Fe Culotta was trying to keep Britney grounded, but Britney was twenty-one years old and no longer in need of a chaperone or a paid companion. After Britney had commented to a reporter, "Look, I'm human. If I screw up, it's because I'm human. If I go out and have a drink or two, it's because I'm human. Why does everyone make such a big fucking deal out of every little thing I do?" Lynne Spears started to get concerned. When Britney asked another reporter, "Does anyone care if I'm having sex? I mean, like, really, does anyone out there really care if I'm having sex?" Lynne became convinced that her daughter had lost control of her public persona entirely. Her polite Southern demeanour had evaporated because she had been pushed into a corner. The rude, diva-like rock star behaviour was not so much a choice as a survival mechanism.

Lynne didn't know what to do. When she spoke to Britney, Britney would smile and hug her and tell her everything was all right and she shouldn't believe a word of what people were saying about her. Britney loved her mother more than anything in the world and did not want to worry her. But Lynne was not reading the tabloids; she was hearing the stories from those in direct daily contact with Britney. Desperate to help, Lynne contacted Justin Timberlake, who was on the road promoting his solo album. She asked him if he could help, if he could talk to Britney. But Justin was not Reg Jones. He had his own career to worry about and he had to endure the same pressures as Britney. He told Lynne that Britney was a sweet girl, but she was an adult and she had to start taking responsibility for herself.

Britney's management, of course, simply denied and denied some more. When Larry Rudolph was asked to comment on the strange behaviour of his superstar client, he said, "She is not having a breakdown. This is a young girl who has been on the most unimaginably wild rollercoaster ride for several years now. She is taking a break for a short time from the public so she can be the private Britney again for a while."

Rudolph had to make such statements to keep the astronomical

Britney Spears is honored with a star on the Hollywood Walk of Fame.

**Britney Spears
and Justin Timberlake**

**Kevin Federline
and Britney Spears**

**Britney Spears and Madonna kiss while performing
an opening act at the 2003 MTV Video Music Awards.**

Britney Spears is spotted carrying her son in New York City on August 27, 2009.

Britney Spears is seen with her manager and current boyfriend Jason Trawick and her children Sean Preston and Jayden James as they board MV Oscar in Woolloomooloo, Sydney on November 15, 2009 in Australia.

Singer Britney Spears is seen walking with her current boyfriend/manager Jason Trawick and sons, Preston and Jayden in Sydney Botantical Gardens on November 14, 2009 in Sydney, Australia.

(L-R) Professional tennis player Alexandra Stevenson and singer Britney Spears at Arthur Ashe Kid's Day benefit at the U.S. Open during August 1999.

Britney Spears poses in a Studio in 1998 in New York City.

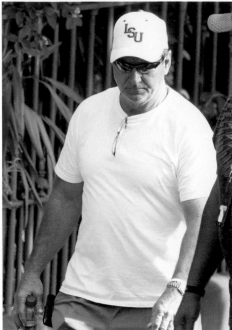

Jamie Spears, father of pop singer Britney Spears, walks near the Park Hyatt Hotel on November 10, 2009 in Melbourne, Australia.

Actress Jamie Lynn Spears attends the premiere of the Warner Bros. film *Nancy Drew* on June 9, 2007 at the Grauman's Chinese Theatre in Hollywood, California.

Britney Spears circa-1999

Britney Spears is seen with her son Jayden James as they disembark the MV Oscar in Woolloomooloo, Sydney on November 15, 2009 in Sydney, Australia

Actress Jamie Lynn Spears (R) and mother Lynne Spears (L) arrive at Sony Pictures' premiere of 'Monster House' held at Mann's Village Theatre on July 17, 2006 in Westwood, California.

TV Personality Paris Hilton and Singer Britney Spears at the 2008 MTV Video Music Awards at Paramount Pictures Studios on September 7, 2008 in Los Angeles, California.

Britney Spears visits Disney World on March 5, 2009 in Orlando, Florida.

Singer Britney Spears and Jason Trawick attend the 52nd Annual GRAMMY
Awards held at Staples Center on January 31, 2010 in Los Angeles, California.

Singer Britney Spears performs on stage during the 2007 MTV Video Music Awards held at The Palms Hotel and Casino on September 9, 2007 in Las Vegas, Nevada.

Singer Britney Spears and actor Colin Farrell arrive at the premiere of 'The Recruit' at the Cinerama Dome on January 28, 2003 in Hollywood, California.

Britney Spears and son Sean Preston in 2006

Paris Hilton and singer Britney Spears attend the Scandinavian Mansion of Style held on December 1, 2007 in Los Angeles, California.

amounts of cash flowing in from fans and sponsors. A lot of people were not just living off Britney—they were getting rich off her. Britney, too, was indulging in the fruits of her labours. L.A. was her oyster; the city was eager to accommodate her every desire. She frequented West Hollywood clubs with her dancers and other "friends" she picked up along the way. Her superstar status bought her instant admission to any club VIP room or party she cared to attend. At these places and events, she mingled with other notables and this made her an even more regular target of the tabloids and gossip columns. She was a latecomer to the celebrity superstar circuit, but now she had entered into it, there was no turning back. At first she was awestruck by the people she was encountering in this exclusive world. She once called everyone she knew to tell them she had just played Ping-Pong with Leonardo DiCaprio. But that changed and she began to get far more comfortable—too comfortable, perhaps—with other big names.

Early in 2003, for example, she had a fling with Irish actor Colin Farrell. Farrell enjoys his life and his success with a vengeance. He's a bad-boy celebrity who carefully cultivates his bad-boy image. To *Playboy* magazine, he quipped, "What's wrong with casual sex? I love casual sex. It's fun, like ordering a pizza." He met Britney just after she broke up with Timberlake. Some reports have it that Farrell asked Britney to be his date for the January 28, 2003 premiere screening of his film *The Recruit* and the after-party at the notorious Chateau Marmont hotel off Sunset Boulevard. Britney giddily agreed, because Farrell was charming and rakish and had a sexy Irish accent and smouldering dark eyes and a reputation for being a guy who liked a lot of "shite." But there are conflicting stories about how they hooked up. A member of Team Britney said that Britney had wanted to meet Farrell and had orchestrated everything herself through one of the producers of *The Recruit*, probably Amanda Cohen. Farrell, however, has said that their meeting was accidental: "I was in the hotel lobby with a bunch of people from Dublin, family and friends that had flown in for the premiere. Britney was there with a few friends as well. We were all having drinks together, chatting. Britney was chatting with me mum. Then it was time to go to the screening. There were five stretch limos waiting in front of the hotel, so we all just piled into them and headed off. When we got to the theater, Britney and I stepped out of the same limo and all of a sudden it meant we were fucking dating."

On the red carpet, they took the Hollywood celeb press by surprise. Photographers snapped away and reporters barked out questions about their "relationship." Britney smiled and Farrell fanned the flames with a wicked smirk, but he insists that they were never really an item: "We met up. We enjoyed each other for a bit. It was what it was. I understand how this stuff works— every little thing is given much greater weight than it has, but in this case, we did what we did and then went back to our lives and careers."

Both left the premiere screening early and separately and met up again at the Chateau Marmont. It was during the after-party that they really sparked rumours. At one point, they both disappeared; they were spotted a while later making out on a terrace like a couple of teenagers. A photographer captured them on film, Colin with his shirt loose and unbuttoned and Britney looking similarly dishevelled. Then a story appeared in the *New York Post* to the effect that the pair had been seen and photographed making out furiously at L.A. nightspot the Troubadour a few nights before the premiere of *The Recruit*. This contradicted their earlier stories. When Britney's camp was approached about it, publicist Lisa Kasteler issued an official response: "They're friends."

It is likely, though, that Colin and Britney had a brief, sexually charged fling. She described him as "the hottest guy in town" and told *W* magazine that she had kissed him and he was "really good." Farrell told a Toronto entertainment journalist that he "could barely keep up with her" but then qualified that with, "Really, though, she's not nearly the innocent virginal girl her PR image suggests, but likewise I am not nearly the bastard that my public image suggests either."

The Colin Farrell/Britney Spears fling ended abruptly in anger and confusion when Colin sent Britney a beautiful gift box. She opened it expectantly only to find a T-shirt that read "I Slept with Colin Farrell and All I Got Was This Lousy T-Shirt." Also tucked into the box was a bumper sticker that read "Honk if You've Slept with Colin Farrell." An angry Britney picked up the phone and dialled his number. "Boy, she blasted me," Farrell laughs. "I got Southern fury on full auto, man. And the more I laughed the angrier she got. When she stopped to take a breath, I tried to explain the humor behind it, and she hung up on me, so that was that." Farrell had the nerve to ask Britney to be his date for his next big premiere, *Daredevil*, which was to take place in L.A. on February 9, but she turned him down with a petulant public comment: "No, I won't be letting him use me to further his career anymore." Farrell was a bit taken aback by the snub, responding, "I think she had other commitments, but that's cool. Everything that happened last time was taken all out of context, but we are still good mates, though."

Britney lost no time in moving on. During a night of clubbing, she met another music sensation, Fred Durst of the band Limp Bizkit. Durst was also a Southerner, from the town of Gastonia, North Carolina, who had surpassed his ambition to become a tattoo artist when he joined the band in 1994. Limp Bizkit had a string of hits featuring loud but precise beats and aggressive lyrics. But by the time he met Britney, in 2003, Durst was paunchy, balding, bearded and tattoo-covered—a generic aging rock star. He had married at twenty and had a daughter. He'd once spent a month or so in jail on an assault charge, because he beat up a man he believed was having an affair with his wife. Durst, in other words, was an unlikely choice for a woman who had once been generally perceived as an innocent Southern belle. He described himself as having "sinned so many ways it's unbelievable. I've robbed stores, I've had plenty of sex, I've lied lots, I've cheated, I've been greedy, I've lusted, everything. I've done it all." When he met Britney, Durst had just split from *Playboy* centrefold Jennifer Rovero, with whom he had a year-and-a-half-old son.

Britney had just been looking for someone to co-write some harder-edged songs with her for her next album. Everyone, including Britney herself, was surprised when word of her association with Durst cropped up on the Limp Bizkit website in early 2003. Durst wrote, "Britney is a sweet, amazing girl. I am really happy to know her right now." Rumours quickly started circulating that they were doing more than writing songs together and reports began to surface of them hanging out in clubs with their hands all over each other; Britney sitting on Fred's lap; Britney and Fred dancing together. After Durst was photographed leaving Britney's house very early one morning, he began addressing the rumours with angry posts on his band's website, such as: "Who really gives a shit if I want to be with Britney. The only person that should really give a shit is Britney. My feelings for Britney are pure and honest." Although Durst reviled the media for invading their privacy, he made things worse by posting news about the two of them on the Web and talking about their relationship to any reporter who would listen.

Durst dipped deep into sleaze in early February, when he made an appearance on Howard Stern's radio show. Not one to beat around the bush, Stern asked Durst directly if he was in a sexual relationship with Britney, who, according to her camp, was still officially a virgin. Durst was there to dish, but he wanted to serve it up his way. He said that he had begun to have tender feelings for Britney when they were collaborating in the studio; then one day he wrote her a romantic letter. He explained that Britney was not just moved by the letter, but she was also turned on by it. She left the studio for a while and "came back dressed in tight pants and a see-through blouse, wearing no bra." Britney, who never went anywhere without her bodyguard and an entourage, suggested that they all head back to her house so they could continue to work in more relaxing surroundings. Durst then told Stern and his millions of listeners that Britney enjoyed oral sex as much as he did, that she loved to "talk dirty," and that she was far from the sweet innocent everyone assumed she was: "She definitely parties too much. She drinks and smokes too much. I think these are all things she picked up, though. Her life is crazy."

Stern egged him on, asking him to describe Britney's body for his listeners. Durst said that Britney had a far better body than his last couple of girlfriends (one of whom was perennial D-lister Carmen Electra). "I like women to have some curves, you know, some softness."

It was clear that Durst was just using Britney to enhance his own public image. Britney's response was to deny any personal involvement with Durst, insisting that they were collaborating professionally, that was it. She told the *Total Request Live* audience, "I don't really know him all that well. He seems like a sweet guy, but he is really not my type at all." But then she let the cat out of the bag. She commented to *GQ* magazine that she had in fact enjoyed a long sexual relationship with Justin Timberlake, adding that it was all right because they were "planning on getting married one day."

But Durst would not be handled and contained. In an interview for British TV, he said to the startled host that Britney Spears was quite aggressive during sex; he then provided some graphic examples. The interview was so vulgar and profane that it was never aired. Realising that he might have gone too far, Durst tried to remedy the situation by telling another journalist, "I play up that pimp thing on purpose. I am not a stereotypical rock star, though. I am a hopeless romantic at heart." Too little too late.

Durst did do one positive thing for Britney: he stated publicly that she didn't have a drug problem. He told a journalist that he'd never seen her use illicit drugs and that "she didn't even ever mention drugs one way or the other." However, this wasn't of much help in the end, because, inexplicably, Britney herself told a reporter, "Let's just say you reach a stage in your life and you are curious. And I was curious at one point. But I am way too focused to ever let anything stop me. Was it a mistake? Yes." With that one brief remark, she all but confirmed that the Miami story, so strenuously denied, had probably been true.

* * *

Britney's PR people dismissed Fred Durst's public utterances as "very junior high." They refuted any suggestion that Britney's personal life was out of control, but the evidence was mounting. There were constant reports of her being seen partying at nightclubs and drinking lots of vodka, usually with a cigarette in her hand. Her management team just said, "Every girl in America relaxes on the weekend like that. What makes what Britney is doing in any way different from what most other girls do?" But Britney was so clearly not "every girl in America." Outside a West Hollywood club, she told a photographer, "I can do anything I want," then climbed into her Mercedes with three other giggling girls and screeched off.

Britney's management, the Jive Records PR department and the Spears family were spinning as fast as they could. The statements they issued in response to all the negative reports about Britney's behaviour were so frequent they were starting to lose their impact. When Britney was on tour or making publicity appearances, her team could maintain a semblance of control over who had access to her and what she was doing. But at this point there was no tour and not a lot of publicity to do, so there was little they could do to prevent Britney from enjoying a taste of rich young Hollywood life.

There was, of course, a huge double standard at work. Colin Farrell and Fred Durst could go from one female conquest to the next. Liaisons with *Playboy* centrefolds, strippers, models, nightclub hostesses—all of that was considered the spoils of success for a male Hollywood celebrity. But if his female counterpart should follow suit, then she was a borderline slut.

* * *

One night at Hollywood's Key Club, Britney watched as a dancer named Columbus Short dazzled everyone with his wicked moves. He was a year younger than Britney, but he had the moves of a far more experienced dancer. Britney invited him to join her little group. The two hit it off at once. One of her dancers reports, "Britney really liked him instantly, not just because of his moves, but because he had a very distinct and interesting personality. He was a nice guy, but he was also very sure of himself and forward, a combination that Britney finds pretty irresistible." Britney asked Short to join her dance team, tour with her after her next album came out and appear in her videos. He was thrilled, of course. Like many talented dancers, he also wanted to make a name for himself as a choreographer. So Columbus became part of Britney's entourage and their connection deepened. The previously quoted dancer recalls that "It didn't start out like she was attracted to him as a man in that way. She really did see him as a great new dance talent that she could have with her onstage. But Britney grew very close to all her dancers. That is very important, because we all spend so much time together we need to really get along; that was how it started with Columbus—just that natural closeness that dancers working together develop." Columbus was looking to Britney to advance his career. He was eager to work with someone dynamic, someone who could help him move up the ladder. Nothing wrong with that—Britney was looking for a talented dancer and Columbus was looking for a good gig.

Britney still believed that she and Justin were destined to be together and continued to hold out hope that they would somehow reconcile. Justin, however, had no intention of ever getting back with Britney and in early April 2003, that became painfully and publicly obvious. Justin was performing and presenting at the Nickelodeon Kids' Choice Awards when he met Cameron Diaz, a fellow presenter. A spark or two passed between them and he asked her to go bowling with him. They quickly became an item and were often photographed with their arms draped around each other or holding hands. Britney, depressed, turned to Columbus Short for comfort. Then photos began appearing of Britney with Columbus and the folks back home began to whisper—Columbus Short is an African American.

In fact, Britney could not have chosen a more stable, respectable and respectful man to lend her the support she so badly needed at this time. Short says that "Britney needed her confidence back. She was emotionally a wreck. She was insecure and she was out of shape. We would talk for hours. She needed someone to listen to her insecurities. She may have needed sex, but that was not what we needed."

After being put through the salacious gossip wringer because of her associations with Farrell and Durst, Britney was looking for someone to trust, someone who wasn't going to take advantage of her and she felt Short was that person. He genuinely liked her and wanted to be her friend. "We never slept together," he says. "And, you know, I heard many times, 'Who turns down Britney Spears?' like I was lying about that, but I wasn't. I respected her as a friend and as an artist; I never looked at her as a sexual object. We had conversations about it, but in the end I saw us as colleagues and to become intimate sexually would have added layers of tension, not just for us but for the rest of the group. That would have wrecked the thing we were best at: being friends."

For a while, there had been no mention of Britney and Columbus in the media. He was an unknown and celebrity journalists were still sorting through the truths, half-truths and fabrications surrounding Britney, Farrell and Durst. As Britney worked on her new album, *In the Zone* and planned the tour following its release, the press finally noticed that a handsome young black man always seemed to be at her side. In the first picture of them to surface, they were just standing together outside a Culver City dance studio where they were rehearsing. In the late summer of 2003, however, Britney and entourage travelled to Rome to shoot a Pepsi commercial. In it, Britney, along with hot new singing sensations Beyoncé and Pink, would play scantily clad gladiators locked in a fight to the death to win the favour of the emperor, played by Enrique Iglesias. The girls would sing a rousing rendition of Queen's "We Will Rock You."

While they were in Rome, Britney and Columbus were snapped by paparazzi on the balcony of a suite at the Hotel Hassler. They were making paper airplanes and flying them towards photographers and "kissing quite romantically," as one Roman newspaper put it; Britney was wearing a T-shirt bearing the motto "Miss B. Haven." Suddenly, everyone wanted to know who Columbus Short was. As the media dug into the story, it was discovered that Columbus had a wife back in L.A. who was eight months pregnant with their first child. Britney reacted calmly. She counselled Columbus on how to handle the rabid scrutiny. "She was really cool," he says. "She taught me how to just ignore it and be cool." When reporters tracked down Short's wife, Brandi, at home in L.A., she, too, responded calmly, stating that her husband and Britney Spears were "friends." "They work together," she added. "The relationship is strictly a professional one."

Back in New York, however, photographers followed Britney and Columbus everywhere. They were seen coming and going from the Trump International Hotel, they were spotted in restaurants and bars and they were shadowed as they tried to shop. Whatever their relationship, Short's wife eventually had enough and divorced him, but he vehemently denied that Britney had had anything to do with it. "We were separated before Britney and I became close," he insisted.

Short eventually moved on. He had worked with Britney for less than two years and many close to her reported that her family was involved with the decision to drop him. But he has always kept to his script. To questions about his relationship with Britney he answers, "I like Britney very much, she is a very cool girl and no matter what anyone says we actually spent the night together in a suite just one time and we weren't alone. A couple of her other female dancer friends were there overnight too." When an *Access Hollywood* reporter asked him about Britney taking him shopping, he shot back, "Listen, I could have milked that cow, if you know what I'm saying. I could have taken advantage of Britney, but I never did, never. Sure I want a $15,000 shirt, but

I want to get it myself, I don't want to be constantly and forever defined by this Britney thing."

* * *

To many, Britney was becoming a Hollywood harlot, a spoiled multimillionaire pop-star diva who cared about nothing and no one but herself. Her defenders were saying she was heading for a major meltdown and that this relationship with a black man, a married hipster, was further evidence of that. But at the time of the release of her fourth studio album, *In the Zone*, Britney was still very happy to be associated with Columbus and one of his close dancer pals. In the liner notes to the album, she wrote, "Kevin and Columbus—we haven't even begun yet." The dancer pal of Short's that Britney mentioned, Kevin, was a struggling young dancer named Kevin Federline.

LIP LOCK

"I wouldn't have turned out this way if I didn't have all those old-fashioned values to rebel against."

–Madonna

The 2003 edition of the MTV Video Music Awards was held on August 28 at Radio City Music Hall in New York, with Chris Rock again hosting the event. The show featured a special performance by Madonna to celebrate the fact that she had been a star performer in the first-ever MTV Video Music Awards. She came onto the stage like the strutting queen of pop culture and performed her hit songs "Like a Virgin" and "Hollywood." Performing with her were the two young women who were now carving out Madonna-like careers of their own and who both cited her as a major influence: Christina Aguilera and Britney Spears. (Apparently, the mantel of Madonna was too broad and heavy to be inherited by one new star—it needed two.)

Britney and Christina had long been living their careers in parallel. Both did *Star Search* and they appeared on *MMC* together. Both had plied their trade at local fairs and sports events early on, though Aguilera had kept at this longer and was now regularly singing the national anthem before Pittsburgh Penguins, Pirates and Steelers games. But as they grew and became professionals, the comparisons seemed to stop, though there never seemed to be any sense of competition between them. Aguilera embraced a diva image and attitude but never took it too far. Like Britney, her first album, self-titled, was a major hit, selling eight million copies in North America alone, with worldwide sales of over seventeen million. Both were nominated in the category of best new artist at the forty-second Grammy Awards in 2000, but Aguilera had won. Since then, there had been a sense that Aguilera's music was not just popular but also more worthy of critical praise than Britney's. She was always seen as a mature performer, albeit a young one. She never had to shake off a bubblegum princess, teenybopper image.

When filmmaker Baz Luhrmann was looking for new artists for his film *Moulin Rouge*, he chose Aguilera, Pink, Mya and Lil' Kim to remake the song "Lady Marmalade." Aguilera had won Latin Grammies for her Spanish albums (*Mi Reflejo* won her best female pop vocal album in 2001) and the collaboration on "Lady Marmalade" won her another Grammy in 2002. Aguilera, though (and also like Britney), was not without her detractors. Many criticised her Latin-influenced songs as nothing more than an attempt to cash in on the then wildly popular Latin music scene, saying she clearly had no real grasp of the Spanish language. (As it happens, Aguilera does speak and understand Spanish. Her dad is from Ecuador).

Aguilera had had her ups and downs as well. She was tangled up with record company and management company lawsuits over contracts and image disagreements. She was trying to resist being sold as a bubblegum pop star along the lines of . . . Britney Spears. Aguilera went the other way with her second album, *Stripped*, a raunchy, lusty album that sold 330,000 copies in its first week of release. She also posed for the cover of *Rolling Stone* practically naked and unapologetically so. Her video for the album's first single, "Dirty," was controversial for its in-your-face sexuality, but she tempered her message by releasing the lovely, classical-music-infused "Beautiful" as the second single from that album and with it won another Grammy for best female pop vocal performance. And when Justin Timberlake was looking for a hot female act to tour with him during the latter half of his *Justified* solo tour, he chose Christina Aguilera.

* * *

On that steamy night in August on the Radio City Music Hall stage, the number began with two little girls (one was Madonna's daughter, Lourdes) dressed like flower girls at a wedding walking around the stage tossing petals into the crowd. Then, on a three-tiered platform stage resembling a wedding cake, a veiled figure rose out of the middle of the platform. She started to sing "Like a Virgin" wearing a lacy, barely there version of a wedding dress and spike-heeled shoes. She pulled back the veil to reveal herself: it was Britney Spears. Britney sang as she descended the stairs and strutted around the stage. Then she stopped singing and another veiled singer dressed similarly entered from stage left and took up the song where Britney left off. The voice was easily identifiable as Christina Aguilera's even before she raised her veil to reveal jet-black locks that contrasted with Britney's blonde. (Christina was not, in fact, Madonna's first choice. She had wanted the combo of Britney and Jennifer Lopez to do the number, but J-Lo turned it down, as she was off celebrating her engagement to Ben Affleck at the time.)

Christina and Britney sang together, strutting and thrusting, writhing sexily around on the stage floor. Then they abruptly stopped and, after a dramatic pause, a black-tuxedo-clad, top-hat-wearing groom—Madonna—rose up out of the top of the wedding-cake stage. She stepped down the stairs singing her song "Hollywood" in spike-heeled, thigh-high leather boots. When she reached the bottom, she, Britney and Christina danced and strutted around the stage. Increasingly, the performance took on a kind of college boy's lesbian fantasy feel as Madonna turned to Christina and bent between her thighs to slip her white garter down her leg; then when Madonna stood back up to face the audience, Christina slid her hand along Madonna's inner thigh. Madonna strutted, Britney and Christina jiggled and thrust. Then they stood abreast of one another for the big moment: Madonna leaned to Britney and Britney leaned to Madonna and they shared an open-mouthed kiss. The MTV camera immediately cut to Justin Timberlake in the audience looking deadpan and unimpressed; it cut back to the stage just as Madonna and Christina were finishing their open-mouthed, tongue-flicking kiss. The crowd was hooting and hollering like they were in a strip joint. Then Missy Elliot came bounding onto the stage and the whole vibe changed, leaving the audience to wonder if they'd really seen what they thought they'd seen.

The next day, even later that evening, the airwaves were abuzz with chatter about the hot Madonna-Britney kiss—there was scarcely any mention of the kiss shared by Madonna and Christina. While the Madonna-Christina kiss seemed like a natural extension of the performance the two highly sexual women were giving, the kiss with Britney was shocking because it seemed like the worldly, crafty temptress was corrupting the sweet, innocent child. Watching the performance, it's clear that Christina is much more at ease vamping and being overtly sexual than Britney is. Britney looks like she's pretending, like she's trying to act like her own version of Madonna but doesn't have the confidence to pull it off.

Fundamentalist Christians had a field day condemning this public display of homosexual behaviour dressed up as entertainment. Britney's public response to the kiss was entirely in line with her squeaky-clean image. Speaking to *Access Hollywood*, she said that her biggest worry was how her parents would react: "I was really kind of nervous about that. I was like, 'Oh my God, my mom. She's going to see this!'" When asked what her parents actually thought of the performance, she said, "Well, my mom actually liked it. And my dad, weirdly enough, he thought it was fine, too. I mean, come on—it's Madonna. If you can kiss any girl in the world, it has to be her."

Britney went on to say she had butterflies in her stomach the whole day leading up to the show. "Oh, I was very nervous and very shy," she related. "Like, honestly, just being with Madonna— she has this presence about her. Like, I mean, I am a shy person to start with, but I was very intimidated and I was, like, not myself. I was not the confident Britney. " As Britney continued to speak about Madonna, it was clear that she had idealised her: "And she just has a way about her, you know? At the same time, it both humbled me and inspired me. And it gave me something to look up to, you know?"

But how did it all come about? Was it spontaneous? Whose

idea was it, anyway? "It was not my idea, no," Britney told *People* magazine. "[Madonna] threw it around a couple of times during rehearsals. She just kind of said, 'You know, just do what you feel in the performance. Just go with it and see what happens,' and that is kind of what happened." And when *Access Hollywood* asked, in true TV celebrity journalist fashion, who the better kisser was, Madonna or Colin Farrell, Britney gushed like a teenager: "Oh my gosh. They are both amazing kissers!"

There was a different version of the story that had Madonna growing frustrated with Britney during rehearsals. Christina was getting the moves down, was getting the whole barely concealed symbolism of it all, but Britney was struggling with it, so Madonna finally said to her, "Just kiss me, Britney. Kiss me!"

Britney had always been fascinated by Madonna and when she became a star she finally met her. While it would be an exaggeration to say they were close, the older woman did feel protective towards the younger singer. Asked by a journalist about Britney and her problems, Madonna snapped, "I find it really irritating that everyone beats up on Britney Spears. I want to do nothing but support her and praise her and wish her all the best. I mean, she is a very young woman. It's shocking. I wish I had my shit that together when I was her age." Madonna was, in fact, a fan. She wore Britney T-shirts, sometimes even onstage. Once, at the Roseland Ballroom in New York, Madonna, wearing leather and a Britney shirt, dedicated her song "What It Feels Like for a Girl" to Britney. When Britney heard that she almost fainted. She said, "She's my idol. For her to dedicate one of my favorite songs of hers to me is incredibly flattering and sweet." Britney, of course, wore Madonna shirts as well. To crown their mutual admiration, Madonna decided to buy Britney a $15,000 diamond necklace with the letter *B* on it to match the one that she herself wore bearing the letter *M*.

At the time of the infamous onstage kiss, Madonna was forty-five years old and the all-time self-reinvention champion, doing so whenever her career needed a boost. Some saw her attachment to Britney as another example of her craftily drawing attention to herself; they insisted that Madonna was feeding off a young star who had now completely eclipsed her in terms of popularity and current album sales. The kiss at the MTV Video Music Awards and their later duet of the steamy French love song "Je t'aime . . . moi non plus" by Serge Gainsbourg and wife Jane Birkin could be seen as a grand publicity stunt to exploit Britney's success. But not everyone was impressed. Fleetwood Mac's Stevie Nicks told Nui Te Koha of the *Herald Sun,* "First of all, Madonna is too old to be kissing someone who is twenty-two and Britney should have been smarter than that. Hopefully she will figure a way out of this hole she has dug for herself." But, as calculating as it might seem, Madonna did try to help Britney out in her own way.

Britney was clearly slipping away from her Southern Baptist belief system and Madonna steered her into something she was passionate about: Kabbalah, a form of Jewish mysticism. Those who follow Kabbalah use deep meditation as a way of connecting with God. Some devotees claim that through this meditation and oneness with God a kind of total universal knowledge and a perfect self-knowledge is reached. Madonna takes it very seriously and has helped finance Kabbalah centres all over the world. She turned Britney on to it to help her through what was clearly a very troubled time. Britney would be seen and photographed wearing her red-string bracelet and carrying her Kabbalah books often in the days and months to come.

* * *

In the Zone was the title of Britney's fourth studio album. It was released on November 18, 2003 and debuted in the number 1 spot on the Billboard 200 album chart. This just solidified Britney's position as a top solo female recording artist; she was the only one to have four albums in a row in the top spot and her first four at that. It took just a week for her to sell over 600,000 copies. This album was the most musically confused of her career. It was easy to see that she was trying to make a transition from the vapid, bubblegum pop sound; she wrote or co-wrote eight of the twelve tracks on the album and co-produced a number of the songs as well.

When asked to describe the music on the album she said, "It should just happen like this one happened, just flow naturally from where I am now, what I am feeling now. I am in the studio just doing my thing and letting it flow. Whatever happens, happens." One of the producers, Lauren Christy, said of the album, "It's not really R&B or dance-based. It just has a really good groove. Lyrically it's a bit different, a bit more grown-up, but not trying to change the world or anything."

The album got mixed reviews, but the UK newspaper the *Guardian* seemed to sum it up best, concluding its review with, "Unlike previous Britney Spears albums, *In the Zone* has no filler and no shoddy cover versions, just 57 varieties of blue chip, hit factory pop. There is Southern hip-hop, deep house, Neptune-style

R&B, the ubiquitous Diwali beat, and most importantly, oodles of Madonna." *Stylus* magazine was more brutal: "Ultimately, *In the Zone* suffers greatly from Britney's uneasy transition from teen tart to sexually powerful woman. Had Britney been in charge of her career direction instead of being mercilessly prostituted by her management, she might have been able to produce something with some semblance of musical vision." Plans were underway to make the tour to support the album, the *Onyx Hotel*, the most spectacular ever mounted by a pop star. At a press conference at a Tokyo hotel on December 12, 2003, Britney promised that fans would see "a whole other side of me."

Like all Britney Spears albums, *In the Zone* has two or three tracks that stand out, but for different reasons. The single "Me against the Music" was the first-ever collaboration between Madonna and Britney—but, in fact, it wasn't really a collaboration at all. Madonna is simply "featured" on the track. But when director Paul Hunter made the video of the song, Madonna was the main attraction. Madonna leads young Britney down into a cavernous underground club. At the end of the journey, Britney reaches up to touch Madonna and Madonna vanishes. The passing-the-torch symbolism was blatant. "Me against the Music" didn't fare as well as expected, but another track on the album, "Toxic," became the biggest Britney had had since ". . . Baby One More Time." Still, the critical coverage of the album focused on two other tracks and once again sex was the reason: "Breathe on Me" and "Touch of My Hand" were controversial because of the sexual content (real or perceived) of their lyrics. Many considered the first a song about oral sex and the second a song about masturbation— Britney was using sex yet again to create buzz and controversy, only this time, like her friend Madonna, she was doing it in an in-your-face fashion. There was no fake, coy shrinking. She was trying to toughen up her image.

* * *

Britney's internal turmoil was now manifesting itself in all sorts of obvious ways. She seemed, in 2003, to be lost, really lost. She didn't know whether to assert herself as a grown-up, independent woman or be a little girl who needed mommy and a legion of handlers to get her from one day to the next. Britney has always been attacked for the clothes she wears both on and offstage, so she went out of her way to dress even more outrageously. On the Carson Daly show on MTV that summer, she wore a miniskirt, oddly colored leg warmers, a rhinestone bow tie, a cropped, midriff-baring T-shirt and a fedora. Many commented that she looked like a stripper in a low-rent strip club with a cigarette dangling from her mouth. Around the same time, she was spotted at a Kentucky Fried Chicken outlet in Malibu wearing low-slung sweatpants and a midriff-baring T-shirt. A tattoo was visible low on her hip. Someone called to her and asked her about the tattoo and as she climbed into her car, she said, "It's a Japanese symbol that means 'mysterious.'" Britney and her *Crossroads* co-star Taryn Manning had gotten identical tattoos one night. The symbol does not mean "mysterious," however; it means "strange."

Viva Las Vegas!

"I think everybody should be pro love."

—Britney Spears

Now that the album was out and a big success and plans for a 2004 tour to begin in March were in place, Britney turned her attention to other business ventures, including launching her own brand of perfume. But first she decided to leave L.A. for a while, leave the glare and head back to Kentwood to spend an extended Christmas holiday with the folks back home in the Tudor mansion she built for Lynne, the house they had christened "Serenity."

Over Christmas that year, Serenity was filled with people— her family members and friends like Reg Jones, who was still hanging around the Spears household years after he and Britney had broken up. There was also another old friend, Jason Alexander, who was home for the holidays. Alexander and Britney had known each other for their entire lives, having played together as toddlers in a day care that Lynne ran. They went to the same school and hung out in the same places long before Britney Jean Spears became "Britney Spears." For some reason, Britney seemed very happy to see Jason, like finding a favourite old pair of jeans you thought you'd thrown out, only to discover they are even more comfortable than you remembered. The world knew what had become of Britney, but she was eager to find out what had become of Jason Alexander. The toddler was now a six-foot-three south-eastern Louisiana College football star, a big, muscular guy you would not want to get into a scrap with (as his arrest record attests). Alexander freely admits that he'd always had a crush on Britney but had never attempted to do anything about it because they moved in very different circles. But one evening, they were hanging out together and Britney started to flirt with him. They shared a bit of a "kiss and cuddle."

One night just before New Year's, Reg, Britney, Bryan and Jason left Serenity and headed to Jason's house to pick up a few bottles. Then they went over to Britney and Bryan's old family home, where Jamie lived. Reg remembers that "Britney was looking pretty wasted by the time we got there." A few hours later, the party was winding down. Bryan fell asleep on the couch, Reg was fading fast on the floor in a corner and, according to Reg, Britney and Jason "were wrapped around each other on the floor in the middle of the room." In the morning, Reg was awakened by Jamie's co-workers arriving to pick him up for work. Jamie cornered Reg and asked where Britney was. Lynne had already called looking for her. "I just pointed in her direction and Jamie went for a look. He came out after seeing Britney and Jason all wrapped around each other and called Miss Lynne."

Minutes later, Lynne came rushing into the house in a rage. First she railed at Jamie, then she woke up the badly hung-over Britney and got her to her feet. Reg says they had a hell of a row and then Lynne hustled Britney into her Lexus and drove off. Back at Serenity, the argument continued, with Britney declaring she was a grown woman and could do whatever she wanted. Britney told Lynne that she needed to keep in mind who had paid for the huge house she lived in and the luxury sedan she drove. Jones recalls, "Miss Lynne did have Britney on a curfew when she was in Kentwood. She would say that Britney was living under her roof in Kentwood and would respect her rules."

Jason Alexander was shocked to get a call from Britney later that day asking him if he wanted to come to Las Vegas with her and a couple of her girlfriends, Elizabeth Jansen and Courtney Brabham. She said she had decided that Kentwood was the last place she wanted to be for New Year's, implying that getting away from Lynne was what she was most interested in. Alexander agreed, not believing his luck.

On New Year's Eve, Britney and her gang checked into a $10,000 a night high-roller suite at the Palms. Britney preferred the Palms (she was quite friendly with members of the Maloof family, who owned the hotel) and particularly liked the hot club there called Rain. At 11:00 p.m. or so, Britney and her friends headed to Rain dressed very casually in jeans and T-shirts. The moment they entered, the vodka began flowing and Jason Alexander began to see firsthand the surreal life Britney led away from Kentwood. Everyone was fawning over Britney; fans mobbed her, asking to have pictures taken with her and hotel security had to keep hustling away autograph-seekers. Britney was a glowing ball of energy at the centre of this Babylonian hub of overindulgence. Jason was dazzled by it, drunk on it. He could not believe that the little Britney he knew in Kentwood could wield this kind of power, that she could carry on with the casual assumption that everything she asked for would be delivered and delivered very quickly. Of course, he was aware of everything she had done, but here he was standing in the midst of it, breathing it in. A Las Vegas radio personality who was at the Palms that night remembers, "They were not unruly or acting like rock stars or anything, they were having a good time. [Britney] was just drinking a lot and enjoying her friends. She would talk to anyone that stopped by. When the New Year rang in she hugged and kissed her male companion [Jason Alexander] passionately and romantically." The party in Rain continued on for several hours and the vodka continued to flow. The Las Vegas radio personality recalls, "At around 3:30 or 4:00, it seemed that the bar was not serving them anymore. Britney was in bad shape—very, very drunk. The man she was with pretty much had to carry her out of the club."

According to Alexander, things between them turned vigorously sexual as soon as they got back into the suite. They hopped into the shower and Britney immediately sank to her knees and performed oral sex on him before they "did it" in "every position you could imagine." The next morning, Britney declared that she was still feeling the need and the sexual smorgasbord continued, with Britney being the aggressive instigator of the fun. They moved to the big bathtub in the suite where they did it again; then they ordered room service. There was more sex play for the rest of the day, until the pair took a break to venture out to a movie. Britney had wanted to see the new Julia Roberts movie, *Mona Lisa Smile*. Once back in the suite, the romp continued and went on, supposedly unabated, until the early-morning hours of January 3, 2004.

This Las Vegas incident is clearly one of Britney's early screams for emotional help. She could have been with any man she chose, but instead she was with a hick from Kentwood who still lived at home and solved even his simplest problems with his fists. Spiriting him off to Las Vegas had rebellion written all over it and it was Lynne she was rebelling against. Lynne had said that Kentwood guys like Reg Jones and Jason Alexander were no longer in her league and she should set her sights much higher, but this created a big conflict for Britney. She herself was a Kentwood hick and so was Lynne; Britney's fame and money seem to have made Lynne feel that they were now better than everyone else. This Las Vegas mess was Britney screaming, "See, Mama—no matter how much we pretend, I ain't better than nobody!"

At around 3:30 on the morning of January 3, Britney asked Jason to marry her. She said it would be the perfect way to end this wild and magical time. Jason was still caught up in the whirlwind of luxury and sexual excess, still trying to decide if he was actually living this or just dreaming it. Naturally, he said yes.

The pair headed to the lobby, where Britney had ordered one of the hotel's lime-green stretch limousines to be made available for her. The driver was actually a bellman, not a proper chauffeur, because of the late hour and the spontaneity of the demand. Britney was wearing ripped jeans and a skimpy black midriff-baring top ("and no undies at all," according to Alexander). On her feet, Nike running shoes; on her head, a baseball cap. The driver was ordered to find them a wedding chapel. He knew of many in the area, but the first two they tried were closed. The third place they tried was called the Little White Wedding Chapel. It never closed. Inside, they were told they first had to go to a twenty-four-hour courthouse to obtain a marriage licence. At the courthouse they both signed the papers—Britney's signature looks like an angry child's, with its big looping letters—then Britney paid the $55 fee and they headed back to the Little White Wedding Chapel, where they signed up for the full wedding package: the ceremony, pictures, a video, flowers, live musical accompaniment by a piano player and a pink garter that Britney slipped over her jeans. The bellman-driver was persuaded, for a handsome tip, to walk Britney down the aisle in the chapel's Michael Jordan Room, where the legendary NBA star was married in 1989. The whole ceremony lasted less than twenty minutes and Britney and Jason were, according to Charlotte Richards, who owns the chapel, "laughing and smiling the whole time." Were they drunk or high? "No sir, we try to stay away from marrying people in that condition, as it will just cause problems later. And if they were either of those things it would be kind of hard to get a licence at the courthouse."

On the ride back to the Palms, Jason insisted that the tradition of the bride taking her husband's name had to be upheld and that Britney Spears was now Britney Alexander. At this point, the driver very cautiously asked if he might say something to the couple; he said that Jason might want to rethink that, because there was a hot new porn star on the L.A. and Las Vegas circuit named Britney Alexander (who had starred in twenty-six films with titles like *Little Naughty Nymphos Part 11*, *Filthy Little Whores Part 9* and *Fresh Young Meat Part 5*).

The newly married couple arrived back at the Palms at around 5:00 a.m. and broke out the champagne. Elizabeth and Courtney sipped the flowing Cristal, but were too stunned to say much of anything. It was decided that after breakfast Britney would call Lynne to let her know what had happened before it came out in the press. Lynne went berserk. Britney kept telling her it was done, so there was nothing to talk her out of. Bryan then got on the phone and demanded to talk to Jason. He told Jason, "this whole fucking thing is going to be annulled right fucking now!" Jason was shocked at the anger directed towards him; all of this, he later told *Access Hollywood*, had been Britney's idea.

While Britney and Jason enjoyed sex as husband and wife for the first time, Lynne was calling up the rest of Team Britney so the wagons could be circled. When Larry Rudolph heard the news, he sent a message to Britney and made plans to travel to Las Vegas immediately. Rudolph's message to Britney read, "Congratulations. You just gave away half your money!"

On their first full day of married life, Britney and Jason had planned to have dinner together at a restaurant in the Palms called the N9NE Steakhouse, but they ended up having to arrange for a bigger table. Lynne Spears had arrived with Bryan, Rudolph was there and so was one of Britney's lawyers, David Chesnoff. Not a moment was wasted discussing why or how this had happened; the focus was entirely on protecting Britney's hundred-million-dollar fortune and creating a story to feed the world press. Jason was treated like a gold digger, even though he'd only done what Britney wanted him to do. He later described Bryan as having been the angriest. He played the protective big brother while the rest were just talking numbers and drawing up a legal document for Jason to sign to extricate Britney from any alimony or financial settlement. The next day at 12:25 p.m., Jason signed the annulment papers, which contained such statements as, "there was no attempt to know each other's likes or dislikes, no attempt to know the desires to have or not have children and each other's desires as to the state of residence. They are so incompatible that there is a want of understanding of each other's actions when entering into this marriage."

Bryan handed Jason an economy-class plane ticket and Jason was driven to the Las Vegas airport, where he had to wait for hours for the flight to take him home. He has maintained ever since that he didn't take a dime off Britney, but rumours later surfaced that he was given half a million dollars to walk away. This seems very unlikely, though. Had he accepted any money, he almost certainly would have had to sign a nondisclosure agreement that would have prevented him from telling his story publicly, which he later did, selling his story to the British tabloid *News of the World*. Alexander later told the BBC, "The whole thing was just so weird. When we were all discussing how to get the marriage ended, she did not even look at me, not once." Team Britney explained to Jason that he would ruin her career if he did not sign these papers and disappear and they had clearly convinced Britney of that as well.

Almost as soon as it hit the wire services, the story turned farcical. Not having heard of the Kentwood Jason Alexander, reporters at first jumped to the conclusion that the groom was the short, pudgy, balding actor who played George Costanza on the sitcom *Seinfeld*. That particular Jason Alexander first heard about the affair when he was getting a coffee. "Some breathless young journalist asked me if it was true that I had married Britney Spears on New Year's Day in Las Vegas," he said while being interviewed for his film *Grand*. "The very question was so completely absurd that I thought it was a joke, so I confirmed the report by saying that we had been keeping our romance secret for years but could no longer hide our love for each other, we needed to share it with the world. I could see that she was scribbling this down. It was all so . . . insane."

The story concocted by Team Britney was that this was just a youthful prank, a joke by a couple of crazy kids that went way too far. It just happened that one of the two was a world-famous pop star. Reg Jones was too close to the people involved to believe that line. "I was totally shocked when I heard what they had done. It was for sure Britney telling her mom that she was not going to be telling her what to do anymore." But Jason Alexander's mother, Doreen Seal, was asked for her opinion by *People* magazine and she towed the official line. "They weren't drunk or anything like that. It was just a moment that got way out of control and there was no one there to stop them." She then made a telling comment: "Britney just wants the kind of normal life that she just can't have."

Virtually everyone from Justin Timberlake on down was asked to comment on the event. The story circulated that Britney had done this as a reaction to the announcement that he and Cameron Diaz were engaged. Timberlake refused to comment; he was in Vail, Colorado, skiing with Diaz. Justin's grandmother, who liked Britney a lot, just said she thought the marriage was "strange." Fellow 'N Sync member Lance Bass was actually in Las Vegas at the same time. He said, "Young people do crazy things here all the time." The one person who seemed conspicuously absent from the public discussion was Jamie, but he was not one to engage in a public discourse on his daughter anyway. In his quiet way, Jamie was probably the only one in the circus who was really worried about his daughter's mental, emotional and physical well-being. As one Kentwood resident says, "[Jamie] was kind of scared for his daughter. He could see that she was in way over her head; there was too much money, too many people around her whispering in her ear."

When it came time to address the issue of the marriage and its annulment on the official Britney Spears website (which Lynne Spears was in charge of), it was lawyer David Chesnoff who made the posting. He wrote, "They are simply two young people who regret what they have done."

Britney kept out of the public eye for a while after the annulment and when she finally re-emerged, she seemed chastened by the whole event. As for Jason Alexander, he would sell his story to the tabloids, make a couple of hundred thousand dollars for his revelations, buy a luxury car and make the rounds of the talk shows and reality shows. He was now, after all, a part of history: he was one half of the shortest celebrity marriage ever—fifty-five hours.

KEVIN

"Kabbalah helped me get rid of a lot of negative influences that were guiding me down the wrong path. There came a point when not even my family or advisers had the answers I needed. Through Kabbalah I was able to look within myself, clear all the negative energy, and turn my life around."

—Britney Spears

Columbus Short once described his friend Kevin Federline to AOL Black Voices columnist Jawn Murray as "the next best thing to a black guy. He has a hip-hop edge to him; he's cool and funky." Britney had seen Kevin with Columbus a few times. Short and Federline worked out at the same dance studio and were good friends. Both had big dreams of becoming dancers and choreographers, maybe even hip-hop stars in their own right. But when Columbus joined Britney's inner circle, such as it was, Kevin remained on the outside looking in. Not that Kevin spent that much time worrying about it; he was doing backup dancing gigs and was on tour himself intermittently.

During the first few months of 2004, between the worldwide public embarrassment of the "fifty-five hours in Vegas" incident and the launch of the *Onyx Hotel* tour, Britney was hanging around dance clubs and rehearsing in dance studios. She was working to get back in shape; her midsection had gotten soft and doughy.

She was also working with Elizabeth Arden on the upcoming launch of her own signature perfume, to be called "Curious."

By early 2004, Britney had known Kevin Federline for almost four years, but only casually. Federline was part of a dance group called LFO, which had toured with Britney briefly a couple of tours back. But she had not noticed him particularly then because she was involved with Justin Timberlake and later Columbus Short. But the friendship with Short brought Federline and Britney into closer and more frequent contact. Britney liked him and once the Las Vegas wedding incident was forgotten, she found herself more and more attracted to this cool dancer. Federline was already with another woman, actress Shar Jackson. They had a young daughter together and another child was on the way. But that didn't stop Britney and Kevin from becoming more and more interested in each other.

A lot has been said and written about Kevin Federline, the street essence he exudes, his tattoos and the hip-hop patois he speaks instead of English, but his origins are quite ordinary. He grew up in Clovis, a suburb of Fresno, in a comfortable and safe neighbourhood with his parents—his dad, Mike, was an auto mechanic who had a reputation for being a laid-back, liberal kind of guy and his mother, Julie, worked in a bank. His parents divorced when he was eight and three years later he and his brother Chris moved to Fresno to live with their dad. Kevin has two step-siblings, Dustin and Nicole. Two things were a constant in Kevin's life: he loved to dance and he really dug girls and they dug him right back. He attended Tenaya Middle School in Clovis and his photo in the yearbook has a caption that reads: "Kevin Federline—Most Likely To Be Seen on *America's Most Wanted.*"

Kevin has always had a way with girls, according to those who knew him back in Clovis. His first girlfriend was Felicia Cabrero; they were both just twelve years old when they began to "go together." "Even then, he would love to dance, break-dancing especially," says Felicia. "I would urge him to explore other kinds of dance as well, because he loved to dance and seemed to have some natural talent for it."

When Felicia changed schools, word got back to her that Kevin had immediately begun seeing other girls, so they broke up, but they remained friends and stayed in contact for years. It was Felicia who suggested that Kevin train, really train, with professionals to hone his skills so he might actually be able to dance professionally one day. When Kevin was fourteen years old, he joined D.A.N.C.E. Empowerment, a not-for-profit organisation that had a youth-with-talent outreach program that used dance to keep youths off the streets and out of trouble. A dancer named Wayne Hurley ran it. Hurley remembers very clearly the day Kevin Federline walked into his studio. He told British author Sean Smith in 2004, "Sure, he was a young guy, acting tough, a lot tougher than he actually was, a bit of a chip on his shoulder." Kevin was at first reluctant to join the group as he was a bit self-conscious, but Hurley encouraged him to do so because, "He had something, something natural, and the girls just loved him." A year later, in 1993, when he was just fifteen, Kevin dropped out of school. He wanted to dance. He spent as much time as he could at D.A.N.C.E. Empowerment while working typical teenage high-school dropout jobs—car wash guy, pizza delivery guy. His involvement with the dance group is what made him start to feel good about himself; he was a popular member of the group and seemed to get better and better as a dancer (later, he would often be described by choreographers as being "talented but not exceptional"). As he filled out, he would literally have to fight girls off; he kept his hair long, sported a thin, Errol Flynn-style moustache and wore superbaggy clothes in the raver style of the day.

Kevin got engaged for the first time when he was just seventeen. Even at this early age he was known as a great lover. His girlfriend, Kerri Whitington, said, "When Kevin and I got engaged, he took me to a park that we loved to hang out in, to the spot where we first kissed, a place where we liked to make love outdoors on warm nights, got down on his knee and proposed." Kerri described him as "exciting and adventurous in bed," but that was actually what led them to break off their engagement shortly after it was announced. Kevin could resist anything but temptation; he would step out with any woman who threw herself at him.

After his engagement to Kerri Whitington came apart, Kevin thought it was time to really roll the dice. He cut his hair, shaved his moustache and headed to L.A. to take his chances in the thriving dance scene there. To go with his new life, he gave himself a new street name: Too Daze. Not long after hitting L.A., he met young, black working actress named Shar (Sharisse) Jackson. She was perhaps best known for her recurring role on the popular cable sitcom *Moesha*; she played Niecy Jackson. Although just still in her early twenties, Shar already had two children. Shar and Kevin connected quickly and she would tell friends that he was "dynamite in bed."

Kevin was going out on auditions from the minute he hit

L.A. and had middling success. He was hired as a backup dancer for Justin Timberlake and then Pink, with whom he eventually toured for over a year. He also worked with Michael Jackson, an artist whom he admired so much he later named one of his children after him (Kaleb Michael Jackson Federline, born July 20, 2004).

Kevin and Shar moved in together and she became pregnant with their first child right away. The couple welcomed their daughter, Kori Madison, into the world on July 31, 2002. Kevin continued as a backup dancer and Shar, who was doing much better than he was, worked constantly in supporting roles in TV and commercials. In late 2003, Shar became pregnant with their second child, Kaleb, right around the time Britney and Kevin's pal Columbus Short were being photographed together. Six months later, Shar got a call from Kevin telling her he "was kind of hanging out with someone"—his way of saying he had found a new woman. The world didn't know it yet, but his new woman was Britney Spears.

The two had been meeting secretly and talking on the phone off and on for months. Britney told her friends that one thing she liked about Kevin was his indifference to her star status, but in fact Britney had the kind of life that Kevin had always dreamed of having. His attitude and the cool he exuded completely bowled her over. As she told *Details* magazine, "Nothing gets to him; that's because he is not one of those shallow motherfucker Hollywood actor guys."

* * *

The *Onyx Hotel* tour was actually conceived as the *In the Zone* tour, but on February 17, 2004, just two weeks before the tour was to begin, Britney and her team were sued for trademark infringement. A clothing company in San Diego claimed that the phrase "in the zone" was part of their corporate identity. A new concept was inspired by the Broadway musical based on the old film *Grand Hotel*, about a day in the life of an iconic Berlin hotel and by Britney's love of the onyx stone. Then, a month after the tour began, a real Onyx Hotel opened in Boston (part of the Kimpton Hotels and Restaurants Group). Their concept for the hotel was developed two years before the tour, but rather than sue, they cleverly decided to promote their hotel by connecting it to the tour, something the Britney camp embraced. Lynne Spears was asked to come in and design a special room at the hotel "reflecting Britney's personality and taste" to be called the Britney Spears Foundation Room. A portion of what guests paid to stay in the room would go to her charity.

The tour kicked off in San Diego on March 2, 2004 and once again Britney was at the centre of a controversy. The tour promoters, Clear Channel Entertainment, announced that people would see a whole new Britney and a very different kind of Britney show. It was not just meant for an older audience, Clear Channel said. They were trying to change the demographic of her audience from families and kids to adults and even "the gay market." The show was impressive and highly erotic, something that brought forth howls of protest from the parents who brought their children to see their idol. The show featured racy costumes—bustiers and panties—and Britney's highly erotic performance of "Touch of My Hand," which she performed in a see-through bathtub wearing a flesh-coloured body suit.

Despite criticism of the show's raunchy tone, dates sold out on every stop on the tour. Just two weeks into the tour, while performing her next-to-last song, "(I Got That) Boom Boom," Britney slipped and injured her knee. She quickly hobbled offstage but, perhaps remembering the Mexico City debacle, she limped back wearing a white robe. She explained to the audience that she had injured her knee and could not finish the concert. She was examined and told she needed rest; she would not be able to resume the tour for at least four or five days. The next few shows, in Chicago and Detroit, were postponed until the end of the tour and Jive Records and Clear Channel told ticketholders that their tickets would be honoured at those shows.

Britney recovered and finished the North American leg of the tour with the makeup Detroit date on April 14. There was a twelve-day break before she headed to London to kick off the European leg on April 26. On April 23, at the Beverly Hills Hotel, Britney introduced her new man to the world, walking out of the hotel with Kevin Federline, who was wearing an oversised T-shirt and a backwards baseball cap. Britney, in tiny denim shorts and a loose-fitting shirt knotted up under her breasts to bare her midriff, was beaming and told the confused photographers (one of whom would say, "Who the fuck is that punk?") that her new man was Kevin Federline, a backup dancer. Britney then declared the little press conference over and she and Kevin strolled past the photographers to her white Mercedes, got in and drove off. Of course, the photographers quickly followed, tailing them all the way to the beach in Santa Monica, about a half hour away. The pair emerged from the car and the horde of photographers was on them within minutes. Britney was happy and playful and jumped on Federline; he piggybacked her across the sand. They sat down on the sand together and cuddled, Britney took off her shirt, revealing a yellow bikini top, looked at the crowd of photographers and said, "You got your pictures, can y'all go away now?"

Suzie Jacks of *US Weekly* said of the incident, "That moment was all about her being seen to take control while seeking the validation of the paparazzi and therefore the watching world." But when the pictures started appearing, the stories that accompanied them had more to do with Federline walking away from a woman with whom he had one child and who was six months pregnant with their second child and about Britney's lack of judgment in taking up with a man who could act with such selfishness.

Two days later, Britney and crew were scheduled to board a plane for England for the jam-packed European leg of the *Onyx Hotel* tour, but she decided that she needed Kevin with her. She called and told him to pack a bag, grab his passport and get to the airport. As she explained to *People* magazine's Todd Gold not long after, "I needed to kiss a lot of frogs before I found my prince. I'm not letting this one out of my sight." She went on to say, "My other loves were all puppy loves. They were like practice for the real thing. This is my happily ever after."

There were shifts in Britney's professional life as well. Bryan Spears was getting more involved in her affairs. He moved from New York to L.A., setting up an office for himself in a beach property Britney owned in Santa Monica in the shadow of the Fairmont Miramar Hotel. Britney bought Bryan a black Mercedes, which he would park near the Fairmont Miramar entrance each morning. This was pretty much the last straw for Larry Rudolph and Johnny Wright. They ended their professional relationships with Britney under which what they would describe as amicable circumstances. Rudolph had been with Britney for nine years. When they publicly announced the dissolution of their relationship, Rudolph said, "Britney and I just came to realise that we have done all that we can do together." Britney's official statement read, "We had a great run. I have appreciated Larry's guidance over the years." Not the most emotional parting of ways for two people who had been so closely involved for so long.

The European leg of the *Onyx Hotel* tour went spectacularly well. The European press had a lot of fun following Britney and Kevin around London, Rotterdam, Stockholm and Berlin as they sought out Big Macs and shopped. During their second stop in London, on May 3, 2004, they exited a shop laden with bags and a reporter shouted out, "Kevin, Kevin, how much of Britney's money did you just spend in there, mate?" Britney played into the paparazzi's hands, reaching over and grabbing Kevin's crotch as they snapped their pictures.

As the tour wound down in early June of 2004, Britney and Kevin went out in Dublin, Ireland and got matching tattoos: lucky dice etched on the insides of their wrists. By the time they boarded their flight home from Dublin, Britney and Kevin had been involved romantically for about three months. They sat together and talked about how amazing it all felt, about children and the future and how they felt about things. Then Britney said to Kevin, "What if I wanted to get married?" He looked at her, waiting for some kind of follow-up. She just said, "Would you marry me?" After a moment, he replied "No." He allowed a brief but dramatic pause and said, "Now, would *you* marry *me*?" Britney laughed and accepted his proposal. The plan was to call everyone and share the blessed news once they were on the ground. Later, Britney would take Kevin to Kentwood to meet the kin.

Things were changing in Kentwood. Lynne now had another little career to look after: Jamie Lynn Spears was one of the stars of Nickelodeon's *Zoey 101*, which required her to divide her time between L.A. and Louisiana (she was still going to Parklane Academy, her siblings' alma mater). Jamie Spears, quietly as always, was undergoing a dramatic transformation. He had left New York and relocated to Los Angeles, where the first thing he did was enter a rehab program to get clear of his alcohol problems. He then bought a sandwich shop on Venice Beach called JJ Chills and pretty much ran it by himself. Before long, it was a thriving little business. Britney had begun contacting him more, spending more time with him, because he was Dad, not a member of the entourage or the business team—just Dad.

News of her engagement to Kevin Federline did not have the same effect on Britney's family as her marriage to Jason Alexander had. They seemed open to meeting Kevin before judging him— perhaps because this time they had been told before the wedding took place.

The couple went shopping for engagement rings. Britney picked out rings made by renowned jewellery designer Cynthia Wolff, which cost in excess of $50,000 each. She paid for them with a credit card that had no limit. The plan was to relax and enjoy their newfound happiness in California for a while, then make the trip to Kentwood. After that, Britney had to shoot the video for her new single, "Outrageous," then go back on the road for the gruelling final leg of the *Onyx Hotel* tour.

Britney really did seem happy with Kevin; she loved his laid-back attitude, his looks—all those qualities that gave him such power over women. One of Kevin's L.A. pals says, "Despite what you read and hear, Kevin is basically a nice guy. He likes to put on an attitude here and there, but so does everyone else out here. If he was a dick, Britney's parents probably would have seen to it that he wasn't around long. But they didn't. They were perfectly all right with him." British author Sean Smith observes, "Kevin is exactly the kind of guy Britney would have ended up with even if she wasn't famous." There even seemed to be a playfulness about her acceptance of the media scrutiny that was now part of her daily life. Just before heading to Kentwood, Britney and Kevin were photographed hanging out in Marina Del Rey, walking together, holding hands and genuinely enjoying each other. Britney was wearing a T-shirt that read "I'm a Virgin," then in small type underneath, "But This Is an Old Shirt."

In Kentwood, astonishingly, Lynne Spears took an instant shine to Federline. She could see how happy Britney was and Federline appeared to be a decent guy, despite the faux-gangsta look he favoured. Britney took Kevin to the home of her late great-grandmother, Lexie. The house is owned by Bryan Spears and the people living in it have maintained the Britney Spears shrine room that Lexie had created when she was alive. It was very important to Britney to ensure that Kevin knew about her, about where she came from—not just what was said about her in *US Weekly*.

Shortly after returning to L.A., Britney and Kevin were interviewed together by *Details* for its February 2005 issue.

Britney described part of her attraction to Kevin was that he was a dancer who had toured and experienced life on the road. He knew the pressures and the sacrifices. In the same interview, she exhibited a new defiance. "I am pretty fed up with people thinking I'm this dumb blonde just because I am, quote, Britney Spears, unquote. People are just way too obsessed with celebrity." Kevin said that he missed Britney when he wasn't with her and she turned and hugged him. Then the interviewer made the mistake of suggesting that Kevin was with Britney for her fame and her money. Kevin didn't answer. Britney did: "Well, time will tell, motherfuckers."

Because of Britney's crazy schedule, the wedding date was left up in the air. She headed first to New York where, on June 8, she was to shoot the video. It would be directed by Dave Meyers, who had done a couple of previous videos with her ("Lucky" and "Boys") and it would feature a cameo by Snoop Dogg. They would start filming on a basketball court and then move to the street outside, where the big dance number was to be shot. During the dance number, on the rain-soaked street, Britney fell awkwardly and grabbed her knee, hollering in pain. The knee started swelling immediately, so she was taken to the nearest hospital. She had an MRI, which revealed that again a piece of cartilage had torn free. She was scheduled for arthroscopic surgery the next day. This injury was more serious than her previous one requiring surgery; there would be a longer recovery and rehabilitation period. Britney had to wear a leg brace for six weeks and undergo up to three months of physiotherapy. That meant the entire third leg of the *Onyx Hotel* tour had to be scrapped. Jive issued a press release saying that the tour suspension was based on doctors' orders and promised that the cancelled shows would be rescheduled.

The injury kept Britney off the road, but it did not keep her out of the studio. She was readying a greatest hits album for Christmas release and recording a couple of new songs for it as well, including a remake of Bobby Brown's "My Prerogative," which is about doing what you want and living your own life and which contains the growling lyric, "Don't tell me what to do!" The album would be a success, selling over six million copies—but, once again, it attracted controversy. On its cover, Britney looks like a porn star in black panties and a black bra with a fur piece around her shoulders.

Britney and Kevin finally set the date for their wedding. It would be a low-key affair for no more than thirty friends and family members and it would be held in the garden of the Studio City home of Jeff Fox, a successful clothing store owner and his wife, Alyson, a wedding planner. The invitations did not mention anything about a wedding, however—it would be "a special event." There had been rumours of a three-hundred-guest wedding to be held in Santa Barbara on October 16 at the luxurious Bacara Resort, but that was just a diversion. Britney was to wear an elegant white strapless dress by designer Monique L'Huiller. Lovely burgundy dresses had been selected for the bridesmaids. Upon arrival, guests were handed an envelope containing the details of the event. Yet despite the careful planning, the occasion almost became a special *non*-event. The sixty-page prenuptial agreement had not been finalised. Britney's lawyer, Laura Wasser, told Kevin's lawyer, Mark Kaplan, that the marriage could not take place until the agreement was signed. Kaplan replied that his client would agree to whatever conditions were laid out in the agreement without question, but Wasser argued most vociferously that no matter what Federline agreed to or promised or swore, if the wedding took place without a signed, binding, prenuptial agreement in place, Federline would be legally entitled to half of Britney's fortune and she, Wasser, would not allow it. Someone suggested that they just fake the wedding for the guests to avoid wrecking the entire day. It would all look legitimate, but there would be no solemnisation, no declaration of "I now pronounce you man and wife." This was agreed to and legal papers were actually drawn up to document the arrangement ("The two parties shall not marry one another on said date, September 18, 2004 and Britney Spears and Kevin Federline both understand and agree that the ceremony the parties intend to participate in shall not be a lawful Californian marriage"). The official civil marriage papers were filed on October 6. Another wrinkle in this arrangement was that both parties had signed a deal with *People* giving the magazine exclusive rights to pictures taken at "the wedding."

The ceremony in the garden was nice. It lasted just fifteen minutes and the couple exchanged platinum rings. *People* photographed the proceedings extensively, as did a documentary crew that was on hand to shoot the ceremony for a reality show that Britney and Kevin had agreed to participate in. Britney's bridesmaids were her friends Courtney Brabham and Elizabeth Jansen, her cousin Laura Lynn, her friend Fe and Jamie Lynn. Lynne was very happy and emotional, declaring that Britney looked "like an angel." Kevin's two children, Kaleb and Kori, had been invited, but they did not attend because the date had been set so quickly. Their mother had already made plans to take them to Disneyland that day and that's where they went.

The party after the ceremony was held at Xes, a nightclub off Sunset Boulevard. Each guest was given a gift bag containing Gap jeans, framed photos of the "newlyweds," silver teardrop key rings and a special cut-out of a Kabbalah term in Hebrew that means "power to heal." As Britney and Kevin headed for the black SUV that would take them to the party, members of the press gathered outside, who had not been told anything about a wedding, real or pretend, suddenly realised what had just happened. They went into a picture-taking frenzy as Britney and Kevin piled into the car and took off.

At Xes, the bridesmaids all wore pink track suits bearing the words "The Maids," while the guys wore blue tracksuits that said "Pimps." Britney's tracksuit said "Mrs. Federline," and Kevin's said "Hers." The party was still going on when word that the wedding was a fake hit the streets and once again the spin doctors jumped in to deny, deny, deny—there had just been a bit of misplaced paperwork and it would be dealt with. After the party, Kevin carried Britney to the car and they were taken to the beautiful Hotel Bel Air, where they would spend the night. They would then head back home with the Kentwood contingent to get out of the public eye for a while before enjoying a proper honeymoon at an exclusive resort in Fiji.

Wanting to start afresh with her new husband and anticipating the family that they had discussed starting right away, Britney decided to buy a new house. She chose a $7.5 million spread in Malibu, which she would renovate to fit her vision of her family home. While waiting for the renovations to be completed, the pair stayed in a $1,500-a-night suite at the Fairmont Miramar in

Santa Monica, Greta Garbo's preferred hotel. The same month as Britney's marriage ceremony, Elizabeth Arden came out with Britney's new fragrance, called Curious. It would take just five months for Curious to rack up over $100 million in sales, shattering the previous sales records for Elizabeth Arden-licenced products. As 2004 drew to a close, Britney's greatest hits album was selling enough copies to solidify her status as one of the best-selling solo acts in the world.

Britney was now asserting her control over her life, her image and her career. But had she really taken control? Had she found a stability that had been woefully absent from her life until now? Or was she still skating on thin ice emotionally? Were success and money and glitz just obscuring her real problems?

SOMEDAY (I WILL UNDERSTAND)

"I don't need Kabbalah no more—my child is my religion."
–Britney Spears

As 2004 turned into 2005, Britney and new husband Kevin Federline were in Kentwood celebrating Christmas and New Year's. One late night in very early January 2005, a tall, good-looking young man popped into the Walmart in McComb. The late hour meant that there were not too many other shoppers in the store. The man strolled up and down the aisles, clearly looking for something. An employee recognised him as the California dancer who had recently married their Britney—Kevin something. "I went over to him and said hello," she recalls. "I didn't make no big deal out of that I knew who he was and stuff. I just asked him if he needed any help, asked him what he was looking for." Kevin Federline looked up from under the bill of his baseball cap and said, "Pregnancy test."

Britney had been telling everyone who would listen that she was enjoying married life very much and couldn't wait to have a child. She told every news source from *Elle* magazine to MTV that once she began to have children, she was going to take a break to devote herself to her new family. It didn't mean she was going to vanish—she had lots of things in the works—but she would budget her time differently.

Britney was pregnant with her first child. After sharing the news with family, they had to decide how and when to announce it to the world. Since the celebrity press is probably the most intrusive and crafty of all, it did not take long for it to notice the fact that Britney was no longer smoking or blasting back vodka shots. Some members of the press began putting two and two together and speculating that Britney was pregnant. The official announcement of the pregnancy came in the form of a mention on her website—Britney would be taking a break, slowing down so she could start a family—but that announcement was not made until she was three months into the pregnancy.

Britney and her family took the pregnancy very seriously and there were some scary moments. Near the end of her first trimester, Britney and Kevin were in Destin, Florida, relaxing when Britney was overcome with abdominal pains. Fearful for the health and safety of her child, Britney rushed to a nearby hospital. She was told that nothing was wrong with the baby and there was no likelihood of a miscarriage, so, on April 12, she announced on her website that she and Federline were expecting.

The couple spent most of the rest of the pregnancy in the Fairmont Miramar in Santa Monica while their Malibu mansion was being readied. In choosing Malibu as their home and the Fairmont Miramar as their temporary residence, Britney was finally accepting that her life was not normal. She was living a crazy life in a crazy business and now that she was about to have a child, she needed protection from the craziness all around her. The Fairmont Miramar has been known as a comfortable haven for stars hiding from their fame ever since the notoriously private Greta Garbo chose it as her residence. Because of its layout and the attention its staff gives to the special privacy needs of the guests, huge stars can be confident that they will not be bothered or photographed there. And Malibu has long been a celebrity enclave of secure, gated beach communities where non-residents are kept away.

While at the Fairmont Miramar, Britney was often seen relaxing by the pool with friends, bottles of water and juice and piles of celebrity magazines. One hotel staff member remembers a cute moment. A vacationing family from England was playing by the pool one day next to Britney and her party. The family's two little girls were splashing in the pool. Britney came to play with them and she asked where they were from. Afterwards, the girls excitedly told their father that they had been playing with Britney Spears. The man looked over at her. Britney's hair had been dyed back to her natural colour, dark brown and the man told his little girls that wasn't really Britney Spears. Britney heard him and went over and said, "Actually, sir, I am."

Britney's friend Madonna sent a trunk full of Kabbalah books to the hotel so Britney could study and meditate. Madonna said that now that she was pregnant, Kaballah and its teachings were more important than ever; one teaching holds that all humanity is connected on both a physical and a metaphysical level. Federline wasn't into Kabbalah and Britney said as much to an interviewer for *Elle* magazine: "I read the Kabbalah books and I meditate on them. Kevin isn't into it as intensely as I am—for some reason, I'm thirsting for it. But he looks at the books every once in awhile." Britney actually had the Hebrew letters *mem, hey* and *shin* tattooed on the back of her neck as part of her devotion to her new faith. The letters form one of the seventy-two names of God in Hebrew and convey "the energy of healing at the deepest and most profound level." However, Britney abandoned Kabbalah six months later when, on September 14, 2005, Sean Preston Federline was delivered by Caesarian section in a comfortable hospital in Santa Monica.

The new mansion in Malibu was in a community nestled at the foot of the Santa Monica Mountains called Serra Retreat. It was, as one would expect, a superstar's house—meaning it was gigantic. Set on two lush acres, it was a Spanish-style mansion with eight bedrooms, a giant swimming pool and a restaurant-size kitchen. Britney made sure there were scented candles everywhere. One of the most important renovations was a near-state-of-the-art recording studio. This represented another way in which Britney was now trying to assert herself. She wanted to write and even produce a lot more of her music; she had decided that her musical efforts would now reflect who she was, not who her record company was telling her she was. One of the first visitors to the home was Jamie. He was bowled over by its size and luxury and asked whether it was a private home or a resort hotel.

Britney and Kevin had agreed in the early days of their relationship to do (for a hefty fee, of course) a reality show called *Britney and Kevin–Chaotic*. So, from their tour of Europe through their wedding day, cameras had followed them everywhere. The network UPN was backing the project and it was to debut in May of 2005. In some of the publicity material for the show, Britney was inspired by a line from "My Prerogative" referring to "truth." The show was initially intended to run for six episodes and it was to mix the reality TV format with documentary footage showing the strange and, well, chaotic life of Britney Spears.

Some of the early footage is bizarre, to say the least. Britney talks constantly about sex and sex positions, asking everyone from her friend Fe to her backup dancers to her bodyguards to bouncers at clubs what their favourite sex position is. Then, when a member of one of her opening acts demands that she answer the same question, Britney giggles and says that she can't answer that question because her family will be watching the show. The show really had nothing to do with Kevin Federline and was never meant to. Originally he was seen as a supporting character who could give the show more texture. The show was about putting the "real" Britney Spears out there for everyone to see, in contrast to the person her managers thought she should be, the person who said what she was supposed to say or just shut up and earned money.

Britney and Kevin–Chaotic was an early, raw example of that new bane of the culture known as the "reality show." Watching it, you get the clear sense that she's trying to play down the pop-star diva, millionaire, spoiled-brat image that surrounded her like a toxic cloud and saying, "See, y'all—I'm just like you." Of course, the rabid Britney fans ate it up. The series began airing on May 17, 2005, but it only ran for five episodes. The final episode, aired on June 14, was about the bizarre faux wedding in Studio City and it ended with the world premiere of the video for Britney's song "Someday (I Will Understand)." So the "reality" show ended its run depicting a fake marriage ceremony. Both Britney and Kevin are credited as executive producers of the show and while it was not a staggering hit like her albums and concerts tours regularly were, it drew between 2 and 3.7 million viewers per episode, which is not bad at all. There is something eerie about the way it shows Britney pursuing Kevin, never the opposite. In the third episode, she tells Kevin that she loves him, but he does not reciprocate. She seems to withdraw, but when she's alone, she turns to the camera and pours out her heart and soul for "comfort." The series clearly shows that Britney is the one who proposed; she's the one who decides everything concerning their relationship and their future. It's almost as if Federline is just along for the ride.

By the fall of 2005, Britney's life seemed to be straightening itself out. She had largely stepped out of the public eye during her pregnancy but was still able to keep herself visible through the reality show and the release of another compilation album in November of 2005 called *B in the Mix: The Remixes*. She was surrounded by family members, who had all pretty much moved out to California, so she no longer felt the pressure and solitude of being surrounded exclusively by agents, managers and lawyers. And she had little Sean Preston and the radical change a new baby brings, no matter what line of work you are in. Britney fully embraced motherhood, but, as any parent will tell you, there is no way to really prepare for the experience. While she was getting used to this major life change, the business of Britney Inc. continued. Since Britney was taking some time off, Kevin thought it might be an opportune time to go into their home studio and try to express himself musically. He was starting to feel a bit self-conscious due to all the talk swirling in the entertainment media about him being a lightweight and a hanger-on—a guy who, at best, was semi-talented. He had gone from hacking around L.A. looking for backup-dancer gigs to living in an eight-bedroom Malibu mansion with a platinum wedding ring on his finger.

Kevin Federline wanted to be known as something other than Mr. Britney Spears. Kevin Federline wanted to try his hand at hip-hop music. Britney was all for it—she wanted him to feel like she was there for him like he was there for her. A friend of Federline's confirms that "Britney, at first, was always telling Kevin that it didn't matter. Fuck all what people said about them or wrote about him. All that mattered was how they felt about each other." Britney was also very supportive of Federline's musical aspirations, helping him lay down his first couple of tracks, "Y'all Ain't Ready" and "PopoZao." But his insecurity would create small cracks in the foundation of their marriage almost as soon as Sean Preston arrived on the scene.

With all the exposure their personal life received as a result of *Chaotic* and with Britney's constant talk about sex on the show, rumours started to circulate that there was a sex tape of Britney and Kevin out there somewhere. *US Weekly* even ran a story claiming that Britney and Kevin were fearful that someone either in her circle or his was about to leak such a tape. Britney's legal squad pounced on *US Weekly* with a multimillion-dollar lawsuit. When Judge Lisa Hart Cole heard the case, she tossed out Britney's claim and the case. In her decision, she stated, "The plaintiff herself [Britney Spears] has put her modern sexuality squarely and profitably, before the public eye. The issue is whether it is defamatory to state that a husband and wife taped themselves engaging in consensual sex. I am ruling that it is not, given the fact that the plaintiff has publicly portrayed herself in a sexual way in performances, in published photographs and in her reality show."

* * *

Although it was not announced for several months, Britney became pregnant with her second child very early in 2006. It was an unplanned pregnancy and Britney told a friend that she was "totally freaked out" by the news and had turned to Lynne for advice on what she should do about it. Lynne told her that unplanned pregnancies are part of "the Lord's plan" and that she should not worry too much about it. Also in early 2006, Kevin's first two singles hit the airwaves. Unlike those of any other struggling L.A. hip-hop artist, his maiden efforts were backed with publicity campaigns and promotional tours. This bothered Britney. She had seen two previous serious relationships destroyed by distances and absences and she was fearful that she and Kevin were about to go down that road. With a new baby and another on the way, Britney was in no position to follow her husband around. The reason she'd attached herself to Federline in the first place was that he was available. Now he was clearly looking for ways to be famous himself. He was doing everything he could to establish himself as a player; he schmoozed people who could give him opportunities and he played the Britney card as often as he could. He was trying to get acting gigs (and he did land a couple, including a guest-starring role on CSI) and he was putting himself out there as a model and product endorser (the San Francisco company Blue Marlin Clothing hired him to model its five-star vintage line of casual wear and the line sold very well in a number of major outlets). But even in these attempts to establish himself, Federline simply looked like he was cashing in on his newfound notoriety by marriage. His appearance on CSI was trumped by Britney's first foray into prime-time network series television when she appeared on Will *and Grace* to guest star in an image-busting role as a closeted lesbian. When the episode aired, reactions to her performance were decidedly mixed. A critic for the *Sun Herald* remarked, "It is impossible to see [Britney Spears] in any role other than her own headline-hugging self." The reviewer for the *Chicago Tribune* wrote that she had "bombed." Still others claimed she'd done a great job and that this was a good career move for her.

She Flew Over The Cuckoo's Nest

"Why are you still taking pictures of me, can't you see I'm crying?"

–Britney Spears

On February 6, 2006, Britney Spears was out with her son Sean Preston. Leaving a store, she was mobbed by photographers. They surrounded her, blocking access to her vehicle. She tried to push her way to the car, telling the paparazzi to please be careful, she had a baby in her arms. Britney and son finally made it to the car and she climbed in and, with Sean Preston in her lap, she fired up the engine and drove off. By the next day, pictures of Britney driving with her child "unsafely" and "illegally" positioned on her lap as she sped away circled the globe and the media snidely called into question her fitness as a mother. All Britney was trying to do was get her child away from the intrusive cameras and to safety. No one bothered to explain the context of the photos.

A month later, news flashed around the world that little Sean Preston had been rushed to the hospital after some sort of household accident at the Federline's "Malibu mansion." Again, the implication was that something untoward had happened. The truth was more banal: Sean Preston had slipped and fallen from his high chair to the floor and Britney, erring on the side of caution, had taken him to the hospital to make sure he was not injured in a way she could not detect. Kids fall down stairs, they roll off beds, they bang their heads on tables, but if it happens to Britney's child, it's news. About a month later another photo damning Britney as a terrible mother was beamed around the globe. This time she was driving in her Mini Cooper with Sean Preston, but his car seat was strapped in facing the wrong way. A photographer in a hovering helicopter snapped that particular photograph over Britney's house. Two days later, while Britney was in New York with Sean Preston, she was photographed with a coffee in one hand and holding Sean Preston with her other arm; the street was wet with rain and she slipped, lost her balance and lost hold of her son. One of her bodyguards reached over and prevented him from falling to the ground. The photographers snapped away. The next day, the latest in the series of photos of Britney as a bad mother ran and was accompanied by comments about the fact that Britney had lost her grip on her child but not her coffee. Britney was being driven to the breaking point.

Back in Malibu, Britney took Sean Preston in the Mini Cooper to an exclusive cluster of shops and cafés called the Malibu Country Mart. Within feet of her driveway, the swarm of photographers who tailed her wherever she was going joined the chase. When she arrived at her destination, she parked and tried to quickly get Sean Preston out of the car and into the café, but the photographers crowded around her car and then blocked her way to the café. With Sean Preston in her arms, she fought her way into the café. Inside, the stress clearly evident on her face, she looked to the staff for help and found that they, too, were taking pictures of her with their cell phones. Britney made her way to a table and sat down. She rested her hand lightly on her baby's head and broke into tears. Britney sat at that table alone with her baby crying uncontrollably while photographers shot photos of her through the window and café workers shot pictures of her from inside. No one asked her if she was okay.

While the photographers certainly share blame for her misery, the fact was that Britney was becoming more emotionally unstable by the day and no matter whose fault it was, her safety and well-being and that of little Sean Preston were at risk. New husband Kevin Federline was not providing her with the emotional support she needed. Her loneliness and isolation grew deeper and deeper. It was obvious to anyone who knew her.

Shortly after the Malibu café meltdown, Britney asked Lynne if she would look after Sean Preston for an afternoon—she just wanted to go out for a drive and be all by herself for a little while. Lynne happily obliged and Britney jumped into the Mini Cooper and drove off. There was no sign of the paparazzi. She went down a coastal road in Malibu and stopped by a local bar called Moonshadows. Moonshadows has an outdoor terrace on a cliff overlooking the crashing surf. (It has become famous as a favourite watering hole of Mel Gibson's; it was here that his infamous night of drinking before his drunken run-in with the California highway patrol began.)

On this day, Britney Spears, the lightning rod of pop culture media attention, strolled alone into the bar, smiled at the bartender and went out onto the terrace. She sat by herself and looked out at the breathtakingly beautiful scenery. She ordered a Malibu and pineapple juice and spoke to no one. Then she ordered another Malibu and pineapple juice, then another and another, downing five drinks in rapid succession. One of the bartending staff says,

"She was really quiet, really in her own little zone. Lots of people recognised her, of course, but for some reason that day, no one, not a single person, approached her that I saw." He adds that when he asked her what she was celebrating, she said, "I'm pregnant again." Britney knew that she was hammered and couldn't drive, so she called her assistant to come and get her. She left her Mini Cooper at Moonshadows to be retrieved later.

In the midst of this strange time, Britney seemed to be able to become the other Britney—the smiling product-endorsing Britney—when required. It was like she was two distinct people: the real Britney, who was falling to pieces; and the pop princess who lived in a glass case waiting to be called upon. During this time, two more fragrances hit stores under her licensing agreement with Elizabeth Arden, earning her a staggering $53 million dollars. In Control and Midnight Fantasy would both be in stores before the end of the year, with In Control hitting stores first, in April. When she commented officially on choosing the name In Control, Britney said, "As I get older, the names go with my age. It's more demanding, it's more sensual, it's black; it's about being in control. That's cool and inspirational. Girls need that."

An expensive TV spot for In Control showed a hotel hallway with Britney and a young man (actor Eric Winter) noticing each other as they head to their respective rooms. They think of each other in their separate rooms and the final image is of her walking towards his room, then looking directly into the camera. The second fragrance, Midnight Fantasy, sold well when it was released in December 2006, but retailers noticed that a much-higher-than-expected number of gift sets was returned after the holidays. Industry analysts attributed this to the negative publicity surrounding Britney's personal life. Britney's behaviour was now causing her value as a brand to suffer.

* * *

Britney had an idealised notion of what being married was supposed to be like and saw marriage and children as a way to establish a kind of normalcy that she'd been desperately seeking since she'd started on the road to stardom so many years ago. But she had already grown extremely disappointed in Kevin Federline as a husband and father. As soon as he was able, he had begun recording and fighting to establish himself as a star in his own right. The public perception was that he was just another in a long line of leeches who attached themselves to Britney to get whatever they could, but a friend of Federline's says that this was not entirely the case. Kevin actually had different intentions from those the tabloids assigned him. The friend insists that "Kevin was really uncomfortable with that talk about him mooching off of Britney, that he was just with her because she was rich and famous . . . that wasn't true at all. He didn't want to live off of her and thought the only way to not do that was to establish himself and to work and to pay his own way. So when he is out there trying to do that, everyone then writes about him that he is neglecting his family and his obligations as a husband and father. If some son of a bitch working in a factory works double shifts to help out his family, do people accuse him of neglecting his family because he is out there working like a slave? Of course not. But they jumped all over Kevin for it."

While that is certainly a viable defence, it doesn't hold up. Britney's view that Kevin now saw a clear opportunity to be a star himself, using her fame and her resources to do it, was more accurate. Federline had moved in with an actress who was doing much better than he was career-wise then left her carrying his second child to take up with the much more famous Britney Spears. People go into performing, especially young, unsophisticated people, with the dream of being famous, being a star. Kevin's actions illustrated that he believed it was his opportunity to go out there and grab it.

For Britney, 2006 consisted mainly of trying to be the mother she dreamed of being, of having the family she dreamed of having and of defending her actions (and her dreams) to millions of people the world over who watched her every move. Photos taken of Britney during this time show her deep sadness; she has a resigned look about her, as if she had now reckoned with the fact that she had, with lots of help and urging along the way, sold her soul for stardom. She wrote a poem and posted it on her website entitled "Remembrance of Who I Am." In it, she spoke of her wish to get to a place of "no more pain, no more chains," of leaving behind "the silly patterns that we follow." Other lines in the poem referred to being "manipulated," "pulled down," and "swallowed . . . by the ones you think you love." She wrote about the Bible and "the sins of the father," and she declared, "what you do you pass down, now wonder why I lost my crown."

During an appearance on *The Late Show with David Letterman* in May, she announced that she was pregnant with her second child. She did her best "Britney" on the show and talked about how happy she was and how magical it all was, but it seemed like an act.

On June 15, 2006, she invited NBC's Matt Lauer into her home for a long, detailed sit-down interview. Lauer pressed Britney on rumours that she and Kevin were already on the verge of divorce and on reports of her showing poor judgment with her child. Britney kept her composure for the most part. She answered all the invasive questions. She explained that when she was with her baby and surrounded by a pack of photographers, her only thought was how to get Sean Preston clear of the commotion. She told Lauer, "You know what? I know I am a good mom, but I'm not perfect. I'm human." She denied that her marriage was in trouble, saying "married life is awesome." She added that she fully supported Kevin in putting together his first album. Oddly, when her composure finally left her it was because of a question Lauer asked about the paparazzi: "What will it take to get the paparazzi to leave you alone." Britney choked up and cried, "I don't know. But that is what I would like—for them to leave me alone." Lauer then asked her if, after all the tumult and upheaval of the past few years, she still believed herself to be lucky and blessed. Britney nodded and said, "Because I have to believe that I am here for a reason." Lauer pressed on, asking what she thought that reason was. "I don't know," said Britney. "I keep searching every day."

Britney accepted an offer from *Harper's Bazaar* magazine to be photographed naked for the cover of its August issue. A quite pregnant Britney sits naked on a concrete block, her legs crossed and her left arm folded across her breasts. Her right arm is bent so her hand shields half her face and she is not smiling—at least, not exactly. In the accompanying article she talks about desperately wanting to get back to work: "I can't wait to do that again. But I really have to take my time and do it right and be safe. Actually, not that safe—when you perform you have to be dangerous.

After this baby, I'm going to get really intense with it." Britney told another journalist that she thought there was nothing wrong with posing naked while pregnant and that the photos were "tasteful."

On September 12, 2006, Jayden James Federline was born in Los Angeles. There were no complications and mother and new son were fine. Britney and Federline, however, rather than celebrating the new addition to their family, drifted further and further apart. Federline showed little respect for Britney; he even seemed resentful. His album, *Playing with Fire*, was released and like his two singles, it was poorly received. He went on the Teen Choice Awards broadcast to perform the first single off the album, called "Lose Control," but that didn't stop many from calling the album the worst in recent music history.

Shortly thereafter, a disturbing video appeared on the Internet showing Britney staggering down an L.A. street drunk, drinking from a can and eating junk food. The video was shot by Federline. Britney looks terrible, she slurs her words and she shouts at Federline, "Stop makin' fun of me Kevin! You're dumb too, you know." Britney's friend Elizabeth Jansen says, "Britney was so sad. She would call Kevin all the time because he never seemed to be around. They would have arguments on the phone. She would try to reason with him, beg him even, to think about her and about their family together, base his decisions on that first then think about his music career. Britney would almost always end up crying after these calls."

* * *

On the morning of November 7, 2006, with Kevin once again out of town, Britney and her legal team (headed again by Laura Wasser) filed for divorce. Court documents revealed that the tried-and-true "irreconcilable differences" was the cause. Britney was asking for physical and legal custody of Sean Preston and Jayden James and requesting that Federline be allowed reasonable visitation rights. Kevin, in New York, was stunned at the news. Sure, there had been arguments and pressures, but there had never been any mention of divorce. Britney had even been telling TV talk show audiences how wonderful married life was.

People who had known Britney for years—and, more importantly, who had known Lynne Spears for years—saw Lynne's hand in this. Early in her marriage to Jamie, Lynne had impulsively filed for divorce then withdrawn the petition just as fast as she'd filed it. It had been a drastic ploy to get Jamie to change his ways and take her concerns seriously. The same technique could very well have been at play here. Britney had reached a point where she needed change—drastic and sudden change. Perhaps if she threatened to kick Kevin off the gravy train he would straighten himself out and start caring about her emotional needs. She could take care of their material needs, but she needed him to be there for her emotionally. But Federline, unlike Jamie, didn't bite, didn't coming running home begging for forgiveness. He got his lawyers to shoot back with a petition of his own. He, too, was seeking physical and legal custody of the boys.

Britney freaked out at the idea that Federline would even think of taking her children away from her; Jayden was just two months old at this point. She headed to New York to meet with her former manager, Larry Rudolph. She and Rudolph were seen skating at Rockefeller Center and having a very serious discussion in a restaurant. Two weeks later, Britney appeared for the first time on the public stage since filing for divorce, acting as the opening presenter on the live telecast of the American Music Awards. As she waited backstage for the show to begin and her name to be announced, she watched the show's opening comedy skit on a big monitor. It featured a Kevin Federline look-alike being nailed into a crate then dropped into the ocean from a crane. Federline, who was now being called K-FedEx, was mocked by a note attached to the crate that read "The world's first no-hit wonder."

Britney had a full-blown freak-out. No one had warned her the show would open like this. She had no time to recover. She was introduced and had to take the stage to present the award. Smiling at the audience, she said a quick "I'm so glad to be here," presented Mary J. Blige with her award and glided off the stage. In tears, she told the show's producers how furious she was that they hadn't warned her about the skit and how cruel it was of them to make fun of her personal troubles; furthermore, obliging her to take the stage right after the skit made it seem like she was endorsing it somehow. The producers didn't know what to do to console her, so they downplayed it, telling her that the crowd thought it was funny and that their laughter showed they were on her side. The Jive Records executives who were on hand demanded that the skit be dropped from the rerun of the show on the West Coast three hours later, but it wasn't. Host Jimmy Kimmel claimed the whole thing was his idea. When he was asked to respond to the ire his great idea caused, he smirked and said, "[Britney and Kevin] both have a great sense of humor."

Britney and her lawyer, Laura Wasser, were concerned that since the skit had been aired on national TV so soon after the divorce filing it would be seen as proof of Britney's arrogance and lack of seriousness about what she had put in motion.

Less than three weeks after filing for divorce and less than eleven weeks after giving birth to her second child, on the night of November 27, 2006, Britney was photographed on the town partying with two of the worst people she could have been seen in public with—two of the most spoiled, vapid, irresponsible and reckless young women our new version of pop culture has chosen to celebrate: Lindsay Lohan and Paris Hilton. They drove around Hollywood in Paris's SUV, welcoming attention from paparazzi at every stop; they climbed out of the vehicle with their breasts spilling out of their tops and Britney was infamously photographed panty-less, her goods on display to every photographer. They went from one club to the next, making a big show of their arrivals and departures, until just past 5:00 a.m. Asked why she was doing the rounds with new friend Britney Spears, Paris Hilton replied, "Who wouldn't want to hang with Britney? She's hot."

Britney and Paris became a regular sight at West Hollywood hot spots like Area, Hyde, the Viper Room, Foxtail and the Abbey. Britney would come in with her sidekick and start drinking immediately, either vodka shots or Jack Daniels and Coke. A large contingent of celebrity press glued themselves to the pair, chasing them in cars and on motorcycles. One night, after a long booze-up and club crawl, a staggering, giggling Britney was photographed wearing a top on which she'd vomited. Britney's exploits had the unfortunate effect of making Kevin Federline look like the more upstanding, responsible parent; surprisingly, he took the high road, remaining quiet and focused. He was in constant touch with Lynne, who was looking after the boys when Britney was out and about.

Kalie Machado, a pretty twenty-three-year old, was hired as Britney's assistant shortly after Britney filed for divorce. She was not supposed to function as Fe did—as a de-facto friend, confidante and chaperone; the days of Britney responding to that sort of thing were long gone. Rather, Kalie was hired to be a personal assistant and, in effect, a witness. Like many of the personal staff engaged by Britney at this time, Kalie would not last long, only about four months, but it was during these months that Britney lost all control. Kalie was with Britney virtually every day from November of 2006 through February of 2007. She was protective of Britney and tried to present things from Britney's point of view when reporting to Lynne or Jamie or even Larry Rudolph, who was again Britney's manager. Kalie was not just an assistant but a defender. As she told US Weekly, "[Britney] was broken-hearted. She was confused and under enormous pressure. Why would going out and getting drunk a few times be considered a meltdown? A lot of people deal with heartbreaks that way."

Another of Britney's assistants, Shannon Funk, a blonde, Paris Hilton look-alike, took a different approach. She claimed to be not just Britney's assistant but also her special shoulder to cry on and her lover. She sold a photo to OK! magazine of her in a swimming pool kissing Britney's neck, which appeared under the headline "Britney's New Lover." Funk and several other young women who were hired as personal assistants ended up selling their stories about Britney to the tabloids and were then called by Federline's lawyers to repeat their tales in court.

And it just got worse. Just after turning twenty-five, just over a month after filing for divorce, Britney agreed to be set up on a blind date. Isaac Cohen was a male model. Some observed that he was like a more refined Kevin Federline, with more handsome, chiselled features. The two seemed to hit it off and almost immediately Cohen was being invited to Britney's house in Malibu. She trusted him and believed that he didn't have an agenda, but after it was over, he sold the details of their six-and-a-half week "relationship" to the British tabloid the *News of the World*.

The pattern was familiar. People who became close to Britney were dazzled by the luxury and the promise of endless, decadent fun. She and Cohen flew to Las Vegas for a romp at one of the most luxurious and exclusive hotel suites in the city: the Hugh Hefner Sky Villa penthouse at the top of the Palms Hotel. The price tag is just north of $20,000 per night and the suite is so big that it has its own gym, giant Jacuzzi and a floor-to-ceiling, wall-to-wall glass window that affords guests the most spectacular view of the Strip there is. Cohen described Britney to the *News of the World* as "amazing" in bed and said how adventurous she was. He referred to the weekend as an "al fresco sex romp." But he also said, "Once the sex stopped she was like a lost little girl, unable to cope with life. There were times when she would just weep uncontrollably. She said she would do anything to be a normal person again and was scared that the photos of her partying would be used against her and she would lose custody of her children. It was all incredibly upsetting and I tried to do whatever I could to make sure she had my support. . . . She realised nothing was working, the partying, nothing; it just made her more miserable. Far from being a trashy drunk, the girl I met was shy, sweet and desperately sad and she was beside herself with fear that her boys would be taken away from her. She would cry so hard and cling to me tightly. She was very frightened. I knew that she was with me because she was feeling completely alone. But she was also a romantic, kind and very giving."

* * *

If you were to stroll around Britney's house during this time, you would feel a certain air of poignancy and perhaps regret. Kevin Federline had vacated, but perfectly centred on the living room coffee table was a pristine copy of the *People* magazine featuring their wedding. Framed copies of the various wedding announcements and invitations still hung on the walls. In the hallway, Britney's wedding dress was displayed in a glass cabinet. The sense of loss was palpable.

What helped to sustain Britney was her love for her children. Those who were with Britney and her kids away from the spotlight paint a portrait of a loving, affectionate, caring mother. Kalie Machado says, "She was hurting a lot and the only real comfort she could get during this time was to have her babies as close to her as possible. No matter what anyone says, she loves those children more than anything else in the world."

Even though Britney had a small platoon of nannies at her disposal, Lynne was always there to help with the kids. Britney still wanted their father to be there, however. "She had lots of help available to her where taking care of the kids was concerned, but she didn't want it," Machado told *People*. "She would call [Kevin Federline's] cell phone constantly and he would never pick up and never return her calls."

Christmas 2006 was fast approaching and Britney was dreading it. The sadness that depressed and lonely people feel is magnified a thousand times during the festive season. Britney didn't want to stay in L.A. over the holidays and decided that she would head to Kentwood to be with her family. There were lots of tears, lots of consoling, lots of frustration. Lynne would later write in her memoir that she wished she had known more about postpartum depression at the time: "I really had no idea just how much agony she was in."

* * *

In retrospect, it seems clear that Britney was suffering from severe postpartum depression, the most extreme version of which is called postpartum psychosis. Its symptoms are "extreme confusion, fatigue, agitation, alterations in mood, feelings of hopelessness and shame, hallucinations and rapid speech or mania." It is a condition that occurs in just one of every thousand births.

GONE BABY GONE

"Is this what you want? Huh? Is this what you want?!"
—Britney Spears

After the Christmas holiday in Kentwood, Britney and Kalie returned to Los Angeles with the children. Shortly thereafter, they all packed up and headed to Las Vegas, the children too, to attend a New Year's Eve Prince concert. Sean Preston and Jayden James were in the care of a nanny at the hotel. After the concert, Britney and Kalie went to Pure, a well-known nightspot. There they drank and danced the New Year in. When asked by *US Weekly* if Britney had gotten drunk, Kalie said, "Well, yes, she got drunk, but she wasn't loud or crazy or obnoxious. She was sad and melancholic. She would be dancing and laughing then something about Kevin would pop into her head and she would just start crying."

Back in Los Angeles, Britney had nothing to do—she was not working on a new album and she didn't have to prepare for a concert or a publicity tour. She felt restless; she needed to constantly be on the move. During the first couple of months of 2007, she and the kids, with Kalie and a nanny, travelled to Las Vegas, then to New York and Miami and then back to Las Vegas. Britney had agreed to put in some time at Pure on January 16; the Pure people wanted her to add cachet to their establishment by hanging out there. She didn't have to sign autographs or do anything at all—she just had to show up and hang out. Just before she was to appear in the lounge, she asked the owners if she could have some private time in the adjoining Pussycat Doll Lounge. Britney, Kalie and a couple of entourage pals, went into the lounge. They locked the door behind them. Britney then told the small group she wanted to play the role of a "hot burlesque dancing queen." She jumped onto the small stage and began to bump and grind and strip for her friends. She never stripped naked, just peeled down to her bra and tight little white shorts. As Machado tells it, "There was nobody else around. She was getting all sexy and having fun onstage. She is a performer. That is what she does."

When she returned home to L.A., Britney ended her brief relationship with Isaac Cohen. He'd seen it coming. It was all over with one phone call. Soon afterwards, he sealed the deal to sell his story to *News of the World*. A week later, Britney's emotional distress was compounded when, on January 27, her aunt, Sandra Covington, died of ovarian cancer. Britney was very close to Sandra and her death cast her further adrift.

Behind the scenes, Britney's lawyer and Kevin's lawyer were trying to work out some kind of amicable agreement. Britney's lawyer tried to broker a joint-custody arrangement. She knew that Federline had some leverage because of her client's reckless behaviour, but she also knew that this leverage was tenuous. She proposed that Federline be given access to his children while the larger issues surrounding the divorce were hammered out. The children would remain living with Britney, but Kevin could have them for three days per week. This was more than Britney felt comfortable with, but it was better than having the children given to Federline full-time on a temporary basis, as he was asking. Reluctantly, Britney agreed to the arrangement.

* * *

One night in late January of 2007, Kalie's cell phone rang. The man on the line said he was a private investigator and that he had been hired by Kevin Federline to collect as much incriminating material as he could on Britney to present at the divorce proceedings. The man claimed that he had met Britney at a party and liked her and had decided that he didn't want to hurt her. He offered to turn all the material over to Britney through Kalie, but Kalie had to agree to meet him in person. Kalie naively agreed to meet the man at a Santa Monica coffee shop a few hours later, but she asked a friend to join her for safety reasons and to have a witness to the meeting. At the coffee shop, the man introduced himself as Osama "Sam" Lutfi. He presented himself as a mysterious but powerful man. He told Kalie not to write down his licence plate number because it was a stolen plate and could not be traced to him. The meeting lasted less than half an hour. Lutfi began by asking detailed questions about Britney's house, who lived there and when people were likely to be out. Kalie was uncomfortable and asked for the information she had been promised. Lutfi produced nothing. Kalie later told *Rolling Stone*, "Then he started telling me that he knew for a fact that I was under investigation. He said that we were always being followed and that the house was bugged." At that point, Kalie and her friend left the meeting. Kalie called Larry Rudolph right away. He told her she was crazy for meeting this creep in the first place and that she should just forget it—the man was just another Hollywood delusional yahoo.

* * *

Britney had become obsessed with Diana, Princess of Wales and was reading books about her life. She identified strongly with the changes that had occurred in Diana's life after she became a public figure—the isolation and the loneliness—and was fascinated by the fact that she'd likely been killed as a result of the media attention surrounding her. Britney also studied a book entitled *Conversations with God*; she was looking for guidance, but she got nothing from any of these books except a greater sense of confusion about her life.

She would tell her close friends Courtney Brabham and Elizabeth Jansen that she felt the constant media scrutiny was killing her, but she would then say that if she were ever to lose the ability to perform and enjoy the attention and energy the fans gave her, that would kill her, too. She said that she wanted to go and live on a little tropical island where no one knew her, but she wanted to be able to come back every couple of years to make a record and do some touring. She spoke of wanting to leave show business entirely and just be a waitress in a small town.

The constant pressure, the depression, the confusion was reaching a breaking point. Lynne, Jamie, Larry Rudolph and others who were professionally and personally close to Britney wanted to attempt an intervention. They believed that at the root of Britney's behaviour problems was her partying, drinking and casual drug use. They decided they would try to convince her to check into a rehab facility. The one they chose was, ironically, called Crossroads and it was located on the lush Caribbean island of Antigua. Britney was angry and completely rejected the idea. She eventually relented, but she left Crossroads before she'd even been there a day. She headed back to L.A. on February 16 not just in emotional turmoil but also in a seething rage at her inner circle.

Two days later, on the night of Friday, February 18, 2007, Britney was being driven by two bodyguards through Tarzana, just outside Los Angeles. A large pack of paparazzi followed close on their bumper. All of a sudden, Britney told the driver to pull over in front of a place called Esther's Hair Salon, owned and operated by one Esther Tognozzi. The paparazzi collected outside, wondering what was up. Inside, Britney told Esther that she wanted all her hair shaved off. She was sick of the look and her extensions were uncomfortably tight. Though a bit star-struck and flustered, Esther understood that it isn't unusual for women with long hair to want a radical hairstyle change when they are in emotional turmoil. It's a way of effecting immediate and visible change in your life. You look different, so maybe you'll feel different. Good stylists always try to talk the client out of it, as most regret the impulse. Esther explained to Britney that she should think it over first, but Britney was adamant and told her with a smile that she wanted it taken "right on down." With the photographers massing outside her window, two bodyguards at the door and the world's biggest pop superstar in her chair, Esther was feeling a bit of pressure herself, but she continued to try to talk Britney out of the radical thing she was suggesting. Then Esther turned away for a moment to ask the bodyguards if they could back her up. Britney jumped out of the chair, grabbed the electric clippers and began shearing her head. The photographers outside were delirious; this was more than they could have dreamed of. Esther just stood and watched. The bodyguards were alarmed— they weren't sure what she was doing or whether she was doing harm to herself.

Once her entire head was shaved and hair lay in piles at her feet, Britney sat back down in the chair. Esther recalls, "She had a funny look on her face. She said quietly that her mom was going to be really mad at her. Then she started crying, not hysterically, just kind of, like, with a resignation. I didn't know what to do, so I tried to make her feel a bit better by telling her she had a lovely-shaped head."

Before her head was even fully shorn, the photographers had sent out shots of her taking the clippers to herself, which were transmitted to news agencies all over the world. Within minutes, images of Britney "going nuts" were on the Internet. As she left Esther's with her bodyguards, she noticed a tattoo parlour next door called Body and Soul and told the bodyguards that she was going in to get a "tatt." They waited and watched as she got a small tattoo on her hip. The tattoo artist told her that her new bald look was cool and asked her why she had decided to do it. Britney replied, "I don't want anyone touching me. I am tired of everyone touching me."

Lynne Spears had to see all this splashed over the media before she could get to Britney and talk to her. Elizabeth Jansen recalls that Britney had been talking a lot about how her mother was putting pressure on her to stop going out and drinking: "She would tell Britney to just sit back and think about how it looks when she's photographed partying while Kevin has committed to not going out on the town during this tough time. It made Britney think that even her mother was turning on her, even though that wasn't true." Kalie adds, "Britney had tried to shave her head a couple of times. She told me she was going to do it. I told her it wasn't a good idea and she didn't listen. But I wasn't with her this time."

No one seemed to know what was happening to Britney. Stories began to circulate that her behaviour was due in part to dependence on a prescription medication that she had been getting for years, but up until now had only used sparingly. Larry Rudolph was trying to impress upon her that in this business image and perception was everything and that if she didn't get it together fast, her career was over. Lynne was genuinely concerned about her daughter and she would often meet with Britney's girlfriends and Kalie to get reports on Britney's behaviour when Britney was away from home. Lynne, Jamie and Bryan were imploring her to seek professional help, but the more they pushed, the angrier Britney became and the tensions between them escalated.

* * *

Just after shaving her head, Britney left her house in Malibu and headed to the ultra hip L.A. hotel the Mondrian. She was alone and wearing a conspicuous blonde wig. At the reception desk, she asked for a suite. She had no cash or credit cards and she was told that she couldn't check in without identification. Britney then began wailing and crying, repeating over and over, "Nobody wants me anymore, nobody wants me anymore." It took a couple of young girls, complete strangers, to calm her down. They put their arms around her and took her to the pool patio. Britney stripped off her clothes, revealing a skimpy bikini and sat down on the steps leading into the pool. Then she began shaving her legs. A pool attendant who was on duty that day says, "She really looked kind of strange—not high or drunk, but kind of out [of] it. Someone else went over to her and told her that, for sanitary and health reasons, she really must stop doing what she was doing." Britney complied, went and sat on a lounge chair and resumed shaving her legs. After that, she posed for pictures and signed autographs for a group of fans who were also hanging out at the pool. Just days before, she had been crying to be left alone and now she was reaching out to strangers.

Lynne, Larry Rudolph and Britney's corporate team again tried to get Britney into a substance-abuse program. They had decided that the relationship between Kalie Machado and Britney was unhealthy, so Lynne ordered Kalie to keep her distance. One source close to Britney says, "Britney would call Kalie a lot because Britney trusted her and liked her, but Kalie had been told she was not allowed to take calls from Britney anymore because she was what they called, in rehab terms, an enabler."

By the time Britney had shaved her head, Kalie had been fired. Six days prior to that crazy night in Tarzana, Kalie was in New York with Britney and got an angry phone call from Lynne Spears. Kalie says, "She was angry and asking me what I was doing there with Britney. I wasn't sure what she meant, because I was Britney's personal assistant. Where else would I be than with her? Lynne continued to yell at me that my being always with Britney, being her friend, was giving her permission to go out and party all the time when she really should be home being a mom to her two children. She called me an enabler and ordered me to return to Los Angeles. I wasn't sure what was going on. I worked for Britney, but Lynne was ordering me around. I did do what Lynne said, though, because from what I had been seeing and Lynne's angry tone, it felt like something serious was going on and I better stay out of it." Back in L.A., Kalie was told to "take a few days off." She wouldn't see Britney again, because her employment had been effectively terminated.

On February 20, 2007, Britney was again persuaded to enter a substance-abuse program. This time, it was in her neighbourhood: the ultra luxurious celebrity rehab centre, Promises, in Malibu. Though it was reported that Britney checked into the centre willingly, a source close to her says, "Well, she walked into the place on her own, but she certainly did not want to be there and didn't believe she needed to be there."

Promises is for "people who are used to being surrounded by luxury." It resembles a first-class resort. Its website says, "The beauty of the natural surroundings inspires a sense of awe and gratitude that encourages the recovery process" and promises that "Guests will be treated to gourmet meals, flat panel TVs, a fireplace, phone and Internet access and numerous patios and sitting areas. Promises Malibu is within a private gated community to help remove the distractions of everyday life, prevent unexpected visitors and allow individuals to concentrate on overcoming the issues they must deal with."

Britney checked herself out less than twenty-four hours. Elizabeth Jansen claims that she missed her children, but her other old friend, Courtney Brabham, says that Britney was living in fear of what Lynne and Kevin Federline were doing behind her back. Lynne and Kevin were in touch often, mostly to discuss the boys' care. There is no reason, however, to believe that anything sinister was going on. Lynne believed that booze, prescription drugs and recreational narcotics were fuelling Britney's problems and that Britney was taking an immature rebellious stand against her mother when she denied her problems and refused treatment. Lynne also believed that working with Kevin was the only way to ensure that the needs of the children were addressed.

When Britney checked herself out of Promises, Kevin immediately petitioned the court for an emergency hearing to seek full temporary legal and physical custody of Sean Preston and Jayden James. He took this action after speaking with Lynne. For Lynne, this represented a kind of tough love for her daughter, but it was misdirected—Britney's real problems were not even being investigated, let alone treated. When Britney heard of the petition she went straight to Federline's house and confronted him. A source close to Federline says Kevin kept his cool and was sympathetic and reasonable. He hadn't wanted the divorce in the first place. He told her he was acting in the children's best interest and that if she agreed to go back to Promises and stay there for the full thirty-day cycle of treatment, he would withdraw his petition for custody. One of Kevin's close friends says this demand had been the idea of Lynne and Larry Rudolph.

As Britney left Federline's home in her white Mercedes, she was once more swarmed by a horde of paparazzi, who followed her car closely. Suddenly, she slammed on the brakes and jumped out of the car wielding a large green umbrella like a baseball bat. She charged at the first carful of photographers, an SUV and began beating the car with the umbrella, grunting and screaming, putting every ounce of her energy into each swing. When she was spent, she got back into the Mercedes and drove away.

The next day, she checked back into Promises and the petition for an emergency custody hearing was withdrawn. Before returning to Promises, Britney had a long conversation with Jamie, who said he was trying to stay focused on his little girl and her pain and how to make it go away. He told her he believed that she needed what Promises could give her. One of Britney's friends says, "She was totally freaked out. She couldn't understand why everyone was trying to force her into rehab without hearing what she had to say about it."

The answer, quite simply, was that Rudolph and the corporate side of Team Britney knew that their hundred-million-dollar asset was in a freefall, losing value fast and that they needed to find a way to reverse the trend. Britney's public image suffered more damage with each bout of strange behaviour. Everyone thought that if they could just get her through rehab, then they could proclaim that she had conquered the demons of drugs and alcohol and her public would feel inclined to like her again. There was a lot riding on this and Britney's handlers tried very hard to make her feel the urgency of the situation. But their efforts may only have made things worse for her. As Brabham puts it, "Britney said many times during this rough period that the pressure her manager was putting on her was literally making her feel like she was losing her mind."

On March 21, 2007, after a month of treatment, Britney left Promises. She summed up the experience by saying, "I've done my time." The first people she wanted to see were her children.

Rudolph issued a statement that Britney had checked out of Promises "after successfully completing their program." Since she had fulfilled her obligations under her agreement with Federline, a new agreement was put in place: pending finalisation of the divorce, custody of Sean Preston and Jayden James would be divided evenly between their parents. Britney, still deeply resentful, lost no time in exacting retribution against the two people she believed were most responsible for forcing her to go into rehab: Larry Rudolph and her mother. Rudolph was the easiest to deal with—she simply fired him. She couldn't fire her mother, but Lynne knew that any reconciliation would be a long time in coming.

Britney knew that work would have to be part of her recovery. She had done a little bit of preliminary work on a new album and now she set about rounding up some good producers. She also organised a small tour, for which she would perform in six House of Blues nightclubs. She called it the *M&Ms* tour (which stood for Mom and Ms., as she was no longer a Mrs.). The idea was to try some different things on a small scale and see what the response would be. If the word of mouth was good, then they would have something to build on. Dates weren't announced. The first show was booked at the House of Blues in San Diego on May 1, 2007. When word started going around that the act called M&Ms was actually Britney Spears, tickets sold out instantly; scalpers got as much as $500 for a $35 ticket. The tour would visit House of Blues clubs in Anaheim, Los Angeles, Las Vegas and Orlando before finishing on May 20, 2007 at the Mansion Nightclub in Miami. The performances were tight club shows: five songs and no encore. Britney performed in skimpy outfits—pink bras and tiny denim skirts. At one point in each show she would select a male audience member and bring him onstage while she sang the sultry "Breathe on Me." To finish up, she would thank the audience, pose with her dancers and introduce them, then skip off the stage. James Hebert of *USA Today* said in his very positive review of the show, "Britney leaves 'em wanting more."

WHERE DO I GO FROM HERE?

"A lot of insecurities from when I was little are coming up again."
–Britney Spears

When she was feeling really lost, Britney often turned to her official website to reach out to her fans. She did this again in May 2007 to try to explain to her fans what had really been going on in her life, but never in her long and heartfelt message does she come close to admitting she had a substance-abuse problem: "I know everyone thinks that I am playing the victim, but I am not, and I hate what is going on now so much. Maybe this is the reason for this letter. I feel like some of the people in my life made more of some of the issues than was necessary. I also know that they knew I was beginning to use my brain for a change and wanted to cut some ties, but they wanted to be more in control of my life than me." She then bares her soul a bit, writing, "I confess, I was so lost," and ends the post as she might end a letter to a personal friend: "I am sitting here at home and it's 6:25. Both my boys are asleep. I am truly blessed to have them in my life!"

Britney seemed to be dealing with things in a calmer and more considered fashion. She had a new personal assistant, a loyal and personable woman from Kentwood named Alli Sims, whom she had known for many years. She also had a new sense of purpose. She had sidelined her mother, having convinced herself that Lynne was secretly colluding with Kevin Federline against her and the two had stabbed her in the back. While Britney's reaction may have sounded paranoid, there was some justification for it. Lynne and Kevin did talk frequently and Britney was not included in their exchanges. But an associate of Kevin's says it was a bit more complicated than that: Lynne "called Kevin a lot, and she was trying to use him to help her manipulate the whole mess, but it was not really to stab Britney in the back. It was because Lynne wanted Britney to do what she said, and Britney wasn't doing it."

Britney felt no better about her father, who had decided, no doubt with prompting, to go public with his thoughts on what was going on with his daughter to the *New York Post*. It infuriated Britney almost beyond measure that Jamie told the *Post* he wanted to apologise to the fans . . . and to Larry Rudolph! "The Spears family would like to publicly apologise to Larry for our daughter's statements about him. Unfortunately, she blames him and her family for where she is today with her kids and career." Jamie insisted that manipulating Britney into rehab was the right thing to do and that Rudolph had acted almost heroically under the circumstances. "When Larry talked Britney into going into rehab, he was doing what her mother, her father and a team of professionals with over a hundred years of experience knew needed to be done. She was out of control . . . Larry was the one picked by the team to get in there and roll up his sleeves and deliver the message to help save her life."

Britney fired back in public with all the rancor of someone who has been betrayed. She spoke of praying for Jamie when he had gone through difficult times, then she added something strange: "My father and I have never really had a good relationship. It's sad that none of the men in my life know how to accept the love of a real woman."

Britney now went on a tear, firing her bodyguards and her publicity people while declaring that she was sick and tired of having an army of greedy, uncaring people around her who presumed to know what she needed better than she did. She was twenty-five years old now, not fourteen. She had in her corner assistants Shannon Funk and Alli Sims, with whom Britney was close (she liked to call Alli and herself Thelma and Louise). Britney felt that with these two strong young women at her side, she had all the support she needed.

She then concocted a publicity stunt, the sole purpose of which was to publicly humiliate her mother. Lynne had been spending most of her time with Jamie Lynn, now fifteen, on the set of *Zoey 101*, a cute show about an all-boys school coping with going coed. Jamie Lynn, a dead ringer for her big sister, played the lead role of Zoey Brooks and she was doing very well, winning the Kids' Choice Award for favourite television actress in 2006. On June 27, 2007, the show was shooting in Santa Clarita, California, an affluent community just outside of Los Angeles. Lynne was there. Earlier that day, Britney left her house in her sleek black Mercedes and stopped beside a hovering pack of paparazzi. She told them to follow her—she had something they all needed to see. She headed off to Santa Clarita and the paparazzi following as instructed. When they arrived at the set of the show, Britney was allowed in and the paparazzi followed, something only Britney could have arranged for. Britney pulled up to her sister's trailer and got out of the car wearing rubber flip-flops and denim shorts. She paused briefly, almost as if to allow the paparazzi to get into position and ready their cameras, before banging on the trailer door. Lynne answered and Britney dramatically shoved a sheaf of papers into her hands. It was a long, rambling letter she'd written to her mother explaining why she wanted to be left alone and how disappointed she was in her for siding with Federline and Rudolph. Britney then turned and headed back to her car. Lynne said something that caused Britney to stomp back towards her gesturing wildly. Sitting on the trailer stairs, Lynne proceeded to read the letter while Britney harangued her. When Lynne had finished reading, the two exchanged more words. Lynne now looked dejected. Britney went back to her car, but before she drove off, she told the gathered press, "I am praying for her right now. I really hope she gets the help she needs." When Lynne was asked to respond to this latest outburst, she said sadly, "I have a very strong family. Everything will be just fine."

* * *

Work was underway on Britney's first new studio album in three years, *Blackout*, which would contain twelve brand-new songs. Britney wanted to make a quick and grand gesture to show the world that she was back and it was a whole new ball game. Jive Records still was in charge of producing and marketing her albums and they were of the opinion that her reputation would recover immeasurably if her new album was solid, so they concentrated on making it that way. Britney was struck with the idea that she should use a celebrity publication to get her message across. She thought that a feature in the photo-heavy British celebrity magazine *OK!* would be perfect. The piece would be thin on text but filled with glamour photos of her wearing beautiful clothes. Britney used no go-betweens in organising this except for Alli and Shannon. The shoot was set up for July 19, 2007 and it would be overseen by *OK!* editor-in-chief (and celebrity journalist in her own right) Sarah Ivens. Ivens and her style team procured the clothing Britney would wear, borrowing pieces from designers Vera Wang, Zac Posen and Elisha Levine.

When Britney arrived for the shoot that July afternoon, it was immediately obvious to Sarah Ivens that something was wrong. She seemed high and she was sashaying around like a clichéd diva. "Britney and her friends were like spoiled children," Ivens says. "They were intent on running everything but were doing so in such an amateurish manner that it was embarrassing." Britney insisted that her friends do her makeup and hair instead of the professionals *OK!* had hired. She complained about the clothing selection. She didn't like anything. She would wear the clothes because they were here, but she didn't think they were "tight and sexy enough." People who were on the set report that she would disappear into the bathroom without notice. She ordered a fast-food lunch and refused to change out of her expensive borrowed gown while eating, theatrically wiping her dirty hands on the gown. After the photos were taken, Britney gave *OK!* a rambling, disjointed interview then abruptly got up and left with her team, still wearing over $15,000 worth of borrowed clothes and jewelry. She had allowed her dog to soil another expensive gown and left it in a heap on the floor.

"I couldn't believe what was happening," says Ivens. "I have been working in the industry for eleven years and attended countless photo shoots in London, New York and L.A., but I've never had anyone walk out. It was so disrespectful. Such a lack of good manners. No matter how big a celebrity you are, that kind of behaviour is not acceptable." Ivens went back to her office and wrote a scathing article about all that had occurred that day. The "Britney comeback" piece would not be happening. Ivens explains, "I wanted to provide a wake-up call for [Britney] and for the people around her."

The article provided Kevin Federline and his lawyer, Mark Kaplan, with fresh ammunition against Britney. The divorce proceedings were concluded and sealed on July 30, 2007, but this new bit of craziness led them to petition the court to amend the custody arrangement and shift custody of Sean Preston and Jayden James from 50-50 to 70-30 in Kevin's favor. His petition stated simply that it was clear for all to see that Britney was not in any condition to care for children and that he could and would do a better job.

* * *

According to the divorce papers, even though she was not touring and hadn't released any new music in a couple of years, Britney was still earning $737,868 per month. Federline had no income at all except the $20,000 per month in spousal support he had been temporarily awarded pending finalisation of the divorce. In view of this, he and his lawyers were not just demanding greater custody of the children, they were also demanding that Britney pay all the legal bills for both sides because she could afford it and he couldn't. Federline and Kaplan knew that Britney was deeply attached to her children and feared losing them above all else.

To put added pressure on her, Kaplan declared his intention to call on her nanny, her assistants, her bodyguards—anyone and everyone in her inner circle—to give sworn statements about her behaviour. This tactic was intended to scare Britney into approving an amended arrangement without another court proceeding.

* * *

MTV usually loved to have Britney perform at their Video Music Awards because she always provided something that would guarantee that the ceremony would be talked about all over the world the next day. But in 2007, MTV wasn't so sure. Jive Records wanted Britney to be on the show badly to hype the imminent release of *Blackout*. But MTV executives wondered aloud if Britney was up to it. Which Britney would show up? Would it be the Britney who wowed audiences during her House of Blues shows, or would it be the Britney who was at the disastrous *OK!* shoot? MTV made two deal-breaker demands of Jive. One was that Britney had to rehearse for five solid weeks so the number would be impeccable; the other was that she had to have a manager who they could deal with, not someone Britney had met in a club or a friend from Kentwood. For this single performance, MTV was demanding that Britney have a real, experienced manager. A final condition that Jive found a bit hard to swallow but had to agree to nonetheless was that the fee for Britney's appearance would be paid only after the successful completion of the arrangement—after the show was broadcast.

When Jive execs sat Britney down to explain the lay of the land to her she was at first delighted to be doing the show again.

They explained the rehearsal part and she agreed that it was a good idea; she wanted to get back into top form. In response to the next condition, she roared, "What do I need a manager for?!" The Jive people told her that MTV thought that because she would be appearing in the big opening number, a major spectacle, it would be easier for her to concentrate on her performance if she had solid, experienced help behind the scenes. Britney resisted at first, but the excitement of getting onstage again, performing again, trumped her distaste for managers. She smiled and said, "Okay, set it up. I'll do it." Jive selected Jeff Kwatinetz, an agent and manager who had been in the film and music industry for quite a while. His agency was called The Firm.

The show was to be held on September 9, 2007, but the location had shifted from Radio City Music Hall in New York to a place Britney knew well: the Palms Hotel and Casino in Las Vegas. Rehearsals took place in L.A. and went well at first; Britney was fired up and worked with even more intensity and creativity than she had for the House of Blues shows. Kwatinetz, the Jive team and MTV executives were on the job as well, putting a sense of organisation and routine back into Britney's life. One of the casualties of this effort was Alli Sims. She disappeared from Britney's life almost immediately. According to Courtney Brabham, "Britney needed an assistant, not a pal to have around all the time to party with. When Alli was out of the picture, Britney just worked. All she would do was work on the routine all day. Even when we asked her if she wanted to go out after work, she would say that she wanted to get the number down first. That was all she was thinking about." Kwatinetz hired a woman named Michelle Dupont to replace Alli. Michelle was a professional, not a friend.

Britney's team also made sure that the best and best known, of the Hollywood celebrity pamper artists were also at her disposal. Her outfit was to be designed by Trish Somerville (who had been working with Christina Aguilera) and Hollywood superstylist Ken Paves was brought in to do her hair, which was still suffering the effects of her self-administered makeover.

After putting in a couple of weeks of serious work on the "Gimme More" number, however, Britney started to slip. She started not showing up for rehearsals, telling her new inner circle that she had the routine down solid and it was stupid to just keep going over it. The team tried to impress upon her that not only was this about maintaining concentration and discipline, but it was also part of her deal with MTV. A week and a half before the show, MTV executives came to take a look at the routine. And Britney delivered. The MTV team left feeling they could exhale once again.

When it came time to fly to Las Vegas, on September 6, a private plane was arranged for Britney and her squad, but Britney declared that she would not get on the plane without Alli Sims. Reluctantly, her handlers sent for Alli and told her in no uncertain terms what they expected of her. The next day, Britney was scheduled to do one final camera rehearsal, a run-through of the number with attention paid to camera positioning. The crew was a bit bewildered by Britney's lack of effort. She had the number down precisely but was neither sharp nor focused. Something didn't feel right.

On Saturday, September 8, the itinerary that Alli (and, to lesser extent, Michelle Dupont, whom Britney was largely ignoring now) would guide Britney through was simple. They would attend the MTV Video Music Awards preshow party at the Hard Rock Hotel and there Britney would do interviews and photo ops with the other stars. From the party they would return to the Palms and go to the suite, where Britney could unwind, relax and get it together for her important performance the next day. But it didn't even come close to happening that way. After leaving the preshow party at the Hard Rock Hotel, Britney and Alli hit the Strip. Their first stop was the Beatles Bar near the Hard Rock Hotel, but they heard that the real action was at club Jet in the Mirage, where P. Diddy and his crew were holed up in the VIP section. Once ensconced there, Britney began drinking heavily and steadily. At 2:00 a.m., P. Diddy told Britney that she should give it up for the evening and said to Alli that she should take Britney home to sleep it off. But Britney wanted to stay with P. Diddy and his record producer pals. They drank at Jet for another hour before taking the party to one of the high-roller suites at the Mirage. Britney and Alli were seen leaving the hotel after 4:00 a.m.

When Britney and Alli finally got back to the Palms, it was close to 5:00 a.m. Britney slept until just after noon. While she dozed, MTV executives were hearing the stories of the partying the night before from the many people who witnessed it. They were angry and nervous and made several calls to Britney's manager and to Jive demanding to know if Britney could be counted on to perform. Publicly, all concerned put on a brave face and said everything was fine and that Britney was so well rehearsed there was no way anything would go wrong.

When Britney was up and ready to head down to the venue, though, it was clear that she was feeling the effects of the night before. She told Alli that once she was in her well-stocked dressing room, "I don't want anyone near me." So Alli turned away Jive PR people, even Michelle Dupont, who had been hired to ensure that just this sort of thing didn't happen. Clearly, Britney was feeling lousy and battling nerves.

Curtain time was getting closer and closer. Britney had to get ready, which meant that her ban on visitors had to be lifted so her stylists and makeup people could do their thing. They were greeted by a surly Britney, who, dancer Chase Benz remembers, was "a mess of nerves. She was a wreck. She could not seem to calm down and it felt like she didn't want to do this show anymore." When Bryan Spears showed up, Britney was relieved and seemed to pull herself together, but that lasted only moments—until Justin Timberlake stopped by to wish her well. Justin was now the picture of pop success and his by-all-accounts sincere smile could only have made Britney more nervous about all she had to prove that evening.

When hairstylist Ken Paves arrived, Britney began behaving like an imperious child, loudly proclaiming, "I don't like him I want her to do it." She pointed at Paves's assistant. The assistant tried to explain to Britney that she wasn't sure what to do; she didn't have the expertise that Ken did, especially given the state of Britney's hair. The task of getting her hair and her extensions looking right was daunting. As Paves tried to calm Britney, she felt patronised. She angrily instructed one of her two bodyguards to throw him out and a stunned Paves was tossed out of the dressing room. The extensions were thrown out with him.

When MTV executives in the auditorium heard that there had been a physical altercation in the dressing room, they grabbed Kwatinetz and a Jive person and told them to speak to Britney right away and come back with assurances that this was not going to turn into a big public mess. Kwatinetz, Michelle Dupont and a couple of Jive people got inside the dressing room. Britney calmly told them that Paves's attitude had rubbed her the wrong way. Kwatinetz explained that she would have to deal with that for just a little while, because he had the custom-made hair extensions she needed. Britney shrugged and said, "Okay, he can come back." But Paves now wanted none of it, refusing to open the door of his suite or answer his phone. Everyone frantically tried to figure out what to do. Alli was sent to the salon in the Palms to see if they had any emergency extensions and the hairstylist for Canadian singer Nelly Furtado said she would be willing to help. Team Britney gratefully accepted and Britney's hair was finally done. It looked okay, but it was not what they had planned for her appearance. Next, they had to get Britney into her dress—a sleek Trish Somerville number. Britney gave Alli instructions to clear the room because she wanted to dress alone and have a few minutes to herself. It was now less than half an hour to show time. MTV people, Kwatinetz, Michelle, Jive Records people all stood outside the dressing room anxiously waiting (one Jive person says he was "just wishing it would all be over with. The tension was awful").

Finally, with less than ten minutes to go, Britney emerged. The jaws of those waiting outside her door collectively dropped. Everyone was speechless. Then someone gasped, "What the fuck?"

Britney had tossed aside the Trish Somerville outfit and donned a black bra, black fishnet stockings and black shorts that were too tight and accentuated her soft midriff. One of the MTV floor manager's assistants (who spoke on the condition that his name not be used) says, "There was a real panic, not just because of the way she was dressed, but [because] she seemed unfocused. When someone asked her why she'd changed costumes at the last minute, it was her assistant [Alli] who answered, saying something like, 'Brit has decided she really wants to just go for it.'" Kwatinetz tried to convince her to put the Trish Somerville outfit back on because they had an arrangement with the designer, but no dice. The floor manager's assistant recalls, "It was time to get her out there onstage; I was yelling at them, 'It's too fucking late!'"

It was indeed show time. As rehearsed, the opening number was dramatic. Britney was supposed to sneer sexily into the camera and snarl (lip-synching), "It's Britney, bitch!" Everyone got into position. Britney was on her mark in front of the camera, the music started, the line was heard... but Britney did not mouth the words. She just stood there. Then, as the number started, it was clear that disaster had struck. This was a new low for Britney. She looked flabby in her costume and all her dance moves, even just the strut across the stage, were awkward and mistimed. Her lip-synching was, to be kind, out of synch. The audience was in shock. This was a spectacular public embarrassment. There were a few mean-spirited laughs, but most in the audience just felt sorry for her.

Backstage after the number, Britney, completely winded by her effort, was very anxious. She ordered an MTV floor assistant to set up a playback on a nearby monitor. After viewing her performance, she became inconsolable. Wracked with sobs, she threw a hoodie on over her costume and bolted. Alli followed, as did a hotel security man. Britney walked briskly, in a panic, to the first door she could find—a fire exit that led to a closed-off second of the casino. On the casino floor, she rushed around looking for another exit, but all she could see was the entrance to the restaurant Guardino's, which was closed. She ducked under a barrier, ran up to the second floor of the restaurant and sat weeping with her back against the wall. Alli and the security officer stayed nearby but gave her the space she needed. For the better part of an hour, Britney sat alone and cried, occasionally sending text messages on her cell phone. When at last she collected herself and stood up, she told Alli that she wanted to leave Las Vegas right away.

The postmortem on her performance began. The stars in attendance at the show offered their comments to the media. "It was like watching a public execution," said Green Day's Billie Joe Armstrong. Kanye West remarked, "I felt so bad for her. I said to myself 'Man, this is a dirty game.'" The official reaction from Jive records was simple and dismissive: "It wasn't a ten, but at least she performed."

A week later, Jeff Kwatinez and his talent agency The Firm, along with Michelle Dupont, resigned. Lawyer Laura Wasser also cut her ties with Britney, issuing a rather disingenuous public statement: "I don't want anyone to perceive this as an act of dumping Britney. In many lawyer-client relationships there is just a time for fresh blood."

Britney was now adrift emotionally, psychologically and professionally. She had been abandoned by her support team. Even those who were used to catering to the outrageous whims of the rich and famous no longer wanted to deal with her. This left her open to being victimised by the parasites who feed on

Hollywood's rich and vulnerable. In Britney's case, the parasite was Sam Lutfi. He had been seen meeting with Alli Sims at West Hollywood restaurants even before the debacle in Las Vegas. This strange man also approached Lynne Spears and, without telling her that he had Britney in his sights, made her a bizarre offer of partnership in a company he represented that planned to sell cheap jewelry on a TV shopping channel. Lynne liked the idea, but nothing came of it.

The armies of well-paid lawyers and managers who had guided Britney thus far had insulated her from the true bottom feeders of the world. Now the professionals had gone and so had her friends. Former personal assistant and party pal Shannon Funk reported that Britney was now even resorting to paying people to hang out with her. She craved the company of people who would reassure her that she was a star and that everything was going to be all right. But, of course, it wasn't.

BETRAYAL

"I don't know who to trust. Look what happens when I trust somebody."

—Britney Spears

On September 17, 2007, another hearing was scheduled in Los Angeles Superior Court in the matter of the custody of Britney's two children. Kevin Federline's concern, apparently genuine, that Britney was in a precarious state and incapable of caring for the children was mounting. Enter Tony Barretto, a physically imposing man whom Britney had hired as a bodyguard in March of 2007. In May, he had been fired. On this day in September, he showed up at the courthouse with his lawyer, the high-powered and very media savvy Gloria Allred. Allred stood before the gathered reporters and said that her client was very reluctant to come forward and get embroiled in this custody fight, but what he had witnessed and—what he would swear to in a statement—made him fearful for the safety and well-being of Sean Preston and Jayden James. She explained that Barretto was a father himself, so he felt that speaking out was the right thing to do.

Of Barretto's claims, the most serious was that he had seen Britney behaving in a way that he interpreted as suicidal. He described what he felt was evidence of mental illness and attested to drug and alcohol abuse. When pressed to cite specific incidents to illustrate his claims, Barretto described a night at the Mondrian Hotel in Los Angeles. Britney had been on a date with a musician she had met while in rehab at Promises. Hours into the date, Barretto and his bodyguard partner were called to come and get Britney. They found her in a room in the hotel and she was barely conscious, her skin waxy and pale. He said that there were liquor bottles and cigarette butts and "a glass pipe used to smoke crystal meth" in the room. Britney's legal team was caught completely off-guard by Barretto and did not challenge him. Barretto's testimony led Commissioner Scott Gordon, who was administering the case, to order Britney to undergo random drug testing and to instruct her and Federline to make use of a program called Parenting without Conflict, which provides counselling for warring parents. Commissioner Gordon also ordered that a re-evaluation of the custody arrangement be made because Britney had demonstrated a habitual use of controlled substances and alcohol. After giving his testimony, Barretto went so far as to file a claim of child abuse with the L.A. County Department of Children and Family Services. Department representatives met with Barretto to hear his story of instability and substance abuse.

Barretto next hit the media circuit, where he told his story to everyone from Larry King to Matt Lauer to British tabloid *News of the World*. But talk-show host and lawyer Greta Van Susteren, on her Fox show *On the Record with Greta Van Susteren*, challenged Barretto's story. Van Susteren, who had become famous as a CNN commentator during the O.J. Simpson trial, asked Barretto if he had ever personally witnessed Britney Spears using drugs. He answered, "I have seen her with alcohol, but I have never seen her use drugs, no." Van Susteren got him to admit that Britney's binge drinking was something he had only witnessed occasionally and had never seen her drink in front of her children. Appearing on Van Susteren's show shortly afterwards, Gloria Allred insisted that Barretto had indeed seen Britney use drugs twice, had often seen her abuse alcohol and had frequently seen her under the influence of alcohol in front of her children. Commissioner Gordon said that he needed time to further evaluate the matter and in the interim Britney had to adhere strictly to the series of conditions he had laid out. Failure to do so would certainly influence his decision significantly.

On August 6, 2007, Britney was involved in a minor traffic incident. She caught another car with her bumper while trying to park and avoid some paparazzi who were in her way. The two boys were with her. Because she walked away, she was charged with misdemeanour hit and run. Later it was discovered that she did not have a valid California driver's licence. On October 1, 2007, after a private meeting between the lawyers for both sides, Commissioner Gordon explained to Britney that her failure to have a valid California driver's licence and to provide proof of compliance with a drug test constituted a breach of the simple conditions he'd laid out during the last hearing. He had no choice but to order Sean Preston and Jayden James into the temporary full custody of Kevin Federline, with Britney getting visitation rights. Britney had taken the written driver's exam, so she was able to get a licence the next day.

Gordon scheduled a second, more formal, closed-door hearing for the afternoon of October 3, 2007, during which both parties could present their views on the matter before Britney was ordered to deliver her children to Kevin. On October 3, Britney was photographed buying gas at a filling station then stopping off for a coffee at a Malibu Starbuck's while her lawyers and Federline and his lawyers attended the hearing. There was a slight delay in the proceedings while everyone waited to see if Britney would arrive, but she didn't. A temporary change to the custody arrangement was ordered pending a deep, much more serious evaluation of Britney's state of mind and state of being. A court spokesperson addressed the mob of reporters outside and told them that Federline had been given temporary full custody of the children and that Britney would have visitation rights. Commissioner Gordon had stipulated that the visits had to be supervised and Britney was allowed two per week. One of the boys' nannies was to bring Sean Preston and Jayden James to Federline in two days' time. Contributing to this decision was a report from Lisa Hacker, the counsellor assigned to the case. Britney had reacted poorly to her, taking exception to being told how to mother her kids. Hacker's report was both positive and negative. She noted that there was a clear indication of love and devotion on the part of Britney and not a shred of evidence of abuse or neglect. But she observed that when Britney was with her children, she was usually focused on her own activities. Hacker concluded that Britney was not cognisant of the harm that her behaviour could do to otherwise healthy and stable children.

Britney's law firm, Trope and Trope, decided it was time to hit back and they enlisted the help of an organisation called Family Care Monitoring Services, which had been established in 1986 to assist in contentious custody battles. Their mandate is to view the situation from the child's perspective and to help organise and supervise visitation; they have a long history of dealing successfully with even the nastiest of custody battles.

The custody hearings, depositions, rulings and orders would go on for the next several months and the power balance would shift each time the case was re-examined.

* * *

Britney's entourage was changing. She still had Alli Sims, but Alli had decided that she was no longer comfortable as a paid assistant, so she just stayed around as a friend. Through Alli, Britney had finally met Sam Lutfi and she'd promptly taken him on as a paid assistant with a certain managerial authority. She told everyone that Lutfi was a great guy—just what she needed. Lynne was suspicious of him, however, remembering the strange offer he had made to her months before. A quick investigation revealed that Lutfi was a stalker and several legal complaints had been filed against him by people whom he had harassed verbally and electronically. Now Lufti had penetrated Britney's circle and was helping her to make decisions about her life and her career.

Britney had started to suffer from insomnia. One night, unable to sleep, she called the director of the Millennium Dance Complex, Robert Baker, whom she had known since 1998 when she started using the facility. She told him that she wanted to dance and asked him if he could open up the complex for her because she needed to get herself back in shape and wanted to get right at it. Baker agreed and an hour later Britney showed up with Sam Lutfi.

Baker observed a strange relationship between the two. Lutfi would act very managerial, then moments later they would be goofing around or acting like they were having a lovers' spat. This episode of midnight dancing, however, seemed to inspire Britney. She became a regular at Millennium again and, Baker observes, "You could see that she was in a groove. She wanted back in the game, but there were also moments of wanting to tone it all down. I remember one night she came to me and was adamant that I allow her to be a teacher. She wanted to teach children to dance."

Baker set up a program for little girls (and his own young son) that ran for a number of weeks and was called the Millennium Junior Program. It was a closed, private set of lessons and the name Britney Spears was not connected with it. Once the kids were assembled in the studio, Britney would just arrive. The little girls were stunned and delighted, but this was not playtime. Britney put them through a rigorous dance workout to music other than her own. After each class, she would hug each child and give individualised words of encouragement. According to Baker, "She was fantastic with the kids and they loved her. It was wonderful seeing her interacting with the kids, because there was no judgment, no baggage, just energy flowing back and forth and lots of fun."

Then, just after her twenty-sixth birthday, in December 2007, Britney became romantically involved with Adnan Ghalib, a British-born photographer who was a member of the paparazzi horde who sat outside her house day every day. Ghalib had the reputation among his colleagues as a guy with delusions of grandeur. He made a living shooting pictures of Britney, but he wanted more. He had often spoken to his photographer pals about having a relationship with Britney. He would say things like, "She's a really great person," and "I'm desperate to get to know her better." He also would do little things to attract her attention and ingratiate himself to her—he would open doors for her and once he even gassed up her car for her.

On September 19, he helped "protect" Britney (as he put it) from some of his own colleagues after they had hemmed her in with their vehicles in the parking lot of a Quiznos sandwich shop. He shouted and cajoled, directing them to move their cars. In early December, she was accosted by photographers in front of a hotel and Ghalib physically shoved some paparazzi aside to allow her get to her car. Before getting in, she briefly put her arm around him. On December 23, Britney again found herself in a parking lot shut off from her car by tabloid photographers. This time, she went to Ghalib's car and shouted through the window for him to let her in. Once inside the car, she got him to take her to the luxurious Peninsula Hotel, where she rented a huge suite for herself and a room that she said was for a new assistant. (By this time, Britney was no longer living in her Malibu mansion; she had taken up residence in another mansion on the beach at the exclusive Malibu Colony. She'd also bought herself a mansion in a gated community called the Summit off Mulholland Drive, but she tended to divide her time between the Malibu Colony and a number of exclusive L.A. hotels.)

On this particular night, Ghalib and Britney hung out in the big suite and talked from 11:00 p.m. until early the next morning. Sneaking out at dawn, Ghalib shocked his colleagues waiting outside; they had never imagined he would come so close to fulfilling his aspirations to get close to Britney. After Ghalib got home, he received a text message from Britney asking him to return to the suite. So Ghalib went back. Over the next few weeks, they saw each other often. In contrast to her usual pattern, this was not a boozy, sex-filled romp. The two seemed to be having the closest thing to a normal relationship that Britney could have. She often went to his apartment in West Hollywood and they were even able to sneak out to a movie together, like a real couple going on a date.

While Ghalib never spoke publicly about his short time with Britney, he freely discussed her with his colleagues and must certainly have understood that the members of his paparazzi circle would be quick to pass on anything he said to the media. Yet he insisted that he'd behaved in a respectful, gentlemanly way. When asked about the sexual nature of their relationship, he replied, "There isn't one. This is pretty fragile, pretty raw. I am not going to take advantage of that."

But perhaps his fellow paparazzi shouldn't have been flabbergasted that Ghalib had actually been able to insinuate himself into Britney's life. It had become apparent that as much as Britney claimed to dread the paparazzi, she had also grown very used to having them around. She went to her favourite Starbuck's in Malibu for a mocha frappuccino with almost clockwork regularity, knowing that the photographers would follow her. It was as though the mob of photographers that greeted her each day had become an audience whose energy she needed to feed off. Celebrity photographer Daniel Alvarado remarks, "When you started seeing Britney hanging around with Paris Hilton and Lindsay Lohan, you knew that Britney, too, had become addicted to the paparazzi like they had. Paris Hilton actually calls or has someone call the various photo agencies to tell them where she will be and when. She can't live without the paparazzi; they give her life whatever little meaning it has. Britney was getting that way as well."

* * *

The enigmatic and shadowy Sam Lutfi was also still very much a part of Britney's scene as 2007 turned into 2008. He saw himself as Britney's main confidant, protector and friend, so he was disturbed by the fact that she was sneaking around with a member of the paparazzi. He was also trying to get Lynne back into Britney's life because he felt that Britney needed her mother. Britney, apparently, had started to feel the same way. Adnan Ghalib says that one night near Christmas, Britney was at his apartment and told him that all she really wanted was to hold her two sons and talk to her mama.

Shortly after this, it came to light that Ghalib was married to model Azzlyn Berry. Berry filed for divorce once she heard about Ghalib's relationship with Britney, but whatever feelings Britney had for Ghalib cooled rapidly after she found out about his marriage. They continued to see each other for a while and he continued to express his deep respect and caring, but the relationship was soon over.

* * *

On January 3, 2008, Britney was at home and her children were visiting. She had reportedly been suffering for the last four days from anxiety and insomnia exacerbated by the prescription drugs she was using to make herself feel better. It had been a long day. She had spent much of it at the offices of Kevin's lawyer answering questions in preparation for yet another custody hearing. Lutfi had been with her. It was reported that she started crying once she was outside.

The children's visit had gone well. Lutfi was in the house, as was Paula Strong, the court-appointed monitor from Family Care Monitoring Services. There was also a maid present. At about 7:00 p.m., just before the boys were to be picked up and returned to their father, Britney broke down after a heated phone conversation with Federline. She began crying and screaming, convinced that if she let the children go, Federline would never allow her to see them again. When bodyguard Lonnie Jones arrived at the door to get the children, Britney became frantic and refused to relinquish them. Strong and Lutfi pleaded with her, telling her that she was only going to make matters worse with this outburst and that she must calm down. Finally, Jones was able to gently lift Sean Preston into his arms and take him outside to the waiting SUV. At that point, however, Britney became hysterical and ran with Jayden James in her arms to an upstairs bathroom and locked the door. She sat on the floor cradling Jayden James and crying uncontrollably. Jones called Federline, who called his lawyers. The lawyers called Strong and told her that the child was at risk and she had no choice but to call the police. Strong called 911 and within minutes several police cars and an ambulance had pulled up in front of the mansion in the gated Summit community. Some three hours into the incident, there were no fewer than six news media helicopters circling the house, their spotlights dancing below. Somehow, the paparazzi were there in droves as well, despite the fact that the house was in a gated community.

Lutfi called Lynne in Kentwood. She called Jamie and Bryan. At first, both shrugged it off, saying it was just that weirdo Lutfi being melodramatic. Within a half hour, however, live news reports were being issued from Britney's front lawn that she was holding one or both of her children hostage in her mansion.

Inside the locked bathroom, Britney was growing more and more disoriented. She had no idea of the firestorm going on outside but was scared to death because she was talking to LAPD officers through the door. The standoff continued until about 10:00 p.m., when Federline's lawyer, Mark Kaplan, arrived on the scene and managed to get Britney to open the door. She asked for her "vitamins," the word she used for the prescription drugs she was taking. She was emotionally drained and physically exhausted. After opening the door, she'd huddled in the corner wearing nothing but panties; when a police officer held a sweater out to her, she slurred, "Don't cover me up. I'm fucking hot." Jayden James was taken from her and whisked away. Britney was placed on a gurney with her arms and legs tied down and slid into an ambulance looking very confused. The ambulance transported her to Cedars Sinai Hospital in Beverly Hills under police escort. She was admitted under a seventy-two-hour paper, which meant that for her own safety she was ordered to stay for that length of time so that doctors could fully evaluate her. Enter famous TV psychologist Phil McGraw—"Dr. Phil." Lynne Spears had been talking to him about all things Britney for quite a while and she had grown close to him and his wife, Robin. At Lynne's request, McGraw went to the hospital to see Britney. The welcome he received from Britney was reportedly "unenthusiastic," and he described their conversation as "limited." McGraw later admitted that not only had he not been of much help, but he may have also made things worse. Jamie came to visit, as, of course, did Lufti. Adnan Ghalib showed up looking very concerned. Now that Britney had dried out and rested up, she told everyone who came to see her that she was just fine.

The staff psychiatric specialists determined that she was not a threat to anyone, including herself and would not need further evaluation or committal. She was allowed to leave the hospital after just under twenty-four hours. The retinue of photographers outside was now double its usual size. Both Britney's houses were under paparazzi siege and photographers had even staked out a few of her favourite hotels just in case. Not wanting to deal with any of this, Britney called Ghalib and asked him to take her to Palm Springs for a few days. (It was in Palm Springs that, according to Ghalib, the pair would become sexually involved.) While Britney was away, Federline's attorney, Mark Kaplan, arranged for his client to be granted emergency sole custody of the children. Kaplan issued a statement to the media saying that it was not Federline's wish or intention to keep the children out of their mother's life completely, he just wanted to provide them with a stable environment.

Britney spent several peaceful days in Palm Springs, during which time she was able to relax and calm down, but on the drive home her anxiety about what she was going back to overcame her. She abruptly told Ghalib to turn the car around; she wanted to spend a few days in Mexico before returning. Ghalib did as he was told. They drove for four hours to the beach community of Rosarito, Mexico, where they checked into an inexpensive hotel under assumed names.

Britney was in heaven, enjoying an anonymity that she had not known in a decade. Ghalib began calling and texting his pals back in L.A., feeding them stories, which rapidly hit the airways and cyberspace. The inevitable headlines appeared: "Britney Spears and boyfriend Adnan Ghalib are in Mexico and planning to marry there," and the like. Word of what Ghalib was doing reached an infuriated Britney and a day after arriving in Mexico, she was travelling back to L.A.

Back in Los Angeles, both Lynne and Jamie were worrying about Sam Lutfi and his role in their daughter's life. Lutfi had been angry when Britney took off without him to Palm Springs and he went completely ballistic when he heard about the Mexican getaway. He was calling Lynne constantly and with each call Lynne grew more worried about just how much authority this strange person had been given over Britney's affairs. Jamie decided it was time he stepped in.

* * *

On January 14, there was a hearing to determine custody of Sean Preston and Jayden James for the foreseeable future. The scene outside the courthouse was shocking: there were over a hundred camera crews from news agencies all over the world. Federline and Kaplan arrived right on time. Britney showed up a bit late in an armoured black Escalade. Lutfi and Ghalib got out on either side and then Britney exited and they were immediately crushed by photographers. Britney panicked and called out, "Get me back in the car! I need to get back in the car!" The two men helped her back in and they drove slowly off. Britney did not return to the hearing.

The hearing was a crushing defeat for Britney: Kevin's emergency sole custody of the children was extended until further notice. Britney was accorded no visitation rights; she would not even be allowed to see her children. Outside the courthouse, Kevin looked on respectfully as Kaplan did the talking. He said that this was nothing to celebrate and that Kevin wanted nothing more than to one day share parenting duties with Britney.

Meanwhile, Britney's Escalade led a parade of paparazzi to the San Fernando Valley and, strangely, to the Little Brown Church, the nondenominational church in Studio City where Ronald Reagan had been married. Once Britney was inside with Ghalib and Lutfi, a church spokesperson came out to tell the paparazzi that the church remained open twenty-four hours a day and everyone was welcome to the comfort and safe haven it offered. Eventually, Britney and her entourage returned to her home, where she could reflect on the full significance of what had happened that day.

* * *

In the midst of all this trauma and confusion, some aspects of Britney's life were going well—very well, in fact. Her new album, *Blackout*, debuted at number 2 on the Billboard charts and the singles "Gimme More," the haunting "Piece of Me," and "Break the Ice" had all sold very well. Britney participated in an MTV promotion called "Britney Spears Wants a Piece of You," a contest in which participants could use MTV's video remixer to cut their own versions of "Piece of Me." The winner was picked by MTV, Jive Records and Britney Spears. The album got solid reviews. *Rolling Stone* proclaimed that Britney "continues to crank out the best pop booty jams"; *Entertainment Weekly* called it a "perfectly serviceable dance album"; the *Guardian* in England called it "bold and exciting." So, at this dark point in her life when she had lost so much—including her most precious possession: her children—Britney still had one thing to hold onto: her music. It was her lifeline. But she needed help to pull herself to shore. And it would come from an unlikely source.

JAMIE

"All this nonsense stops now."

–Jamie Spears

On January 14, 2008, Britney and her entourage, paparazzi in tow, stopped at a Rite Aid drugstore. She and boyfriend Adnan Ghalib went in, followed by photographers and purchased a home pregnancy test. Britney was heard to say, "I just know I'm pregnant. I got a feeling in my tummy. I know I'm pregnant." At home, Britney took the test. She was not pregnant.

But she was on edge and volatile. Vanessa Grigoriadis of *Rolling Stone* wrote that on a shopping trip with Ghalib to the Westfield Topanga Mall, Britney tried on clothes, tossed the rejects aside and threw the ones she wanted to buy to Ghalib. A large crowd gathered around her. Young girls, including some store employees, were taking pictures and calling out her name. Britney finally tossed her black American Express card to Ghalib and told him to pay for the merchandise; she wanted to get out of there. But the card would not clear. When the cashier went to the changing room to explain this to Britney, she began screaming and crying and yelling, "Fuck these bitches! These idiots can't do anything right!" She tossed a Coke bottle onto the floor and Coke splashed all over the heaped clothing. Then she whipped out another credit card and shoved it at the cashier. This one went through. Ghalib gathered up her stuff and they pushed through the crowd. Britney was crying and her face was red and smeared with makeup. She kept screaming, "Fuck you! Fuck you! Fuck, Fuck, Fuck!" at the top of her lungs. A young woman said something to her about being from the South also, but Britney snarled at Ghalib, "I don't want her talking to me." She then turned to the startled young woman and said, "I don't know who you think I am, bitch! But I am not that person!"

* * *

The lives of the members of the Spears family, with Britney in the lead, were giving new meaning to the word "chaotic." Sam Lutfi was insinuating himself deeper and deeper into Britney's affairs and telling Lynne that Britney would kill herself if he wasn't around to support and guide her. Lynne and Britney were again at odds and it had just gone public that Britney's little sister, Jamie Lynn, age sixteen, was pregnant. The rest of the family was questioning Lynne's judgment, because she had sold exclusive rights to *OK!* magazine to take photos of the pregnant teen for a million dollars.

Jamie decided he had had enough. He contacted his legal advisers, including lawyer Andrew Wallette and asked them to establish an emergency conservatorship to give him complete control over Britney's assets. This was not something that the courts would grant lightly. Jamie would have to make a convincing and compelling case that the situation was dire and emergency measures were necessary. He had an uphill battle before him, but events would help him out.

On the night of January 28, 2008, Britney was discovered sitting on the stone stoop outside her house with her little dog London in her lap. She had clearly been crying and seemed not to notice the photographers surrounding her and snapping pictures. She just sat there with a vacant look on her face. After the photographers had had their fill, a female reporter approached her and asked if she was okay. Britney looked blankly at her and said, "I'm fine. I'm just sitting here for once enjoying my dog." But things were not fine. Britney had fled the house to get away from the now crazily overbearing Sam Lutfi, who was yelling at her that she needed to pay more attention to him and allow him to be her life coach. Strangely, several paparazzi had for several weeks been keeping Jamie abreast of what was happening to Britney. They now called Jamie to report on Lufti and Jamie called Lynne.

Britney sat outside in a daze for about a half an hour before heading inside, but she rushed out of the house again almost immediately and asked one of the paparazzi, Felipe Tiexiera, if he would drive her somewhere away from the house. As the two drove off, Jamie and Lynne (accompanied by a friend named Jackie) were hurrying, separately, to Britney's house. There they got into a very aggressive argument with Lutfi. Jamie was particularly angry and demanded to know what qualifications Lutfi had. Jamie and Lynne then asked Lufti why he felt it necessary to be with Britney twenty-four hours a day.

The horde of paparazzi was growing outside. Word was out that something explosive might be in the offing. And it was. Just minutes later, one of Britney's bodyguards, who seemed to be taking orders from Lutfi, escorted Jamie out of the house. Jamie got into his truck and drove away looking angry. Not long after

Jamie left, Britney returned, accompanied by Adnan Ghalib. Inside, the tension continued. In affidavits later sworn out to support Jamie's conservatorship case and his application for a restraining order against Lutfi, Lynne said, "[Lutfi] then told Jackie and me that we needed to do whatever he tells us." Lutfi continued to argue that only he truly knew Britney and cared about her and that they had better accept it because they had no choice in the matter. Lutfi then ejected Ghalib from the house, but before Ghalib had even reached his car, Lutfi had already sent him a crazed text message, which Ghalib promptly showed to his paparazzi pals. It read: "You need to cease all contact with her completely. I've tried to work with you helping her but you didn't do as asked. The only way to help now is to disappear. She's never been this way before."

Following this incident, Jamie had Andrew Wallette issue a restraining order against Lufti. On January 30, 2008, Lutfi called Lynne ranting and raving that he had been given top-secret information that Britney was about to be forcibly committed to a psychiatric facility and that he would intervene. Lynne and Jackie rushed over to Britney's house to make sure she was all right. She seemed out of sorts, but coherent and alert. Then a group of LAPD officers entered the house with a document in hand, followed by ambulance attendants with a gurney. Lynne and Jackie stepped between the cops and Britney. The lead police officer explained to them that Britney Jean Spears was being "detained under a 5150 involuntary psychiatric hold." After asking a few more questions, Lynne told Britney not to struggle, to go along with it. Everything would be fine. Britney climbed onto the gurney and was strapped down and wheeled out of the house. The army of photographers on the ground and in the sky recorded the event. They followed the ambulance as closely as the police would allow all the way to the UCLA Medical Center, where Britney was once again committed on a seventy-two-hour paper. Lynne was told that she was not allowed to ride with Britney in the ambulance, so she made her way to the hospital on her own.

When Lynne pulled up, Jamie was there too and the scene was frantic. Lutfi was already there trying to get to Britney. In Britney's room, Lynne, who had not been forewarned by Jamie that it was he who had instigated the commital, accused Lutfi of being responsible for it and insisted that he'd done it to further isolate and control Britney. This precipitated a shouting match between the two. Doctors cleared the room and told Lynne and Jamie that it was best that they leave the facility to cool down and let them help their daughter. They then barred everyone, including Lutfi, from Britney's room. Lutfi protested that he was all that was keeping Britney sane and must be allowed to be with her, but this fell on deaf ears.

The next day, Judge Reva Goetz granted Jamie conservatorship over his daughter's affairs and assets. Then the following day, February 1, 2008, a restraining order was issued against Sam Lutfi. He was not to go near Britney's home or her person and was to have no telephone contact with her. Britney remained in the care of the psychiatric team at the UCLA Medical Center for the full run of the seventy-two-hour paper and she voluntarily stayed in treatment for four more days after the order expired. She was released from the facility on February 8.

Jamie had, up until this point, kept a low profile. He had been preoccupied with his own alcohol problems and, besides, he didn't really understand the world Britney inhabited. He now worked to understand it and to help Britney to understand it too. Jamie was ill-prepared to deal with Britney's complex financial affairs and the level of attention her every move attracted. But he did his best. He and his advisers established a schedule for Britney that was designed to structure her life, to calm her down and get her to a place where the courts would no longer feel it necessary to keep her from her children. They also focused on helping her to recharge her creative batteries so she could get back to doing the thing she loved most: performing. Jamie assembled a reliable team to support her. He brought Big Rob, her first and most loyal and trusted bodyguard, back into the fold and reinstated Larry Rudolph as her manager—it would be his third time.

Relations between Britney and Jive Records had deteriorated considerably, but they were still intact and Rudolph set about making them solid once again. One of the things he arranged, with the help of agent Jason Trawick of the William Morris Agency, was a guest-starring role for Britney on the popular sitcom *How I Met Your Mother*. The episode she appeared in, "Ten Sessions," was broadcast on March 24 and it earned the highest ratings in the show's history; so Britney was asked to make an encore appearance a couple of months later. Plans were also put in place for Britney to record a new album and plan for a new world tour. The idea was to signal to the world that she had made it to the clearing in a very dark and dense forest.

But Britney was not yet completely out of the woods. She was still experiencing mood swings and would overreact when she felt she was being pressured. She also expressed discomfort with the way her father had taken control of her life and her career. For years, she had spoken publicly of feeling like a prisoner and the new conservatorship arrangement underscored that. She would soon be twenty-seven, but she felt she was being treated like a child. In fact, that was exactly how she was being treated and necessarily so. Both of her parents had stated in a conservatorship hearing that their daughter was really "a twenty-six-year-old little girl."

* * *

On July 18, 2008, the custody arrangement was finalised— or, at least, settled once again. It gave Federline sole custody of the children and restored Britney's visitation rights; her time with the boys would increase based on her personal conduct. Under the prenuptial agreement, Federline was entitled to a one-million-dollar payout and $20,000 per month in spousal and child support; he would get an additional $5,000 per month if he went on tour with Britney so she could still see the children when she was on the road. Britney was ordered to pay Kevin's legal bills for the proceedings, which were reportedly in the $250,000 range.

As work on her new album, cheekily titled *Circus*, progressed, it was clear that Britney was still of value to Jive Records. Plans for her massive new tour and stage show were set to be unveiled later in 2008, around the time of her birthday. But in the midst of all this reparation and rebuilding, there was still Lutfi to deal with. He refused to accept his ejection from Britney's life and during the late summer of 2008 he tried to launch a legal challenge to Jamie's conservatorship. He first approached California State

Attorney General Edmund Brown with a rambling letter—written by lawyer and Lutfi associate Jon Eardley—charging that Britney opposed the conservatorship, had never been told about it and was in hospital undergoing psychiatric treatment when it was executed. Eardley claimed he was "orally authorized" by Britney to file for a notice of removal. The attorney general refused to intervene and said that in his view the courts had acted appropriately. Eardley had tried to launch an appeal of the conservatorship order a couple of months earlier, in March, but the judge had told him that such orders were subject only to petition, not appeal and threw it out.

Another legal shot was fired on Jamie's authority, this time by Adam Streisand, a lawyer Britney had authorised to speak on her behalf. Through the court arrangement with Jamie, a lawyer named Sam Inghams had been appointed to oversee her legal affairs, but Britney had replaced him with Streisand. Attorney Streisand's petition stated that "Ms. Spears has expressed the strong desire that her father not be appointed conservator. He has been estranged from her and this has caused her stress." This, too, was tossed out by the judge, who determined that Britney "lacked the capacity to retain counsel or organize her affairs herself." So the conservatorship stayed in place.

* * *

As September rolled around, so did the MTV Video Music Awards. Once again, Britney Spears, despite the debacle of the previous year, was asked to open the show. It was a bold decision and in some ways an act of kindness on MTV's part, although the producers did stipulate that Britney's performance be pre-taped. The event was held on September 7, 2008 at Paramount Studios in L.A. The host was the acerbic and controversial British comedian Russell Brand. By the end of the proceedings, extraordinarily, Britney, who was in attendance, was declared the big winner of the night. After being nominated sixteen times in previous years, she won three awards: video of the year, best female video and best pop video, all for "Piece of Me." Many saw it as a glorious redemption for Britney. Looked at more circumspectly, however, it could be considered proof that the recording industry will forgive just about any transgression as long as the transgressor is still able to sell records. There was also a feeling that she had been kicked around by the media and used and abused by charlatans—that she had suffered enough public humiliation. As if to send a message that all was forgiven, as Britney left the stage after winning her third award of the evening, the audience of fans and industry professionals gave her a standing ovation.

On September 26, 2008, Jive Records released the first single from *Circus*. The track, "Womanizer," headed straight to number 1 on the Hot 100 chart; it was the first single of hers to top that chart since ". . . Baby One More Time." Jive announced that *Circus* would be released on December 2, 2008, Britney's twenty-seventh birthday and gave details on her massive new tour.

A new kind of positive energy surrounded Britney now. She even was able to win a small legal victory after seeing so many decisions go against her. When the charge of driving without a licence went before Judge James Steele in L.A. Superior Court on October 21, 2008, the case was dismissed outright; Britney argued, through lawyer Michael Flanagan, that since she did have a valid Louisiana driver's licence, she was not required to have a valid California licence.

The same month, however, Judge Reva Goetz made Jamie's temporary conservatorship arrangement permanent, with certain conditions. Lawyer Andrew Wallette would act as co conservator in some areas (due partly to Jamie's former bankruptcy). But the arrangement was now firm. The judge determined that Britney had demonstrated an inability to "manage her financial resources or resist fraud and undue influences." The order also stated that she did not object to the arrangement. Compensation for Jamie's role as conservator was set at $10,000 per month (which would later be raised to $16,000 a month), with an $800 per month office-expence account. In January 2009, Jamie and Wallette obtained restraining orders against Sam Lutfi, Adnan Ghalib and lawyer Jon Eardley. The court determined that there was clear evidence that they were actively involved in a conspiracy to gain control of Britney's money and her affairs. Lutfi and Ghalib were ordered not to contact Britney or come within 250 yards of her.

* * *

As she turned twenty-seven, Britney could look back on the train wreck of the past several years. Had it all really happened, or had it been one long nightmare? Of course it had happened; every minute had been documented for all to see. Now, though, it was past and all of her energy could be directed forward. *Circus* was released on schedule and she was back in top form. The album debuted in the number 1 spot on the Billboard Top 200 list and it would sell a whopping 505,000 copies in the first week alone.

This feat would lead her, a week after her MTV Video Music Awards triumph, to enter the *Guinness Book of World Records* as the youngest female artist in history to have five albums debut at number 1.

Circus was generally a critical success as well. Much attention was paid to one controversial song title, "If U Seek Amy," because of its rather obvious double entendre, bolstered by an equally racy video. The massive *Circus Starring Britney Spears* tour was set to begin in March 2009.

* * *

On February 27, 2009, Britney made a special trip as a way of touching off her big comeback tour. As the tour's sixteen truckloads of equipment were being set up in New Orleans, a private jet carrying Britney, her two children and her entourage touched down at the small airport in McComb, Mississippi, where the whole journey had begun. There to greet her was a small group of photographers—nothing like the horde she was used to. She was there to see family and old friends, some twenty of whom would be in New Orleans in the front row for the kick-off show of the new tour. It was a nice touch and a sentimental way to mark her return.

Amid all the talk of a comeback, there were voices of dissension, as well. A few figures from Britney's past said that this was happening too fast and that shoving her back into the scene so soon after her spectacular collapse was dangerous. These people thought that the same old Hollywood thinking was again at work: her handlers wanted her back out there earning money for everyone and she would be fine with it. One of those voices of dissent was her old music manager Johnny Wright. "I wish her nothing but the best," he said. "But she is being thrown back into the money machine again. At the beginning, she knew she could quit at any time. Now she has 170 people living off her. Her father has quit his job to live off her. Her mother has lived off her daughters for years. She is back in that place of having no choice."

Wright's point is well taken. While releasing a comeback album on her birthday, winning awards and gearing up for a big new tour helped her to shake off the past and broadcast a healthy new image to her fans, it wasn't the whole story. The timing of *Circus*, both the album and the tour, had little to do with sentiment and almost everything to do with contractual obligations. Britney was obligated to deliver an album by a certain date and to support it with a tour. And she has always been one to do what's required, no matter the price.

On the night of March 3, 2009, Britney arrived at the New Orleans Arena in a black Escalade, ninety minutes before show time. She went straight to her dressing room to get ready. She was happy and eager and full of the good kind of nervous energy, the kind one gets before a good performance. Just before they went onstage, Britney gathered her dancers in a circle, put her arms around the two closest to her and asked God to bless them all and help them to give all the good people out there a great show. They took the stage to thunderous screaming and applause. Jamie, Lynne, Sean Preston and Jayden James were seated in the front row. The show unfolded without a hitch and at the end of the encore performance of "Womanizer," Britney punched the air in an "I did it!" salute and called out, "Thank you New Orleans! I love you guys! Did y'all have a good time?" While critics claimed that she wasn't the wild performer she'd been five or six years before, that she wasn't in as good physical condition and that her moves weren't as well timed, the consensus was that she was back and that given all she had been through, she was remarkable.

The Circus Starring Britney Spears tour was a spectacular success, earning almost a hundred million dollars worldwide. *Forbes* magazine would report that between June 2008 and June 2009, she had earned over $35 million. During the tour, Jive Records announced that Britney would record a new studio album that would be as bold as anything she had ever attempted and that the target date for worldwide release was May 2010. On November 24, 2009, Jive released a compilation album of Britney songs, *The Singles Collection*. On it was the chart-topping "3," a raunchy song about the joys of three-way sex.

Watching Britney perform during the *Circus* tour, it was hard not to marvel that she was there at all. It was as though she had never descended to the depths of despair. She seemed so strong, as if she would never again be vulnerable to the temptations and pressures that had dragged her down in the first place. Yes, Britney was back, but the dangers still lurked—it would be irresponsible to ignore them. So while on tour, Britney, who was obligated to have biweekly therapy sessions, had a psychologist travelling with her.

It has been suggested, but denied, that the tour psychologist was also there to monitor Britney's intake of the medications that controlled her depression and anxiety. Part of her treatment was to take three common but powerful psychotropic drugs: Adderall,

Seroquel and Risperdal. These drugs, in combination with the antidepressants she was already taking, created a vicious cycle. For example, she had to take Adderall, a stimulant, to counteract the effects of the powerful anti-anxiety medication Risperdal.

When it became known that sizable quantities of Risperdal and Seroquel had been found in Britney's homes, it led to speculation that she was suffering from bipolar disorder. Naturally, no one at UCLA Medical Center would discuss the details of her treatment; the official word was that she had accepted treatment and was responding to it.

TWENTY-TEN FORWARD

"I'm probably the loneliest person in the world."

–Britney Spears

Around the time Britney met Kevin Federline, she also met a man, a good friend of her brother Bryan's, named Jason Trawick. Over the years, Britney would run into Trawick, usually with Bryan and she even once told Bryan that she had a bit of a crush on him. Trawick is an agent with the William Morris Agency in Los Angeles. Hillary Duff and Taylor Swift are his clients.

Since 2006, he had been informally helping Bryan with some aspects of Britney's representation and at one point, in December 2007, Britney had gone on a double date with Trawick, Bryan and Bryan's girlfriend, but there were no sparks then. Trawick was overweight and not very outgoing. After Jamie took over Britney's affairs, Trawick helped him as well and he was officially appointed Britney's agent in late 2008. As Trawick began to spend more time with the Spears family, Britney suggested he work out at her home gym and get her stylist, Kim Vo, to give him a makeover. Jason did: he slimmed down, got his hair cut and coloured and grew a fashionably scruffy beard; he took to dressing more stylishly. Britney began to look at him as more than just another person on her payroll. Rumour had it that Lynne had also prodded Trawick to clean himself up because she thought he would be a good catch for Britney.

In March of 2009, Trawick began a casual "relationship" with Britney, who was ten years his junior. In May, during a break in the *Circus* tour, Trawick joined the Spears family for a getaway in the Bahamas. He and Britney were seen enjoying each other's company and appeared to be very much at ease with one another. Jamie admitted that he quite liked Jason and Lynne gushed about him to *US Weekly*'s Kevin O'Leary: "He's the kind of man you would dream of your daughter marrying. The kids love him, and he's stable." A Los Angeles radio personality commented that Trawick was the "the first guy Britney has dated since Justin Timberlake that actually has a job." A smitten Britney told her parents in June that she wanted to marry Trawick because he made her feel "safe and loved" and that this was the first relationship she'd ever had that felt real. With Jason, she said, she could talk about anything. Ed Alonso, a magician on her tour, says that Britney had been stabilised "by a good group of people around her, family and friends; and whenever she needs to just talk to someone she knows who will actually listen to her, she always calls [Trawick] first."

The romance was blooming and for the next few months, Trawick accompanied Britney and often her kids, almost everywhere. He was there on their September visit to the Sugar Factory candy store in the Las Vegas Mirage Hotel and was seen cradling a worn-out Jayden James in his arms when the excitement grew too much for him. A couple of nights later, the couple was spotted having dinner in the Beverly Hills restaurant Bond St. When the *Circus* tour moved on to Australia, Kevin Federline went along to look after the boys when they weren't with Britney and Trawick was on board as well. Jason was photographed with Britney taking Sean Preston and Jayden James on a three-hour sailboat tour of Sydney Harbour and after the tour he helped Britney wind down for a few days at the Tides Resort in Zihuatanejo, Mexico. They capped off the year by celebrating Britney's twenty-eighth birthday together with a shopping spree in West Hollywood followed by a romantic dinner at the Little Door restaurant.

When the January 2010 issue of *Elle* magazine hit the stands in December, Britney and her sons were featured on the cover. The photo is one of the best ever taken of Britney; she looks healthy, even radiant and she exudes happiness. Now it seemed that Britney had achieved a perfect comeback. She had a fistful of new awards, a successful tour and album and a new, caring man in her life.

On January 22, 2010, Britney appeared in a Los Angeles court to challenge her father's conservatorship once again. She had been telling her dancer friends that her father's tight control over every aspect of her life was getting embarrassing and she had grown quite tired of it. But in trying to give the impression that she had reached a new level of personal responsibility, she fell short of the mark. She sashayed into the courtroom wearing a miniskirt and big sunglasses and looking like she was on her way to meet Paris Hilton for a night of clubbing. She was smiling and she carried a file folder. Judge Reva Goetz refused her request. The judge's reasoning was that Britney had flourished under conservatorship; it appeared to have been exactly what she needed. Britney argued that while she appreciated what her father and others had done for her, she was all right now and she didn't know why she had to be on a strict $1,500 dollar a week allowance while her father was taking $4,000 a week for himself. It was her money, she argued. She wondered aloud how long she would have to go on paying for her mistakes. Judge Goetz was unmoved and said that while she could see how the conservatorship might pose certain inconveniences for her, the benefits far outweighed them.

On January 31, 2010, despite being ruffled by tabloid rumours that Trawick had stepped out on her, Britney brought him with her to the Grammy Awards ceremony at the Staples Center in Los Angeles. She was nominated for a Grammy in the category of best dance recording for her song "Womanizer," though she lost out to Lady Ga-Ga. Britney was all smiles when the cameras were on her. She looked good in her Dolce and Gabbana bodysuit and fishnets. Afterwards, she and Jason headed back to Miami, where she was recording a new album.

* * *

In February 2010, there was further evidence that the big Britney Spears comeback spin was in full, furious force. Britney scored a sponsorship deal with the company Candies, which sells everything from clothing to jewellery to candy to furniture. The company was launching a new ad campaign that would go into heavy rotation in April 2010, with special focus on the magazines *Seventeen* and *Teen Vogue*. The main image in the campaign would be Britney, smiling innocently at the camera, wearing pink hot pants and a tasteful white top.

Renowned celebrity photographers Annie Leibowitz, Mark Seliger and Terry Richardson were hired to shoot Britney for the ads. Everyone seemed to hit it off during the shoot, which took place on a soundstage on the Paramount Pictures lot. Britney was on her best behaviour, polite and attentive, although a makeup assistant did report that she appeared "docile and mellow, almost unnaturally so."

There was lots of pink in the photos. Seliger's shots featured a pink Harley Davidson and a pink burlesque-house backdrop. Richardson chose to shoot Britney against a solid-white backdrop using such props as a pink teddy bear. Leibowitz selected an industrial theme. While the photos are certainly sexy, they seem to evoke a younger Britney, the coltish girl at the outset of her career. It was almost as though they were attempting to erase the troublesome events of the intervening years and reacquaint the world with the curvy, sexy Britney everyone loved.

Shortly after the shoot, Britney went to spend some time with her sister, Jamie Lynn. The two rarely saw each other. Jamie Lynn says, "I am really proud of my sister, and she is real proud of me, too, but we are both busy with our careers and never seem to be in the same spot at the same time." The sisters were spotted in West Hollywood having lunch on February 20, 2010; then they headed back to Calabasas, near Malibu, where Britney was renovating a home she had just bought.

At the Calabasas estate, Britney showed Jamie Lynn the improvements she was making to the house, which would reportedly cost over $700,000. These improvements were approved by Jamie Spears, who, under to the conservatorship arrangement, had to sanction any expenditures Britney made in excess of her allowance. These expenditures would include some $100,000 for special Venetian plasterwork for the walls, $100,000 for master bathroom alterations, $150,000 for furniture, $200,000 for artwork and $150,000 for home-entertainment electronics.

Epilogue

So here we are. Britney has been a superstar—an award-winning, record-shattering, mega-earning pop star—for over a decade and she is just twenty-eight years old. But in a way, she has no more rights and freedoms now than she had when she was a child doing *The All New Mickey Mouse Club* and she had a chaperone and a tutor and all of her earnings went into a trust. In a sense, the Britney Spears story is the classic "Be careful what you wish for" scenario with a little "The only thing worse than not getting what you want is getting everything you want" thrown in for good measure.

It's been a rocky road for Britney. Hollywood, with its ravenous appetite for celebrity gossip and its worship of wealth and excess of every kind, has come close to eating her alive. Too many in Britney's inner and outer circles were content to overlook her suffering and her obvious cries for help because their personal interest lay in keeping the river of gold flowing and she was the source. Lost and neglected inside the staggering success achieved at such a young age was a real person named Britney Jean Spears and she has had to battle her way out of the juggernaut that she and those around her created. She now seems to have won that battle, although she has the scars to show for it. She's poised at a new beginning, a bit older and a bit wiser. Her job now is to try to pick up all the broken pieces and reassemble herself into a stronger, revitalised whole.

Imagine that comeback for a moment: a real comeback, a return from a voluntary retreat, a return to sanity and stability with her talents and creative energies fully recharged. When that happens, the only people who will have the right to cling to her will be two little boys named Sean Preston and Jayden James. Think of the music she will produce then. Instead of snarling songs about people who steal her soul and drive her crazy, she'll sing songs about reflection and renewal and the grace that comes from redemption.